ANTHONY STORR

MUSIC
AND THE MIND

'*Music's the medicine of the mind*'
JOHN LOGAN (1744–88)

Ballantine Books • New York

This edition published by arrangement with The Free Press, a division of Macmillan, Inc.

Library of Congress Catalog Card Number: 93-90047

ISBN: 0-345-38318-4

Cover illustration by James Yang

Manufactured in the United States of America

First Ballantine Books Edition: November 1993

10 9 8 7 6 5 4 3 2 1

FOR
SOPHIA, POLLY, AND EMMA
WHO SHARE MY LOVE
OF MUSIC

Contents

Acknowledgements

I would like to thank all those with whom I have discussed this book for their help. My wife Catherine Peters has read more than one version of the typescript and, as always, has made a number of valuable comments. My publishers, Erwin Glikes of The Free Press and Stuart Proffitt of HarperCollins, have made many useful suggestions. I am particularly grateful to Patrick Gardiner for his expert criticism of the chapter on Schopenhauer; and to Lucy Warrack for her penetrating remarks on both Nietzsche and Schopenhauer. Professor Margaret Bent tactfully eliminated some of my grosser errors in the early part of the book. I gained much encouragement from the comments of Bruce Phillips, who was kind enough to read the whole typescript. Professor Brian Trowell and Jeremy Montagu allowed me to pick their brains on technical points, and Hugo Cole was equally helpful in the same connection. Dr Kay R. Jamison's psychological knowledge and insight have been invaluable. Ellen Dissanayake kindly allowed me to quote from her unpublished work, and so did Frances Berenson. Dr Robert Barton informed me of a paper on animal communication which proved illuminating. Stephen Englehard provided useful references and criticism. Rebecca Wilson proved herself an expert copy-editor. Old men forget, and there may be other people whom I have omitted to thank. To them I can only offer apologies.

Introduction

Since music is the only language with the contradictory attributes of being at once intelligible
and untranslatable, the musical creator is a being
comparable to the gods, and music itself the
supreme mystery of the science of man.

CLAUDE LÉVI-STRAUSS[1]

Today, more people listen to music than ever before in the history of the world. The audience has increased enormously since the Second World War. Recordings, radio, and even television, have made music available to a wider range of the population than anyone could have predicted fifty years ago. In spite of dire warnings that recordings might empty opera houses and concert halls, the audience for live performances has also multiplied.

This book reflects my personal preference in that it is primarily concerned with classical or Western 'art' music, rather than with 'popular' music. That these two varieties of music should have become so divergent is regrettable. The demand for accessible musical entertainment grew during the latter half of the nineteenth century in response to the increased wealth of the middle class. It was met by Offenbach, both Johann Strausses, Chabrier, Sullivan, and other gifted composers of light music which still enchants us today. The tradition was carried on into the twentieth century by composers of the stature of Gershwin, Jerome Kern, and Irving Berlin. It is only since the 1950s that the gap between classical and popular music has widened into a canyon which is nearly unbridgeable.

In spite of its widespread diffusion, music remains an enigma. Music for those who love it is so important that to be deprived of it would constitute a cruel and unusual punishment. Moreover, the perception of music as a central part of life is not confined to professionals or even to gifted amateurs. It is true that those who have studied the techniques of musical composition can more thoroughly appreciate the structure of a musical work than those who have not. It is also true that people who can play an instrument, or who can sing, can actively participate in music in ways which enrich their understanding of it. Playing in a string quartet, or even singing as one anonymous voice in a large choir, are both life-enhancing activities which those who take part in them find irreplaceable. But even listeners who cannot read musical notation and who have never attempted to learn an instrument may be so deeply affected that, for them, any day which passes without being seriously involved with music in one way or another is a day wasted.

In the context of contemporary Western culture, this is puzzling. Many people assume that the arts are luxuries rather than necessities, and that words or pictures are the only means by which influence can be exerted on the human mind. Those who do not appreciate music think that it has no significance other than providing ephemeral pleasure. They consider it a gloss upon the surface of life; a harmless indulgence rather than a necessity. This, no doubt, is why our present politicians seldom accord music a prominent place in their plans for education. Today, when education is becoming increasingly utilitarian, directed toward obtaining gainful employment rather than toward enriching personal experience, music is likely to be treated as an 'extra' in the school curriculum which only affluent parents can afford, and which need not be provided for pupils who are not obviously 'musical' by nature. The idea that music is so powerful that it can actually affect both individuals and the state for good or ill has disappeared. In a culture dominated by the visual and the verbal, the significance of music is perplexing, and is therefore underestimated. Both musicians and lovers of music who are not professionally trained *know* that great music brings us more than sensuous pleasure, although sensuous pleasure is certainly part of musical experience. Yet what it brings is hard to define. This book is an exploratory search; an attempt to discover what it is about music that so profoundly affects us, and why it is such an important part of our culture.

CHAPTER I

ORIGINS AND
COLLECTIVE FUNCTIONS

Music is so naturally united with us that we cannot
be free from it even if we so desired.

BOETHIUS[1]

No culture so far discovered lacks music. Making music appears to
be one of the fundamental activities of mankind; as characteristically human as drawing and painting. The survival of
Palaeolithic cave-paintings bears witness to the antiquity of this
form of art; and some of these paintings depict people dancing.
Flutes made of bone found in these caves suggest that they danced
to some form of music. But, because music itself only survives
when the invention of a system of notation has made a written
record possible, or else when a living member of a culture recreates
the sounds and rhythms which have been handed down to him by
his forebears, we have no information about prehistoric music. We
are therefore accustomed to regarding drawing and painting as
integral parts of the life of early man, but less inclined to think of
music in the same way. However, music, or musical sounds of
some variety, are so interwoven with human life that they probably
played a greater part in prehistory than can ever be determined.

When biologists consider complex human activities such as the
arts, they tend to assume that their compelling qualities are
derivations of basic drives. If any given activity can be seen to aid
survival or facilitate adaptation to the environment, or to be derived
from behaviour which does so, it 'makes sense' in biological terms.
For example, the art of painting may originate from the human
need to comprehend the external world through vision; an
achievement which makes it possible to act upon the environment

I

or influence it in ways which promote survival. The Palaeolithic artists who drew and painted animals on the walls of their caves were using their artistic skills for practical reasons. Drawing is a form of abstraction which may be compared with the formation of verbal concepts. It enables the draughtsman to study an object in its absence; to experiment with various images of it, and thus, at least in phantasy, to exert power over it. These artists were magicians, who painted and drew animals in order to exercise magical charms upon them. By capturing the image of the animal, early humans probably felt that they could partially control it. Since the act of drawing sharpens the perceptions of the artist by making him pay detailed attention to the forms he is trying to depict, the Palaeolithic painter did in reality learn to know his prey more accurately, and therefore increased his chances of being successful in the hunt. The art historian Herbert Read wrote:

> Far from being an expenditure of surplus energy, as earlier theories have supposed, art, at the dawn of human culture, was a key to survival, a sharpening of the faculties essential to the struggle for existence. Art, in my opinion, has remained a key to survival.[2]

The art of literature probably derived from that of the primitive story-teller. He was not merely providing entertainment, but passing down to his listeners a tradition of who they were, where they had come from, and what their lives signified. By making sense and order out of his listeners' existence, he was enhancing their feeling of personal worth in the scheme of things and therefore increasing their capacity to deal effectively with the social tasks and relationships which made up their lives. The myths of a society usually embody its traditional values and moral norms. Repetition of these myths therefore reinforces the coherence and unity of the society, as well as giving each individual a sense of meaning and purpose. Both painting and literature can be understood as having developed from activities which, originally, were adaptively useful.

But what use is music? Music can certainly be regarded as a form of communication between people; but what it communicates is not obvious. Music is not usually representational: it does not sharpen our perception of the external world, nor, allowing for some notable exceptions,* does it generally imitate it. Nor is music propositional: it does not put forward theories about the world or convey information in the same way as does language.

There are two conventional ways in which one can approach the problem of the significance of music in human life. One is to examine its origins. Music today is highly developed, complex, various and sophisticated. If we could understand how it began, perhaps we could better understand its fundamental meaning. The second way is to examine how music has actually been used. What functions has music served in different societies throughout history?

There is no general agreement about the origins of music. Music has only tenuous links with the world of nature. Nature is full of sound, and some of nature's sounds, such as running water, may give us considerable pleasure. A survey of sound preferences amongst people in New Zealand, Canada, Jamaica and Switzerland revealed that none disliked the sounds of brooks, rivers and waterfalls, and that a high proportion enjoyed them.[3] But nature's sounds, with the exception of bird-song and some other calls between animals, are irregular noises rather than the sustained notes of definable pitch which go to form music. This is why the sounds of which Western music is composed are referred to as 'tones': they are separable units with constant auditory waveforms which can be repeated and reproduced.

Although science can define the differences between tones in terms of pitch, loudness, timbre, and waveform, it cannot portray the relation between tones which constitutes music. Whilst there is still considerable dispute concerning the origins, purpose, and significance of music, there is general agreement that it is only remotely related to the sounds and rhythms of the natural world. Absence of external association makes music unique amongst the arts; but since music is closely linked with human emotions, it cannot be regarded as no more than a disembodied system of relationships between sounds. Music has often been compared with mathematics; but, as G. H. Hardy pointed out, 'Music can be used to stimulate mass emotion, while mathematics cannot.'[4]

*For example, Haydn's *The Creation*, Beethoven's 'Pastoral' Symphony, Delius's *On Hearing the First Cuckoo in Spring*, Strauss's *Sinfonia Domestica*.

If music were merely a series of artificial constructs comparable with decorative visual patterns, it would induce a mild aesthetic pleasure, but nothing more. Yet music can penetrate the core of our physical being. It can make us weep, or give us intense pleasure. Music, like being in love, can temporarily transform our whole existence. But the links between the art of music and the reality of human emotions are difficult to define; so difficult that, as we shall see, many distinguished musicians have abandoned any attempt to do so, and have tried to persuade us that musical works consist of disembodied patterns of sound which have no connection with other forms of human experience.

Can music be related to the sounds made by other species? The most obviously 'musical' of such sounds are those found in bird-song. Birds employ both noises and tones in their singing; but the proportion of definable tones is often high enough for some people to rate some bird-songs as 'music'. Bird-song has a number of different functions. By locating the singer, it both advertises a territory as desirable, and also acts as a warning to rivals. Birds in search of a mate sing more vigorously than those who are already mated, thus supporting Darwin's notion that song was originally a sexual invitation. Bird-song is predominantly a male activity, dependent upon the production of the male sex hormone, testosterone, although duets between male and female occur in some species. Given sufficient testosterone, female birds who do not usually sing will master the same repertoire of songs as the male.[5]

Charles Hartshorne, the American ornithologist and philosopher, claims that bird-song shows variation of both pitch and tempo: accelerando, crescendo, diminuendo, change of key, and variations on a theme. Some birds, like the Wood thrush *Hylochicla mustelina*, have a repertoire of as many as nine songs which can follow each other in a variety of different combinations. Hartshorne argues:

> Bird songs resemble human music both in the sound patterns and in the behavior setting. Songs illustrate the aesthetic mean between chaotic irregularity and monotonous regularity . . . The essential difference from human music is in the brief temporal span of the

bird's repeatable patterns, commonly three seconds or less, with an upper limit of about fifteen seconds. This limitation conforms to the concept of primitive musicality. Every simple musical device, even transposition and simultaneous harmony, occurs in bird music.[6]

He goes on to state that birds sing far more than is biologically necessary for the various forms of communication. He suggests that bird-song has partially escaped from practical usage to become an activity which is engaged in for its own sake: an expression of avian *joie de vivre*.

Singing repels rival males, but only when nearby; and it attracts mates. It is persisted in without any obvious immediate result, and hence must be largely self-rewarding. It expresses no one limited emotional attitude and conveys more information than mere chirps or squeaks. In all these ways song functions like music.[7]

Other observers disagree, claiming that bird-song is so biologically demanding that it is unlikely to be produced unless it is serving some useful function.

Is it possible that human music originated from the imitation of bird-song? Géza Révész, who was a professor of Psychology at the University of Amsterdam and a friend of Béla Bartók, dismisses this possibility on two counts. First, if human music really began in this way, we should be able to point to examples of music resembling bird-song in isolated pre-literate communities. Instead, we find complex rhythmic patterns bearing no resemblance to avian music. Second, bird-song is not easily imitated. Slowing down modern recordings of bird-songs has demonstrated that they are even more complicated than previously supposed; but one only has to listen to a thrush singing in the garden to realize that imitation of his song is technically difficult. Liszt's 'Légende' for solo piano, 'St François d'Assise: La Prédication aux oiseaux', manages to suggest the twittering of birds in ways which are both ingenious and musically convincing. I have heard a tape of American bird-song which persuasively suggests that Dvořák incorporated themes derived from it following his sojourn in the Czech community in Spillville, Iowa. Olivier Messiaen made more use of bird-song in his music than any other composer. But these are sophisticated, late developments in the history of music. It is probable that early man took very little notice of bird-song, since it bore scant relevance to his immediate concerns.[8]

Lévi-Strauss affirms that music is in a special category compared with the other arts, and also agrees that bird-song cannot be the origin of human music.

> If, through lack of verisimilitude, we dismiss the whistling of the wind through the reeds of the Nile, which is referred to by Diodorus, we are left with little but bird song – Lucretius' *liquidas avium voces* – that can serve as a natural model for music. Although ornithologists and acousticians agree about the musicality of the sounds uttered by birds, the gratuitous and unverifiable hypothesis of the existence of a genetic relation between bird song and music is hardly worth discussing.[9]

Stravinsky points out that natural sounds, like the murmur of the breeze in the trees, the rippling of a brook or the song of a bird, *suggest* music to us but are not themselves music: 'I conclude that tonal elements become music only by virtue of their being organized, and that such organization presupposes a conscious human act.'[10]

It is not surprising that Stravinsky emphasizes organization as the leading feature of music, since he himself was one of the most meticulous, orderly, and obsessionally neat composers in the history of music. But his emphatic statement is surely right. Bird-song has some elements of music in it, but, although variations upon inherited patterns occur, it is too obviously dependent upon in-built templates to be compared with human music.

In general, music bears so little resemblance to the sounds made by other species that some scholars regard it as an entirely separate phenomenon. This is the view of the ethnomusicologist John Blacking, who was, until his untimely death, Professor of Social Anthropology at the Queen's University of Belfast, as well as being an accomplished musician.

> There is so much music in the world that it is reasonable to suppose that music, like language and possibly religion, is a species-specific

trait of man. Essential physiological and cognitive processes that generate musical composition and performance may even be genetically inherited, and therefore present in almost every human being.[11]

If music is indeed species-specific, there might seem to be little point in comparing it with the sounds made by other species. But those who have studied the sounds made by subhuman primates, and who have discovered what functions these sounds serve, find interesting parallels with human music. Gelada monkeys produce a wide variety of sounds of different pitches which accompany all their social interactions. They also use many different rhythms, accents, and types of vocalization. The particular type of sound which an individual produces indicates his emotional state at the time and, in the longer term, aids the development of stable bonds between different individuals. When tensions between individuals exist, these can sometimes be resolved by synchronizing and co-ordinating vocal expressions.

Human beings, like geladas, also use rhythm and melody to resolve emotional conflicts. This is perhaps the main social function served by group singing in people . . . Music is the 'language' of emotional and physiological arousal. A culturally agreed-upon pattern of rhythm and melody, i.e., a song, that is sung together, provides a shared form of emotion that, at least during the course of the song, carries along the participants so that they experience their bodies responding emotionally in very similar ways. This is the source of the feeling of solidarity and good will that comes with choral singing: people's physiological arousals are in synchrony and in harmony, at least for a brief period. It seems possible that during the course of human evolution the use of rhythm and melody for the purposes of speaking sentences grew directly out of its use in choral singing. It also seems likely that geladas singing their sound sequences together synchronously and harmoniously also perhaps experience such a temporary physiological synchrony.[12]

We shall return to the subject of group arousal in the next chapter. Meanwhile, let us consider some other speculations about the origin of music.

One theory is that music developed from the lalling of infants. All infants babble, even if they are born deaf or blind. During the first year of life, babbling includes tones as well as approximations to words: the precursors of music and language cannot be separated. According to the Harvard psychologist Howard Gardner, who has conducted research into the musical development of small children:

> The first melodic fragments produced by children around the age of a year or fifteen months have no strong musical identity. Their undulating patterns, going up and down over a very brief interval or ambitus, are more reminiscent of waves than of particular pitch attacks. Indeed, a quantum leap, in an almost literal sense, occurs at about the age of a year and a half, when for the first time children can intentionally produce discrete pitches. It is as if diffuse babbling had been supplanted by stressed words.[13]

During the next year, children make habitual use of discrete pitches, chiefly using seconds, minor thirds, and major thirds. By the age of two or two and a half, children are beginning to notice and learn songs sung by others. Révész is quite sure that the lalling melodies produced by children in their second year are already conditioned by songs which they have picked up from the environment or by other music to which they have been exposed.[14] If lalling melodies are in fact dependent upon musical input from the environment, it is obviously inadmissible to suggest that music itself developed from infant lalling.

Ellen Dissanayake, who teaches at the New School for Social Research in New York and who has lived in Sri Lanka, Nigeria, and Papua New Guinea, persuasively argues that music originated in the ritualized verbal exchanges which go on between mothers and babies during the first year of life. In this type of interchange, the most important components of language are those which are concerned with emotional expressiveness rather than with conveying factual information. Metre, rhythm, pitch, volume, lengthening of vowel sounds, tone of voice, and other variables are all characteristic of a type of utterance which has much in common with poetry. She writes:

No matter how important lexico-grammatical meaning eventually becomes, the human brain is first organized or programmed to respond to emotional/intonational aspects of the human voice.[15]

Since infants in the womb react both to unstructured noise and to music with movements which their mothers can feel, it seems likely that auditory perception prompts the baby's first realization that there is something beyond itself to which it is nevertheless related. After birth, vocal interchange between mother and infant continues to reinforce mutual attachment, although vision soon becomes equally important. The crooning, cooing tones and rhythms which most mothers use when addressing babies are initially more significant in cementing the relationship between them than the words which accompany these vocalizations. This type of communication continues throughout childhood. If, for example, I play with a child of eighteen months who can only utter a few words, we can communicate in all kinds of ways which require no words at all. It is probable that both of us will make noises: we will chuckle, grunt, and make the kinds of sounds which accompany chasing and hiding games. We may establish, at least for the time being, a relationship which is quite intimate, but nothing which passes between us needs to be expressed in words. Moreover, although relationships between adults usually involve verbal interchange, they do not always do so. We can establish relationships with people who do not speak the same language, and our closest physical relationships need not make use of words, although they usually do so. Many people regard physical intimacy with another person as impossible to verbalize, as deeper than anything which words can convey.

Linguistic analysts distinguish *prosodic* features of speech from *syntactic*: stress, pitch, volume, emphasis, and any other features conveying emotional significance, as opposed to grammatical structure or literal meaning. There are many similarities between prosodic communication and music. Infants respond to the rhythm, pitch, intensity, and timbre of the mother's voice; all of which are part of music.

Such elements are manifestly important in poetry, but they can also be in prose. As a modern example, we can consider James

Joyce's experiments with the *sound* of words which are particularly evident in his later works.

> But even in his earliest stories the meaning of a word did not necessarily depend on the object it denoted but on the sonority and intonation of the speaker's voice; for even then Joyce addressed the listener rather than the reader.[16]

It will be recalled that Joyce had an excellent voice and considered becoming a professional singer. He described using the technical resources of music in writing the Sirens chapter of *Ulysses*. Joyce portrays Molly Bloom as comprehending the hurdy-gurdy boy without understanding a word of his language.

One popular Victorian notion was that music gradually developed from *adult* speech through a separation of the prosodic elements from the syntactic. William Pole wrote in *The Philosophy of Music*:

> The earliest forms of music probably arose out of the natural inflections of the voice in speaking. It would be very easy to *sustain* the sound of the voice on one particular note, and to follow this by another sustained note at a higher or lower pitch. This, however rude, would constitute *music*.
>
> We may further easily conceive that several persons might be led to join in a rude chant of this kind. If one acted as leader, others, guided by the natural instinct of their ears, would imitate him, and thus we might get a combined unison song.[17]

Dr Pole's original lectures, on which his book is based, were given in 1877, and bear the impress of their time, with frequent references to savages, barbarians, and the like. Although *The Philosophy of Music* is still useful, Pole shows little appreciation of the fact that music amongst pre-literate peoples might be as complex as our own. Twenty years earlier, in 1857, Herbert Spencer had advanced a similar theory of the origins of music, which was published in *Fraser's Magazine*.*

Spencer noted that when speech became emotional the sounds

*Pole makes passing reference to this in one footnote, but makes no acknowledgement to Spencer.

produced spanned a greater tonal range and thus came closer to music. He therefore proposed that the sounds of excited speech became gradually uncoupled from the words which accompanied them, and so came to exist as separate sound entities, forming a 'language' of their own.

Darwin came to an opposite conclusion. He supposed that music *preceded* speech and arose as an elaboration of mating calls. He observed that male animals which possess a vocal apparatus generally use their voices most when under the influence of sexual feelings. A sound which was originally used to attract the attention of a potential mate might gradually be modified, elaborated, and intensified.

The suspicion does not appear improbable that the progenitors of man, either the males or the females, or both sexes, before they had acquired the power of expressing their mutual love in articulate language, endeavoured to charm each other with musical notes and rhythm. The impassioned orator, bard, or musician, when with his various tones and cadences he excites the strongest emotions in his hearers, little suspects that he uses the same means by which, at an extremely remote period, his half-human ancestors aroused each other's ardent passions during their mutual courtship and rivalry.[18]

Géza Révész reproduced another theory of the origin of music, which was first advanced by Carl Stumpf, although Révész makes no direct acknowledgement to this earlier author. It is based on the perception that the singing voice has greater carrying power than the speaking voice. Early man, Révész supposes, when wishing to communicate with his fellows at a distance, discovered that he could do so more effectively by using a singing voice rather than a speaking voice. Révész affirms that giving vent to loud, resounding signals produces pleasure, and remembers his own delight in making his voice ring out into wide open spaces. He assumes that such calls can pass over into song quite easily. In other words, he tries to derive all music from the yodel.

It is true that musical sounds are used by pre-literate people for communication at a distance, and that wind instruments of considerable carrying power have been invented for this purpose.

Allegedly, the Mura Indians of the Amazon communicate with each other across the great rivers in a special musical language which they play on a three-holed flageolet.[19] Signalling by means of drums and horns is a widespread practice in Africa and elsewhere. Even so, communication using musical sounds is not itself music, and there is no direct evidence that such signals became transmuted into music.

Révész's theory also fails to account for the rhythmic element in music, which ethnomusicologists find to be fundamentally important. Neither Révész nor Darwin nor Spencer are able to tell us *why* music became attractive to early men or their descendants.[20]

Jean-Jacques Rousseau, who was not only a revolutionary social theorist but also an accomplished composer, argued that musical sounds accompanied or preceded speech as we know it. In his biography of Rousseau, Maurice Cranston recounts from the *Essai sur l'origine des langues* Rousseau's theory that

> men first spoke to each other in order to express their passions, and that at the early stages of human society there was no distinct speech apart from song. Earliest languages, he suggests, were chanted; they were melodic and poetic rather than prosaic and practical. He also claims that it was men's passions rather than their needs which prompted their first utterances, for passions would drive men towards others, whereas the necessities of life would impel each to seek his satisfaction alone. 'It is not hunger or thirst, but love, hatred, pity and anger which drew from men their first vocal utterances.' Primitive men sing to one another in order to express their feelings before they come to speak to one another in order to express their thoughts.[21]

John Blacking claims that singing and dancing preceded the development of verbal interchange.

> There is evidence that early human species were able to dance and sing several hundred thousand years before *homo sapiens sapiens* emerged with the capacity for speech as we now know it.[22]

It may even have been the case, as the eighteenth-century Italian philosopher Giambattista Vico suggested, that human beings danced before they walked. He also thought that poetry came before prose, and that men naturally embodied their feelings, attitudes, and thoughts in symbols. The metaphorical use of language, according to Vico, preceded the literal or scientific; and he is not the only philosopher to think this. Heidegger wrote:

> Poetry proper is never merely a higher mode (*melos*) of everyday language. It is rather the reverse: everyday language is a forgotten and therefore used-up poem, from which there hardly resounds a call any longer.[23]

The objective language generally used by scientists and philosophers, which is concerned with conceptual thought and with demonstration and proof rather than with evocation, and which usually avoids metaphor as far as possible, is quite different from the 'musical' language used by poets, by the pre-literate, or even by those who are not highly educated in the Western tradition. 'The magnet loves iron' is not a scientific explanation of magnetism, but is a naturally anthropomorphic way of speaking found the world over.

> A world in which men naturally talk of the lips of a vase, the teeth of a plough, the mouth of a river, a neck of land, handfuls of one thing, the heart of another, veins of minerals, bowels of the earth, murmuring waves, whistling winds and smiling skies, groaning tables and weeping willows* – such a world must be deeply and systematically different from any in which such phrases are felt, even remotely, to be metaphorical, as contrasted with so-called literal speech. This is one of Vico's most revolutionary discoveries.[24]

As Isaiah Berlin points out, all the metaphors listed above are taken from the human body. When human beings looked upon the external world and tried to describe it, it was natural that they did so in terms of their own subjective, physical experience. The language of science had not yet become dissociated from the language of poetry and music, and the notion that the phenomena of the external world could only be understood if anthropomorphism was excluded had not yet developed. The behaviourist idea that human

*All these examples are taken directly from Vico's *Scienza Nuova*.

13

beings can only properly be comprehended when their actions are observed with scientific objectivity rather than assessed by means of empathic understanding was far in the future. Vico would have agreed with John Blacking in supposing that a people's music is one important key to understanding their culture and their relationships.

In ancient Greece, which is usually considered to be the birthplace of Western civilization, music was both ubiquitous and supremely important. Although we know little about how Greek music actually sounded, classical scholars refer to it as 'an art which was woven into the very texture of their lives'.[25]

As in our culture, elaborate instrumental skills were the preserve of professional musicians; but the Greeks considered that instruction in singing and in playing the lyre should be a regular part of education for every freeborn citizen. Music was an important feature of domestic celebrations, feasts, and religious rituals, and musical competitions were held alongside athletic contests. Poetry and music went hand in hand: the poetry of Homer, for example, was originally recited to the accompaniment of the lyre.

For the Greeks, music and poetry were inseparable. The poet and the composer were frequently the same person, so that often words and music were created together. The Greek word *melos* indicated both lyric poetry and the music to which a poem is set: it is the origin of our word 'melody'. It is worth noting that, in spite of its mathematical connections, music accompanied the subjective language of poetry rather than the objective language of intellectual argument. We can imagine *The Odyssey* being chanted to musical accompaniment; we cannot imagine *The Republic* being similarly treated.

> First of all, early poetry was song. The difference between song and speech is a matter of discontinuities of pitch. In ordinary speech, we are constantly changing pitch, even in the pronunciation of a single syllable. But in song, the change of pitch is discrete and discontinuous. Speech reels around all over a certain portion of an octave (in relaxed speech about a fifth). Song steps from note to note on strict and delimited feet over a more extended range.
>
> Modern poetry is a hybrid. It has the metrical feet of song with the pitch glissandos of speech. But ancient poetry is much closer to

song. Accents were not by intensity stressed as in our ordinary speech, but by pitch. In ancient Greece, this pitch is thought to have been precisely the interval of a fifth above the ground note of the poem, so that on the notes of our scale, dactyls would go GCC, GCC, with no extra emphasis on the G. Moreover, the three extra accents, acute, circumflex, and grave, were, as their notations ´, ^, `, imply, a rising pitch within the syllable, a rising and falling on the same syllable, and a falling pitch respectively. The result was a poetry sung like plainsong with various auditory ornamentation that gave it beautiful variety.[26]

The Greek word for this is μουσική. It cannot easily be translated; for it signifies musically determined verse, or music and poetry in one. Whereas modern Western verse is primarily linguistic, words which may or may not be set to music,

The ancient Greek verse line behaved differently. Here the musical rhythm was contained within the language itself. The musical-rhythmic structure was completely determined by the language. There was no room for an independent musical-rhythmic setting; nothing could be added or changed.[27]

Gradually, the musical component shrank, to be replaced by a system of accents; that is, by dynamic stresses which bore little relation to the original rhythm and which were not intoned at different pitches. Thrasybulos Georgiades, from whose book *Music and Language* I have just quoted, thinks that the original μουσική was replaced by prose and music as separate forms. Linguistically determined poetry followed, with verse rhythms governed by stress rather than pitch. It then became possible to set both prose and poetry to music in the ways familiar to us. So language and music could be recombined where this was thought appropriate, as, for example, in the Christian liturgy; but only after their initial unity had been disrupted and their independence from each other had been established.

Rousseau may well have been right in thinking that there was no distinct speech apart from song at the beginning of history. The psychoanalyst Anton Ehrenzweig, himself an accomplished musician, wrote:

It is not unreasonable to speculate that speech and music have descended from a common origin in a primitive language which was neither speaking nor singing, but something of both. Later this primeval language would have split into different branches; music would have retained the articulation mainly by pitch (scale) and duration (rhythm), while language chose the articulation mainly by tone colour (vowels and consonants). Language moreover happened to become the vehicle of rational thought and so underwent further influences. Music has become a symbolic language of the unconscious mind whose symbolism we shall never be able to fathom.[28]

If song and speech were initially more closely linked, and then became separated, it is understandable that the differences in their functions became accentuated. One can imagine that, as prose became less metaphorical, less anthropomorphic, more objective, and more precise, people would use this kind of speech for conveying information and expounding ideas, whilst reserving poetic and musical communication for religious and other rituals. However, even the speech used by scientists and mathematicians to explain and convey their ideas is never entirely devoid of varieties of tone, emphasis, and pitch. If this were the case it would be so monotonous that no one would listen to it.

Today, we are accustomed to listening to instrumental music which has no necessary connection with the human voice or with public ceremonies. We have also developed language to the point at which it can be used for scientific description or for conceptual thought without prosody, metaphor, or the expression of subjective feeling. Seen from the perspective of history, these changes are recent. I think that they are also connected. If we consider together the ideas of Vico, Rousseau, and Blacking, we can perceive that language and music were originally more closely joined, and that it makes sense to think of music as deriving from a subjective, emotional need for communication with other human beings which is prior to the need for conveying objective information or exchanging ideas.

Ethnomusicologists generally emphasize the *collective* importance of music in the cultures they study. There are a number of cultures which, like that of ancient Greece, do not distinguish music as a separate activity from those which it invariably accompanies.

Singing, dancing, the recitation of poetry, and religious chant are so inseparably linked with music that there is no word for music as such. Indeed, it may be difficult for the observer to determine whether a particular activity includes music or does not. Ceremonial speech may, as in the case of Greek poetry, include rhythmic and melodic patterns which are so much part of it that words and music cannot really be differentiated.

The origins of music may be lost in obscurity but, from its earliest beginnings, it seems to have played an essential part in social interaction. Music habitually accompanies religious and other ceremonies. Some anthropologists have speculated that vocal music may have begun as a special way of communicating with the supernatural, a way which shared many of the features of ordinary speech, but which was also distinctive.[29]

Stravinsky would have agreed with this suggestion. In his Charles Eliot Norton lectures delivered at Harvard in 1939–40 he unequivocally affirms that 'the profound meaning of music and its essential aim . . . is to promote a communion, a union of man with his fellow man and with the Supreme Being.'[30]

In pre-literate societies the arts are usually intimately connected with rituals and ceremonies which are dissociated from the routines of ordinary day-to-day living. As Ellen Dissanayake has cogently observed, the arts are concerned with 'making special'; that is, with underlining and rendering ritualized forms of behaviour.[31] In ritual, words are used metaphorically and symbolically and often reunited with music, which still further charges them with meaning. Raymond Firth, the anthropologist who wrote with such insight about Tikopia and other Pacific communities, states

> Even songs, as a rule, are not composed simply to be listened to for pleasure. They have work to do, to serve as funeral dirges, as accompaniments to dancing, or to serenade a lover.[32]

Pre-literate societies have very little idea of the individual as a separate entity. They regard the individual as indissolubly part of the family, and the family as part of the larger society. Ritual and aesthetic activities are integral parts of social existence, not superstructures or luxuries which only the rich can afford.

Amongst the Venda of the Northern Transvaal, music plays an important part in initiation ceremonies, work, dancing, religious worship, political protest – in fact in every collective activity. Especially important is *tshikona*, the national dance. This music can only be produced when

> twenty or more men blow differently tuned pipes with a precision that depends on holding one's own part as well as blending with others, and at least four women play different drums in poly-rhythmic harmony.[33]

This description disposes of the notion that the music of rural African societies is less developed or less complex than our own: it is simply different. *Tshikona* is highly valued. It raises the spirits of everyone who participates. Blacking thinks this is because its performance generates the highest degree of individuality in the largest possible community; a combination of opposites rarely achieved. Playing in a modern Western orchestra or singing in a large choir may be enjoyable and uplifting, but neither activity provides much scope for individuality.

Music contributes both to the continuity and the stability of a culture whether pre-literate or not. That ardent collector of folk-songs, Béla Bartók, deploring the changes brought about by the First World War and realizing that the type of music produced by a particular culture is inseparable from the nature of that culture, wrote:

> I had the great privilege to be a close observer of an as yet homogeneous, but unfortunately rapidly disappearing social structure, expressing itself in music.[34]

The triumph of the West and the ease of modern communication have caused the disappearance of different musics, as they have also diminished the number of spoken languages.

John A. Sloboda, a psychologist at the University of Keele, argues that pre-literate cultures may have even more need of music than our own.

Society requires organization for its survival. In our own society we have many complex artefacts which help us to externalize and objectify the organizations we need and value. Primitive cultures have few artefacts, and the organization of the society must be expressed to a greater extent through transient actions and the way people interact with each other. Music, perhaps, provides a unique mnemonic framework within which humans can express, by the temporal organization of sound and gesture, the structure of their knowledge and of social relations. Songs and rhythmically organized poems and sayings form the major repository of knowledge in non-literate cultures. This seems to be because such organized sequences are much easier to remember than the type of prose which literate societies use in books.[35]

Johann Gottfried Herder, supposedly the father of European nationalism, had made a similar observation in the eighteenth century.

All unpolished peoples sing and act; they sing about what they do and thus sing histories. Their songs are the archives of their people, the treasury of their science and religion.[36]

The music of the Australian aboriginals remained free from outside influences, and unknown to the West, until the arrival of the British two centuries ago.

Since all their knowledge, beliefs, and customs, upon whose strict preservation through exact ritual observance the constant renewal of nature (and hence their own survival) was held to depend, were enshrined in and transmitted by their sacred song-cycles, it is reasonable to think that theirs is the oldest extant, still practised music in the world. Since they had no form of writing or notation, oral tradition was the only means of retaining and inculcating their lore, and music therefore provided the essential mnemonic medium. As such it was invested with the utmost power, secrecy, and value.[37]

Bruce Chatwin, in his fascinating book *The Songlines*, demonstrates how songs served to divide up the land, and constituted title-deeds to territory. Each totemic ancestor was believed to have sung as he walked, and to have defined the features of the landscape in so doing. Song was the means by which the different aspects of the world were brought into consciousness, and therefore remembered. As Chatwin observed, aboriginals used songs in the same way as birds to affirm territorial boundaries. Each individual inherited some verses of the Ancestor's song, which also determined the limits of a particular area. The contour of the melody of the song described the contour of the land with which it was associated. As Chatwin's informant told him: 'Music is a memory bank for finding one's way about the world.'[38]

When the tribe met to sing their own song-cycle on ritual occasions, song-owners had to sing their particular verses in the right order. Songs also transcended language barriers and constituted a means of communication between individuals who could not communicate in other ways.

When a culture is under threat, music may become even more significant. Bruno Nettl, Professor of Musicology and Anthropology at the University of Illinois, discussing the music of the Flathead Indians, suggests that

> the uses of music in Flathead culture are mainly to accompany other activities, perhaps in order to validate them as done in a properly Flathead fashion . . . Music supports tribal integrity when many peoples, whites and other Indian tribes, because of the onset of modernization and Westernization, come into a position of influencing the Flathead.[39]

E. O. Wilson, the Harvard socio-biologist, writes that, in primitive cultures,

> Singing and dancing serve to draw groups together, direct the emotions of the people, and prepare them for joint action.[40]

One joint action for which sounds produced by musical instruments may help to prepare people is that of warfare. Attacks upon enemies are often initiated by blowing horns and trumpets which both arouses the aggressiveness of the attackers and is supposed to terrify the enemy.

The Muras and other tribes of the Orinoco region performed wild overtures on horns before commencing their attack; the Samoans blew conch-shells, and the savages of Guiana began their advance with a screech of horns and trumpets.[41]

Such sounds are also used to frighten away evil spirits.

Music can sometimes symbolize rebellion. It may be permissible to express anti-government attitudes in songs, the words of which would invite arrest if they appeared in a newspaper article. Under some regimes, night-club satirists are given a licence denied to the ordinary citizen. The song 'Lilliburlero' became an epitome of anti-Catholic sentiments, and is said to have contributed to the revolution of 1688 and to the subsequent defeat of James II at the Battle of the Boyne.

Continuity and stability are served by tunes which everybody knows; but music can also create new patterns of joint experience. Blacking gives examples of African drum patterns which when combined and performed by several players can create new cultural products.

> Through musical interaction, two people create forms that are greater than the sum of their parts, and make for themselves experiences of empathy that would be unlikely to occur in ordinary social intercourse.[42]

The mnemonic power of music is still evident in modern culture. Many of us remember the words of songs and poems more accurately than we can remember prose. That music facilitates memory has been objectively confirmed by the study of mentally retarded children who can recall more material after it is given to them in a song than after it is read to them as a story.[43]

Some people who are primarily interested in classical music are disturbed to find that they recall the words and lyrics of popular songs more easily than they remember the music which means most to them. I think this is because popular songs are simple, endlessly repeated and difficult to avoid. This also accounts for their nostalgic quality. Anniversary 'evenings out' are seldom accompanied by the 'Eroica'. Repetition can make any type of music memorable. Professional musicians, especially conductors and instrumental soloists, are required to remember huge quantities of classical music, and can usually do so without too much difficulty because they have studied it and played it repeatedly.

In Western societies the importance of music as a means of defining and identifying a culture has declined, but it has not disappeared. Particular pieces of music continue to be associated with particular societies, and come to represent them in the same way as a national flag. 'They are playing our tune' is a phrase which can have a much wider significance than our habitual reference of it to the courtship memories of a mated couple. In Britain we never refer to 'God Save the Queen' as 'our tune'; nevertheless it symbolizes the structure of our society and the allegiance which is still expected of us. It is ironic but not inexplicable that in the USA the same tune is used for 'My Country, 'tis of Thee'. To play the hymn 'Abide With Me' at football matches is in dubious taste; but those who join in singing it feel an enhanced sense of joint participation, even if they do not believe the words which they are singing, or subscribe to the Christian beliefs which the hymn expresses.

It is not surprising that Church leaders have doubted whether the feelings which music arouses are genuinely religious. Music's power to fan the flame of piety may be more apparent than real; more concerned with enhancing group feeling within the congregation than with promoting the individual's relation with God. St Augustine reveals that he was so entranced by the pleasures of sound that he feared that his intellect was sometimes paralysed by the gratification of his senses. On the other hand, the beauty of music could also aid the recovery of faith.

So I waver between the danger that lies in gratifying the sense and the benefits which, as I know, can accrue from singing. Without committing myself to an irrevocable opinion, I am inclined to approve of the custom of singing in church, in order that by indulging the ears weaker spirits may be inspired with feelings of devotion. Yet when I find the singing itself more moving than the truth which it conveys, I confess that this is a grievous sin, and at those times I would prefer not to hear the singer.[44]

It will never be possible to establish the origins of human music with any certainty; however, it seems probable that music developed from the prosodic exchanges between mother and infant which foster the bond between them. From this, it became a form of communication between adult human beings. As the capacity for speech and conceptual thought developed, music became less important as a way of conveying information, but retained its significance as a way of communicating feelings and cementing bonds between individuals, especially in group situations. Today, we are so accustomed to considering the response of the individual to music that we are liable to forget that, for most of its history, music has been predominantly a group activity. Music began by serving communal purposes, of which religious ritual and warfare are two examples. It has continued to be used as an accompaniment to collective activities; as an adjunct to social ceremonies and public occasions. We share these functions of music with pre-literate cultures. In our society, one cannot imagine a Coronation or a State funeral taking place in the absence of music. We know less than we would like about what musical activities went on in the past in private houses; but it is important to recall that the modern concert, in which instrumental music is performed in a public concert hall as a separate entity unaccompanied by voices and in the absence of any ceremony, was not a prominent feature of musical life in England until the late seventeenth century. Since then, music as a distinct form in its own right has continued to grow in importance. During the same period, the performer has become more sharply differentiated from the listener. The individual listener's response to music is a principal theme of this book.

CHAPTER II

MUSIC, BRAIN AND BODY

Human attitudes and specifically human ways of
thinking about the world are the results of dance
and song.

JOHN BLACKING[1]

Music brings about similar physical responses in different people at
the same time. This is why it is able to draw groups together and
create a sense of unity. It does not matter that a dirge or funeral
march may be appreciated in a different way by a musician and by
an unsophisticated listener. They will certainly be sharing some
aspects of the same physical experience at the same moment, as well
as sharing the emotions aroused by the funeral itself. Music has the
effect of intensifying or underlining the emotion which a particular
event calls forth, by simultaneously co-ordinating the emotions of a
group of people.

It must be emphasized that making music is an activity which is
rooted in the body. Blacking believes that 'feeling with the body' is
as close as anyone can get to resonating with another person.

Many, if not all, of music's essential processes can be found in the
constitution of the human body and in patterns of interaction of
bodies in society . . . When I lived with the Venda, I began to
understand how music can become an intricate part of the development of mind, body, and harmonious social relationships.[2]

It is generally agreed that music causes increased *arousal* in those
who are interested in it and who therefore listen to it with some
degree of concentration. By arousal, I mean a condition of
heightened alertness, awareness, interest, and excitement: a gen-

24

erally enhanced state of being. This is at its minimum in sleep and at its maximum when human beings are experiencing powerful emotions like intense grief, rage, or sexual excitement. Extreme states of arousal are usually felt as painful or unpleasant; but milder degrees of arousal are eagerly sought as life-enhancing. We all crave some degree of excitement in our lives; and if stimuli from the environment are lacking, we seek them out if we are free to do so. Not all music is designed to cause arousal. Satie wrote music designed only to provide a comforting background. This has been succeeded by the kind of 'wallpaper' music played in elevators, which soothes some people and provokes fury in others. However, this is an exception and not the kind of listening being discussed at this point. Lullabies may send children to sleep; but we listen to Chopin's *Berceuse* or the *Wiegenlieder* of Brahms and Schubert with rapt attention.

Arousal manifests itself in various physiological changes, many of which can be measured. The electro-encephalogram shows changes in the amplitude and frequency of the brain waves which it records. During arousal, the electrical resistance of the skin is diminished; the pupil of the eye dilates; the respiratory rate may become either faster or slower, or else become irregular. Blood-pressure tends to rise, as does the heart rate. There is an increase in muscular tone, which may be accompanied by physical restlessness. In general, the changes are those which one would expect in an animal preparing for action; whether it be flight, fight, or mating. They are the same changes recorded by the polygraph or 'lie detector' which demonstrates arousal in the form of anxiety, but which, contrary to popular belief, cannot prove guilt or innocence.

Recordings of muscle 'action potentials' on another instrument, the electro-myograph, show marked increases in electrical activity in the leg muscles whilst listening to music, even when the subject has been told not to move. In the concert hall, the physical restlessness induced by arousal is often insufficiently controlled. Some people feel impelled to beat time with their feet or drum with their fingers, thereby disturbing other listeners. There are tracings recording the increase in Herbert von Karajan's pulse-rate while conducting Beethoven's Overture, *Leonora* No. 3. Interestingly, his pulse-rate showed the greatest increase during those passages which most moved him emotionally, and not during those in which he was making the greatest physical effort. It is also worth noting that recordings of his pulse-rate whilst piloting and landing a jet aircraft showed much smaller fluctuations than when he was conducting.[3] Music is said to soothe the savage breast, but it may also powerfully excite it.

What seems certain is that there is a closer relation between *hearing* and emotional arousal than there is between *seeing* and emotional arousal. Why else would the makers of moving pictures insist on using music? We are so used to hearing music throughout a film that a short period of silence has a shock effect; and movie-makers sometimes use silence as a precursor to some particularly horrific incident. But a love scene in a film is almost inconceivable without music. Even in the days of silent films a pianist had to be hired to intensify and bring out the emotional significance of the different episodes. A friend of mine, visiting the Grand Canyon for the first time, found himself disappointed at his lack of response to this awesome sight. After a while, he realized that he had seen the Grand Canyon many times on the cinema screen and never without music. Because his sight of the real thing lacked such musical accompaniment, his arousal level was less intense than it had been in the cinema.

Seeing a wounded animal or suffering person who is silent may produce little emotional response in the observer. But once they start to scream, the onlooker is usually powerfully moved. At an emotional level, there is something 'deeper' about hearing than seeing; and something about hearing other people which fosters human relationships even more than seeing them. Hence, people who become profoundly deaf often seem to be even more cut off from others than those who are blind. Certainly, they are more likely to become suspicious of their nearest and dearest. Deafness, more than blindness, is apt to provoke paranoid delusions of being disparaged, deceived, and cheated.

Why is hearing so deeply associated with emotion and with our relationship with our fellow human beings? Is there any connection with the fact that, at the beginning of life, we can hear before we can see? Our first experience of hearing takes place in the womb, long before we leap into the dangerous world and begin to look at it.

David Burrows, who teaches music at New York University, writes:

> An unborn child may startle in the womb at the sound of a door slamming shut. The rich warm cacophony of the womb has been recorded: the mother's heartbeat and breathing are among the earliest indications babies have of the existence of a world beyond their own skin.[4]

A dark world is frightening. Nightmares and infantile fears coalesce with rational anxieties when we come home at night through unlit streets. But a silent world is even more terrifying. Is no one there, nothing going on at all? We seldom experience total silence, except in the artificial conditions of those special rooms in psychological laboratories in which darkness is combined with sound-proofing to exclude input to our senses as completely as possible. As Burrows points out, we are dependent on background sound of which we are hardly conscious for our sense of life continuing. A silent world is a dead world. If 'earliest' and 'deepest' are in fact related, as psychoanalysts have tended to assume, the priority of hearing in the emotional hierarchy is not entirely surprising; but I think it unlikely that this is the whole explanation.

The details of the physiological responses outlined above need not detain us. We have all experienced them, and we are all aware that the condition of arousal can be exciting or distressing according to its intensity. The important point to recognize in this context is that, with a few exceptions, the physical state of arousal accompanying different emotional states is remarkably similar. Sexual arousal and aggressive arousal have in common fourteen physiological changes. The Kinsey team found that there were only four respects in which the physiology of anger differed from the physiology of sex. Although there are rather more physiological differences between the state of fear and the states of anger and sexual arousal, fear still shares nine of the same items of physiological change with the other two, including increase in pulse-rate, increase in blood-pressure, and increase in muscular tension.[5]

It is easy to appreciate that we enjoy becoming sexually aroused; less easy to acknowledge that we like being frightened, and still less easy to accept that we may welcome the excitement of being angry. But many people enjoy the fear induced by ghost stories or horror films; and some will admit that 'justified' wrath against an enemy is exhilarating. The fact is that human beings are so constituted that they crave arousal just as much as they crave its opposite, sleep. Whilst we may deliberately and reasonably affirm that we want our morning newspaper to contain no accounts of disasters, there is no doubt that tragedy is stimulating, as the proprietors of the tabloids know only too well.

One of Freud's cardinal errors was to suppose that what human beings most wanted was a state of tranquillity following the discharge of all tensions. He treated powerful emotions as an intrusion, whether they were instigated by stimuli from without or caused by instinctual impulses from within. For Freud, the main function of the central nervous system was to see that the tensions caused by such emotions were discharged, either directly or indirectly, as soon as possible. He called this dominating feature of mental life the Nirvana principle. In Freud's scheme, there is no place for 'stimulus hunger'; that is, for the need which human beings have to seek out emotional and intellectual stimuli when they are placed in a monotonous environment or when they have been in a state of tranquillity for so long that they have become bored.[6]

Freud died in 1939. If he had been alive in the 1950s and 1960s, he would have become aware of research into the effects of shielding human beings from as many incoming stimuli as possible. Although Nirvana-like bliss and relief from tension can sometimes be achieved by exposing people to short periods of voluntary isolation in the sound-proof, light-proof rooms already referred to, longer periods of solitary confinement usually lead to desperate efforts to find something stimulating which will relieve monotony. Human beings suffer from stimulus hunger as well as from stimulus overload; and those who have experienced months or years alone in prison cells find that doing mental arithmetic, recalling or writing poetry, or other mental activities, are absolutely necessary if they are not to sink into apathy or despair.[7]

It seems obvious that one reason why people seek to listen to or to participate in music is because music causes arousal, which may be intense at times, but which is seldom unbearably so. When, in *A la Recherche du temps perdu*, Mme Verdurin protests at her husband's suggestion that the pianist shall play a particular sonata in F sharp on the grounds that it will make her ill, we do not believe her, and Proust did not intend us to do so.

'No, no, no, not my sonata!' she screamed, 'I don't want to be made to cry until I get a cold in the head, and neuralgia all down my face, like last time. Thanks very much, I don't intend to repeat that performance. You're all so very kind and considerate, it's easy to see that none of you will have to stay in bed for a week.'[8]

Every concert goer is familiar with the histrionic member of the audience who demonstrates his or her intense sensibilities by sighing, groaning, or clapping ecstatically; and who then looks around with rolling eyes to make sure that these antics have been noticed.

This is not to deny that music can provoke intense, genuine emotional arousal, from ecstatic happiness to floods of tears. This does not happen with everyone. The unmusical person, as one would expect, is less physiologically aroused than the musical person. Even in people to whom music means a great deal, responses vary with their mood. One would not expect a depressed person to respond to music as vigorously as an elated person; although music has been known to break through the carapace of melancholy and enable the depressed person to regain access to the feelings from which he had been alienated.

There is another aspect of arousal which is relevant to music. There is some measure of agreement about the nature of certain well-known musical works, whether they are jolly, uplifting, humorous, martial, impressive, and so on. No one calls Rossini's overture to *The Barber of Seville* tragic; no one thinks of Beethoven's Fifth Symphony as merely pretty. Roger Brown, one of the world's experts on the development of language in children, has also studied reactions to music. His research has demonstrated that there is widespread consensus between listeners about the emotional content of different pieces of music even when these pieces are unknown to, or not identified by, the different listeners.

That is, whether a piece of music is considered poignant, wistful, elegiac, boisterous, rustic and so on, does *not* depend upon previous knowledge of the piece in question, or upon identifying the context in which it was composed.[9]

But it is simplistic and inaccurate to suppose that the emotions expressed in the music – sadness, joy, or whatever other emotion seems displayed – are necessarily those aroused in the listener. Peter Kivy, author of an influential, award-winning book on music, *The Corded Shell*, repeatedly affirms:

> We must separate entirely the claim that music can arouse emotion in us from the claim that music is sometimes sad or angry or fearful . . . a piece of music might move us (in part) because it is expressive of sadness, but it does not move us by making us sad.[10]

Othello's suicide is profoundly moving; but it does not make us feel suicidal. What moves us is the way in which Shakespeare (and Verdi) made sense out of tragedy by making it part of an artistic whole. As Nietzsche realized, even tragedy is an affirmation of life.

In spite of Roger Brown's demonstration that the general emotional tone of a piece of music will probably be similarly perceived by different listeners, there will always be disputes about specific details when criticism is carried further. This does not imply that one listener is more or less perceptive than the other. Both may have experienced arousal; and both will therefore agree that the music has had a powerful effect upon them. It is natural enough, given the varying backgrounds from which listeners come, and the very different life-experiences to which they have been exposed, that what they read or project into any given piece of music may also be rather different. What is interesting is that there is as much consensus as there appears to be.

The idea that music causes a general state of arousal rather than specific emotions partly explains why it has been used to accompany such a wide variety of human activities, including marching, serenading, worship, marriages, funerals, and manual work. Music structures time. By imposing order, music ensures that the emotions aroused by a particular event peak at the same moment. It does not matter that the kind of emotions excited in different individuals may vary. What matters is the general state of arousal and its simultaneity. Because of its capacity to intensify crowd feeling, music has a power akin to that of the orator.

Ellen Dissanayake, in the paper from which I quoted in the last chapter, believes that the importance of physical movement as a constituent of musical behaviour has been underestimated. She points out that children up to the age of four or five find it difficult to sing without moving their hands and feet. The close relationship between music and bodily movement is not confined to pre-literate societies. The composers Roger Sessions and Stravinsky have both stressed the connection with the body; and Stravinsky not only composed superb music for ballet, but also insisted that instrumentalists be visually perceived whilst playing. This may be one reason why so many musicians dislike recorded performance. They want to *see* the players' movements as well as hear the sounds they make.

Stravinsky, in old age, asked:

> What is the 'human measure' in music? . . . My 'human measure' is not only possible, but also exact. It is, first of all, absolutely physical, and it is immediate. I am made bodily ill, for example, by sounds electronically spayed for overtone removal. To me they are a castration threat.[11]

There can be no doubt that seeing the movements which musicians make during live performance is, for many people, an important reason for going to concerts as opposed to listening to music at home on radio or disc. Some of the greatest conductors, like Richard Strauss and Pierre Monteux, kept their physical movements to a minimum; others are more flamboyant. But some listeners confess that their appreciation of a particular work is increased by observing the gestures of a conductor.

There is pleasure to be gained from seeing the co-ordinated bowing of the various string sections, just as there is from seeing other examples of group co-ordination, like gymnastic displays. Virtuoso instrumentalists not only play music which is technically inaccessible to the amateur, but also give people the same sort of pleasure which they gain from seeing a great athlete or juggler in action. This may not be directly connected with the appreciation of music itself; but it does underline the physicality of musical performance.

Debussy wrote:

> The attraction of the virtuoso for the public is very like that of the circus for the crowd. There is always a hope that something dangerous may happen.[12]

This view was shared by the violinist Jascha Heifetz who claimed that every critic was eagerly awaiting an occasion on which his impeccable technique would let him down.

Because music affects people physically and also structures time, it is sometimes used when a group of people are performing repetitive physical actions. Some songs are working songs which alleviate boredom and co-ordinate the actions of threshing, pounding, reaping, and the like. It has been suggested that music originated because rhythmically organized work was discovered to be more efficient; but this sounds like a notion derived from a Protestant, capitalist ethic transposed backward in time. Even if Vico was wrong in supposing that dancing preceded walking, dancing probably antedated organized work; and the rhythmic movements of the dance are usually linked with music.

Our modern equivalent to the use of music in co-ordinating agricultural labour is the provision of music in factories. Opinion is divided as to its effects. Judging from its use in agriculture, one might expect that music would improve performance of the routine operations which are common in factory work. Repetitive movements are less tedious when synchronized with musical rhythms. The provision of music is certainly popular amongst factory workers. However, the heightening of morale is not necessarily accompanied by increase in output. Whilst music probably enhances the performance of routine tasks, especially those in which repetitive physical actions prevail, it tends to interfere with the performance of non-repetitive actions which need thinking about. For example, there is evidence suggesting that music increases the number of errors in typing.[13]

The order which music brings to our experience is rhythmic,

melodic and also harmonic. As the great violinist Yehudi Menuhin puts it:

> Music creates order out of chaos; for rhythm imposes unanimity upon the divergent; melody imposes continuity upon the disjointed, and harmony imposes compatibility upon the incongruous.[14]

The effect which music has upon repetitive physical actions is predominantly rhythmic. Rhythm is rooted in the body in a way which does not apply so strikingly to melody and harmony. Breathing, walking, the heartbeat, and sexual intercourse are all rhythmical aspects of our physical being. In some pre-literate cultures rhythm is so highly developed that Western musicians cannot reproduce its complexities. Grosvenor Cooper and Leonard Meyer, who were both professors of Music at the University of Chicago, begin their book *The Rhythmic Structure of Music* by writing:

> To study rhythm is to study all of music. Rhythm both organizes, and is itself organized by, all the elements which create and shape musical processes.[15]

We take for granted the fact that rhythm imposed from outside has an effect upon our own capacity for organizing our own movements. For instance, a military band playing a march orders our strides and also reduces fatigue.

David, a six-year-old autistic boy, suffered from chronic anxiety and poor visual–motor co-ordination. For nine months, efforts had been made to teach him to tie his shoe-laces without avail. However, it was discovered that his *audio-motor* co-ordination was excellent. He could beat quite complex rhythms on a drum, and was clearly musically gifted. When a student therapist put the process of tying his shoe-laces into a song, David succeeded at the second attempt.

> *A song is a form in time.* David had a special relationship to this element and could comprehend the shoe-tying process when it was organized in time through a song.[16]

The effects of music upon patients with neurological diseases causing movement disorders are sometimes astonishing. Some patients can make voluntary movements to the sound of music which they cannot accomplish without it. The disease known as *paralysis agitans*, or Parkinsonism, causes an inability to co-ordinate and control voluntary movement. In his famous book on sufferers from post-encephalitic Parkinsonism, *Awakenings*, the neurologist Oliver Sacks describes a patient who suffered from recurrent 'crises' characterized by intense excitement, uncontrollable movements, forced repetition of words and phrases, and other symptoms. Dr Sacks writes:

> By far the best treatment of her crises was music, the effects of which were almost uncanny. One minute would see Miss D. compressed, clenched and blocked, or jerking, ticcing and jabbering – like a sort of human bomb; the next, with the sound of music from a wireless or a gramophone, the complete disappearance of all these obstructive-explosive phenomena and their replacement by a blissful ease and flow of movement as Miss D., suddenly freed of her automatisms, smilingly 'conducted' the music, or rose and danced to it.[17]

Dr Sacks later writes of these terrible cases: 'The therapeutic power of music is very remarkable, and may allow an ease of movement otherwise impossible.'[18] One of Dr Sacks's patients who had taught music described herself as 'unmusicked'. When frozen into immobility by the disease, she would remain helplessly unable to move until she was able to recall tunes she had known in her youth. These would suddenly release her ability to move again.

Fortunately, the epidemic disease of *encephalitis lethargica* which caused this type of Parkinsonism has disappeared; and only sporadic cases are now recorded. But Parkinsonism is common in the elderly, and is said to occur in 1 in 200 people over the age of fifty. It is due to loss of cells in the *substantia nigra*; the part of the brain which produces dopamine. This is a chemical neurotransmitter which is involved in the passage of impulses from the brain to the voluntary muscles.

Happily, most of us who listen to music do not do so because we need it as treatment for neurological disease; but the *physical* effects of music are undoubted, and, as we have seen, can be measured in people who are perfectly normal.

Occasionally, music's effect upon the brain can be the opposite of therapeutic. In rare cases, music can provoke an epileptic fit. The neurologist Macdonald Critchley described one patient whose epileptic attacks were exclusively brought on by music. Playing a record of Tchaikovsky's *Valse des Fleurs* caused emotional distress followed by a typical *grand mal*; that is, a major epileptic seizure with convulsive movements, frothing at the lips, and cyanosis.[19] Such attacks are without doubt 'organic'; that is, the result of music as a physical stimulus acting directly on the brain, not secondary to the emotional effects of music. This can be shown by provoking a fit whilst the electro-encephalogram records the electrical activity of the patient's brain.

In most cases of musicogenic epilepsy, the seizures are induced by music played by an orchestra. Less commonly, a single instrument, piano, organ, or the ringing of bells may cause an attack. In very rare instances, even the recall of music can be sufficient provocation. Musicogenic epilepsy raises many unsolved neurological problems which it would be inappropriate to discuss in this context. But this rare phenomenon convincingly demonstrates that music has a direct effect upon the brain.

Music and speech are separately represented in the two hemispheres of the brain. Although there is considerable overlap, as happens with many cerebral functions, language is predominantly processed in the left hemisphere, whilst music is chiefly scanned and appreciated in the right hemisphere. The division of function is not so much between words and music as between logic and emotion. When words are directly linked with emotions, as they are in poetry and song, the right hemisphere is operative. But it is the left hemisphere which deals with the language of conceptual thought. This difference between the hemispheres can be demonstrated in a variety of ways.

It is possible to sedate one hemisphere of the brain whilst leaving the other in a normal state of alertness. If a barbiturate is injected into the left carotid artery, so that the left hemisphere of the brain is sedated, the subject is unable to speak, but can still sing. If the injection is made into the right carotid artery, the person cannot sing, but can speak normally. Stammerers can sometimes sing sentences which they cannot speak; presumably because the stammering pattern is encoded in the left hemisphere, whilst singing is predominantly a right hemispheric activity.

The electrical activity of different parts of the brain can be recorded by means of the electro-encephalogram. It can be demonstrated that, if recordings of speech are played to six-month-old babies, the left hemisphere of the brain will show more electrical activity than the right. But if recordings of music are played, the right hemisphere shows the greater electrical response.

If different melodies are played simultaneously through right and left earphones (so-called 'dichotic listening'), the melody heard through the left earphone will be better recalled than that heard through the right. This is because the left ear has greater representation in the right hemisphere of the brain. The right hemisphere processes the perception of melody more efficiently than the left. If words are similarly presented, the reverse is true since the left hemisphere specializes in processing language.

Patients who have suffered brain damage or disease may lose the ability to understand or make use of language without losing musical competence. The great Soviet neuro-psychologist A. R. Luria studied a composer named Vissarion Shebalin who, following a stroke, suffered from severe sensory aphasia; that is, he was unable to understand the meaning of words. Yet he continued to teach music and composed his fifth symphony which Shostakovich said was brilliant.[20] Luria's famous patient, Zasetsky, whom he studied for many years, received a terrible bullet wound during the Second World War which extensively damaged the left side of his brain. His capacity to use and understand language was at first badly impaired. Amongst many other losses of cerebral function, his spatial perception was grossly distorted and his memory fragmented. Yet he liked music just as much as he had done before he was wounded, and could easily remember the melodies of songs, though not their words.[21]

Howard Gardner reports the case of an American composer who suffered from a form of aphasia which left him with a persistent reading difficulty. But, although he could not understand the meaning of printed words, he had little difficulty with musical notation, and was able to compose music just as well as he could before his aphasia.[22]

The musician portrayed in Oliver Sacks's *The Man Who Mistook His Wife for a Hat* suffered from a brain lesion which, although he could see, made it impossible for him to recognize the essential nature of objects, as the title of the book indicates. Yet his musical abilities were unimpaired: indeed, he could only dress himself, eat a meal, or have a bath, if he did so whilst singing. Music became the only way by which he could structure the external world or find meaning in it.[23] This case might be illuminatingly compared with that of the autistic boy, David, described earlier.

There are very few instances of brain lateralization in other animals, although, interestingly enough, bird-song is one exception. In birds, a functioning left hypoglossal nerve is essential for the production of song.

The development of hemispheric specialization is certainly connected with the development of language as an uniquely human phenomenon. Moreover, language is not only a superior means of communication between human beings, but also an essential tool for understanding and thinking about the world. We do not necessarily think in words. The scanning and sorting of information goes on unconsciously as part of the creative process, and can certainly take place during sleep. There is no reason to confine the use of the term 'thinking' to conscious deliberation. But, if we are to formulate our thoughts, express them, and convey them to our fellows, we must put them into words. Although language appears to be understood by both hemispheres to some extent, formulating thoughts in words, and creating new sentences, are functions of the left hemisphere.

It is worth noting that children with lesions in the right hemisphere may be competent at reading, but poor at communicating their feelings. Their speech is often monotonous and inexpressive, lacking just those emotional/intonational aspects of speech recognized earlier as being important in communication between mothers and infants.

It is probably the case that as a listener to music becomes more sophisticated and therefore more critical, musical perception becomes partly transferred to the left hemisphere. However, when words and music are closely associated, as in the words of songs, it seems that both are lodged together in the right hemisphere as part of a single Gestalt. Since the word order of a song is fixed, the innovative verbal skills which belong in the left hemisphere are not required.

Musical gifts are multiple and not always found together in the same person. There is often a wide discrepancy between musical interest and musical talent. Many of those to whom music is immensely important struggle for years to express themselves as composers or executants without avail. Others who are auditorily gifted, as shown by musical aptitude tests, are not necessarily very interested in music. Teachers of music agree that enthusiasm for music becomes increasingly important for success as a child grows older. Musically gifted children may fail to realize their full potential because their interest in music declines.[24]

It is my impression, and no more than an impression, that this discrepancy between interest and talent is more often encountered in music than in other subjects. For example, those who are not mathematically gifted seldom long to be mathematicians; but musical enthusiasts often confess that their lack of musical talent is their greatest disappointment.

The discrepancy between interest in, and talent for, music may be explicable in terms of hemispheric specialization. We have already observed that critical appreciation of music is partly a function of the left hemisphere. People who score highly on a test of musical aptitude tend to show left hemisphere advantage, regardless of training.[25] Perhaps emotional response to music is chiefly centred in the right hemisphere, whilst executive skills and critical analysis are functions of the left hemisphere. Sloboda quotes the case of a violinist with damage to the left hemisphere who retained some musical abilities whilst suffering impairment of others. A great deal of further research is required to establish the neurological correlates of the varied skills which music requires, but what seems certain is that there is no one centre in the brain which houses them all.

As we pointed out earlier, the language used both by philosophers and scientists is neutral and objective. It eschews the personal, the particular, the emotional, the subjective. No wonder it is principally housed in a separate part of the brain from that concerned with the expressive aspects of music. Whilst it is perfectly possible to study music from a purely objective, intellectual point of view, this approach alone is insufficient.

Any attempt to understand the nature of music must take into account its expressive aspects and the fact that the parts of the brain concerned with the emotional effects of music are distinct from those which have to do with appreciation of its structure. Recordings of blood-pressure, respiration, pulse-rate and other functions controlled by the involuntary, autonomic nervous system taken from the same subject demonstrated that, when he was completely involved with the music there were marked changes in the tracings recording evidence of physiological arousal; when, however, he adopted an analytical, critical attitude, these changes were not apparent.[26]

This is objective confirmation of the art historian Wilhelm Worringer's well-known dichotomy, empathy and abstraction; categories which are just as applicable to music as to the visual arts with which he was primarily concerned.[27] Worringer claimed that modern aesthetics was based upon the behaviour of the contemplating subject. If the subject is to enjoy a work of art, he must absorb himself into it, make himself one with it. But this empathic identification with the work is only one way of approaching it. The other is by way of abstraction. Aesthetic appreciation is also a matter of discovering form and order, which requires detachment from the work. These two attitudes are linked with extraversion and introversion. In individuals, one or other attitude is usually predominant and, when exaggerated, leads to mutual misunderstanding. Empathic identification with a musical work may so emotionally involve the listener that critical judgement becomes impossible. In contrast, an exclusively intellectual, detached approach may make it difficult to appreciate the music's emotional significance. Many disputes both in psychology and in aesthetics arise because each participant claims that whichever attitude he personally adopts is the only valid one.

Although appreciation of a musical work necessarily involves perception of both form and expressive content, it is interesting that the two can be artificially separated. Many years ago, I acted as a 'guinea-pig' for one of my colleagues who was investigating the effects of the drug mescaline. Whilst still under its influence, I listened to music on the radio. The effect was to enhance my emotional responses whilst concurrently abolishing my perception of form. Mescaline made a Mozart string quartet sound as romantic as Tchaikovsky. I was conscious of the throbbing, vibrant quality of the sounds which reached me; of the bite of bow upon string; of a direct appeal to my emotions. In contrast, appreciation of form was greatly impaired. Each time a theme was repeated, it came as a surprise. The themes might be individually entrancing, but their relation with one another had disappeared. All that was left was a series of tunes with no connecting links: a pleasurable experience, but one which also proved disappointing.

My reaction to mescaline convinced me that, in my own case, the part of the brain concerned with emotional responses is different from the part which perceives structure. The evidence suggests that this is true of everyone. The appreciation of music requires both parts, although either may predominate on a particular occasion.

In connection with the perception of form and structure it is worth recalling that the auditory apparatus is itself primarily concerned with symmetry and closely linked with balance. The labyrinth or inner ear contains the complex vestibular organ which orients us to gravity, and provides essential information about the position of our own bodies, by registering acceleration, deceleration, angles of turn et cetera. Such internal feedback is needed if we are to be able to control our own movements and relate them to changes in the environment.

It also makes possible our upright posture. Equilibrium or balance can only be maintained if we are constantly informed about tilts of the body, backward, forward, right or left. A tilt in one direction immediately elicits a compensatory muscular reaction in order to prevent our falling and restore our balance.

From an evolutionary perspective, the vestibular apparatus antedates the auditory system which developed from it. Although the two systems remain functionally separate, the vestibular nerve and the cochlear nerve, which respectively convey information from the vestibular apparatus and the auditory apparatus, run in close parallel.

The auditory system is designed to record the nature and location of vibrations in the air, which we perceive as sounds. Experience tells us which sounds are dangerous or threatening, and which are likely to be harmless. By turning our heads so that the sound in each ear is of equal volume we accurately locate the direction of its origin. Hearing and orientation are closely allied.

We are so accustomed to thinking of sight as the primary sense by which we learn how to find our way around that we are apt to forget that hearing can also be used in this way, as it certainly is by the blind. Repeated visual encounters with a particular area become internalized as a picture which can be recalled at any time and in any place. The tapping sticks of the blind provide an auditory map of the immediate environment based on variations in sound alone which also becomes internalized as a schema.

Anyone who has experienced sea-sickness or who has been drunk knows that impairment of one's sense of balance and equilibrium is extremely unpleasant. In contrast, anything which increases our feeling of being securely balanced and in control of our movements enhances our sense of well-being. Marching soldiers swing their arms symmetrically as they march; and also march better to music. Music can order our muscular system. I believe that it is also able to order our mental contents. A perceptual system originally designed to inform us of spatial relationships by means of imposing symmetry can be incorporated and transformed into a means of structuring our inner world. For example, writers who 'hear' their sentences as if read aloud tend to write better prose than those who merely see them. A writer considering how best to express a particular point may finally exclaim 'I see how to put it.' It is often equally appropriate to say 'I hear how to put it.'

The Greeks of Plato's day considered that the right type of music was a powerful instrument of education which could alter the characters of those who studied it, inclining them toward inner order and harmony. Equally, the wrong type of music could have seriously bad effects. Both Plato and Aristotle shared this view of music, although they did not always agree as to which type of music was beneficial and which harmful. Plato, in *The Republic*, reports Socrates as saying:

And therefore, I said, Glaucon, musical training is a more potent instrument than any other, because rhythm and harmony find their way into the inward places of the soul, on which they mightily fasten, imparting grace, and making the soul of him who is rightly educated graceful, or of him who is ill-educated ungraceful; and also because he who has received this true education of the inner being will most shrewdly perceive omissions or faults in art and nature, and with a true taste, while he praises and rejoices over and receives into his soul the good, and becomes noble and good, he will justly blame and hate the bad, now in the days of his youth, even before he is able to know the reason why; and when reason comes he will recognise and salute the friend with whom his education has made him long familiar.[28]

Plato, who was not averse to strict censorship, wanted to banish from the ideal State styles of music which were sorrowful, plaintive or associated with indolence and drinking. There were only two styles which should be tolerated: one for use in battle or in times of misfortune, when a man's resolve might need boosting; the other to be used in times of peace, when he is either seeking to persuade God or man in moderate fashion, or else himself is yielding to persuasion in an equally balanced way. Such music might be used to represent his prudence and moderation.

These two harmonies I ask you to leave; the strain of necessity and the strain of freedom, the strain of the unfortunate and the strain of the fortunate, the strain of courage, and the strain of temperance; these, I say, leave.[29]

As Glaucon points out, this leaves only the Phrygian and Dorian modes from amongst those in common use. The term 'mode' as employed by the Greeks is difficult to define exactly in modern terms, for it referred both to the scale and also to the type of melody; but the general sense is clear enough.

Aristotle believed that,

men are inclined to be mournful and solemn when they listen to that which is called Mixo-Lydian; but they are in a more relaxed frame of mind when they listen to others, for example the looser modes. A particularly equable feeling, midway between these, is produced, I think, only by the Dorian mode, while the Phrygian puts men into a frenzy of excitement.[30]

Indeed, Aristotle thought Socrates wrong to permit the Phrygian mode to be added to the Dorian, because he believed it to be too orgiastic and emotional. For educational purposes, he recommended the Lydian mode because of its power to combine orderliness with educative influence.

The Phrygian mode, according to the great classical scholar E. R. Dodds, was used both in the Dionysiac rituals of the Archaic Age and later in the Corybantic rituals of the fifth century BC. Both seemed to have been based upon the notion of 'catharsis': that is, upon the idea that individuals could be purged of irrational impulses or cured of madness if they temporarily lost all inhibitions and 'let go' in an ecstatic fashion.[31]

Plato was conservative as well as severe. Socrates says that it was necessary that

> music and gymnastic be preserved in their original form, and no innovation made . . . for any musical innovation is full of danger to the whole State, and ought to be prohibited. So Damon tells me, and I can quite believe him – he says that when modes of music change, the fundamental laws of the State always change with them.[32]

We may not share the Greek view that particular modes have different effects upon listeners. But we recognize that some composers habitually select certain keys when they want to express particular emotions. It is generally agreed that Mozart used G minor to express tragedy or melancholy; for example, the Piano Quartet K. 478, the String Quintet K. 516, the Symphonies K. 183 and K. 550. Perhaps the Greek idea of linking certain modes with particular emotions is not so far from our own perceptions as at first appears.

Plato anticipated, or perhaps invented, the notion of *mens sana in corpore sano* which became the supposed aim of English public school education. What was needed was a proper balance between the physical and mental. He believed that those who simply pursued athletics became violent and uncivilized, whilst those who only exposed themselves to music became soft and feeble. Plato suggested that there are two principles of human nature, the spirited and the philosophical, which are served by gymnastics and music respectively.

> And he who mingles music with gymnastic in the fairest proportions, and best attempers them to the soul, may be rightly called the true musician and harmonist in a far higher sense than the tuner of the strings.[33]

Centuries later, the historian Edward Gibbon makes use of a similar dichotomy. Indeed, he may have learned it from Plato.

> There are two very natural propensities which we may distinguish in the most virtuous and liberal dispositions, the love of pleasure and the love of action . . . To the love of pleasure we may therefore ascribe most of the agreeable, to the love of action we may attribute most of the useful and respectable qualifications. The character in which both the one and the other should be united and harmonized would seem to constitute the most perfect idea of human nature.[34]

Plato wrote in the *Timaeus*:

> All audible musical sound is given us for the sake of harmony, which has motions akin to the orbits in our soul, and which, as anyone who makes intelligent use of the arts knows, is not to be used, as is commonly thought, to give irrational pleasure, but as a heaven-sent ally in reducing to order and harmony any disharmony in the revolutions within us. Rhythm, again, was given us from the same heavenly source to help us in the same way; for most of us lack measure and grace.[35]

Theon of Smyrna, a Platonist who flourished between AD 115 and 140, left a treatise concerning arithmetic, astronomy, and the theory of musical harmony which he called 'Mathematics useful for reading Plato'.

> The Pythagoreans, whom Plato follows in many respects, call music the harmonization of opposites, the unification of disparate things, and the reconciliation of warring elements . . . Music, as they say, is the basis of agreement among things in nature and of the best government in the universe. As a rule it assumes the guise of

harmony in the universe, of lawful government in a state, and of a sensible way of life in the home. It brings together and unites.[36]

It goes without saying that Plato and Aristotle were two of the most intelligent men who have ever lived. Their view of the physical universe has been superseded by modern scientific discoveries, as has that of Newton. But music and art are in a different category. Unlike science, art is not superseded, and nor are views about its meaning and significance. The great music of the past is great today. Bach's *Mass in B minor* has not been displaced by Beethoven's *Missa Solemnis*. Bartók's quartets have not supplanted those of Beethoven. Modern masterpieces of music enlarge our sensibilities; but they do not surpass or replace those masterpieces which have preceded them. The views of Plato and Aristotle on music and the other arts are not outdated. They are not like theories about the physical world which can be proved or disproved. They are as worthy of critical appraisal today as they were when they were first formulated. Although scientific discovery has displaced the Greek view of the universe, the Greek perception of music may have been nearer the truth than our own.

Music is so freely available today that we take it for granted and may underestimate its power for good or ill. The idea that some modes should be forbidden and others encouraged may make us smile. In Britain, we cannot imagine our rulers banning a scale or key, partly because we would think this an unwarranted interference with personal liberty, but also because, as I suggested in the introduction, music is seldom taken seriously by politicians and educationalists who are not themselves musicians. This is not always the case elsewhere. Allan Bloom's well-known attack on American education, *The Closing of the American Mind*, contains a chapter on music in which the author expresses considerable anxiety about the effect which rock music has upon students. Bloom recognizes that great music is powerfully educative, and fears that rock has banished any interest in, or feeling of need for, any other kind of music.

In Stalin's Russia, contemporary European music, including jazz, was virtually banned, and Russian composers were subjected to many restrictions and a flood of instructions. Shostakovich's opera *The Lady Macbeth of Mtsensk* was banned in 1936, and the composer wisely withheld a number of other works which he feared would not conform to the dictates of 'socialist realism'. Although such censorship is deplorable, it does imply some recognition of the power and importance of music in the lives of ordinary people.

The power of music, especially when combined with other emotive events, can be terrifyingly impressive. At the Nuremberg rally of 1936, the thunderous cheers of the vast crowd eventually drowned the music of the massed bands which played Hitler in. But the bands were there long before Hitler appeared, preceding his rhetoric with their rhetoric, preparing the huge gathering for Hitler's appearance, binding them together, arousing their expectations, aiding and abetting Hitler's self-dramatization, making it credible that a *petit bourgeois* failure had turned himself into a Messiah. The Greeks were right in supposing that music can be used for evil ends as well as for good. There can be no doubt that, by heightening crowd emotions and by ensuring that those emotions peak together rather than separately, music can powerfully contribute to the loss of critical judgement, the blind surrender to the feelings of the moment, which is so dangerously characteristic of crowd behaviour.

Rousseau would not have been surprised by Hitler's oratorical style, which accords with his ideas about the development of speech. It is interesting that at the Nuremberg rally, as on many other occasions, Hitler's speech was not intended to convey information but took on the quality of an incantation or chant. Hitler's voice was harsh and unmusical, but he used language in the way it is used in religious ritual. As the historian and German scholar J. P. Stern points out in his perceptive account of this Nuremberg rally, Hitler used a declamatory style superimposed upon near quotations from biblical texts.

> How deeply we feel once more in this hour the miracle that has brought us together! Once you heard the voice of a man, and it spoke to your hearts, it awakened you, and you followed that voice. Year in year out you followed it, without even having seen the speaker; you only heard a voice and followed it.

Now that we meet here, we are all filled with the wonder of this gathering. Not every one of you can see me and I do not see each one of you. But I feel you, and you feel me! It is faith in our nation that has made us little people great, that has made us poor people rich, that has made us wavering, fearful, timid people brave and confident; that has made us erring wanderers clear-sighted and has brought us together!

So you have come this day from your little villages, your market towns, your cities, from mines and factories, or leaving the plough, to this city. You come out of the little world of your daily struggle for life, and of your struggle for Germany and for our nation to experience this feeling for once: Now we are together, we are with him and he is with us, and now we are Germany![37]

Considered intellectually, this speech is rubbish. Considered emotionally, its effect was overwhelming. Hitler was using words to reinforce the effect which the music, the banners, the search-lights, and the processions had already induced. He was both arousing his audience and making them experience the same, or closely similar emotions, simultaneously. Over and over again, Hitler stressed the feeling of unity: unity with him, unity with each other. The language which Hitler used is not the conceptual language which is used for abstract thought or exchange of information. It is rhetoric of a hypnotic persuasiveness, exploiting the basic human need to belong; to feel part of a social group; to be united with one's fellow countrymen. In spite of his harsh voice and his vulgar turns of speech, Hitler's incantatory style affected crowds in rather the same way as can some music. It looks as if Rousseau was right when, in the passage already quoted from Maurice Cranston's biography, he affirmed that 'Earliest lang-uages . . . were chanted; they were melodic and poetic rather than prosaic and practical.'[38]

Hitler's adoration of Wagner's music began early in his life and persisted until his own *Götterdämmerung*-like finale. If he became depressed his friend and financial backer Hanfstaengl, who was also a pianist, would play some Wagner for him and he would respond 'as to an energizing drug'.[39] It is interesting that Hitler's favourite composer is the one most generally recognized to be able to overwhelm people emotionally, for this is what Hitler did with his speeches. There must be people still living who heard Hitler speak who look back upon their emotional response to his oratory with horror. I guess that only an exceptionally detached, independent-minded intellectual could have attended events like the Nuremberg rallies without being temporarily swept off his feet.

Today, we are beginning to understand some of the physiological mechanisms by means of which music affects us. But the human brain is immensely complex and our knowledge of how music impinges upon it is incomplete and elementary. We know that how the brain develops is partly determined by the external stimuli to which it is exposed. It would not surprise me to learn that exposure to music with a reasonably complicated structure facilitates the establishment of neural networks which improve cerebral function. This has not yet been demonstrated; but we can affirm with confidence that Plato and Aristotle were right. Music is a powerful instrument of education which can be used for good or ill, and we should ensure that everyone in our society is given the opportunity of participating in a wide range of different kinds of music.

CHAPTER III

BASIC PATTERNS

The Musical Scale is not one, not 'natural', nor even founded necessarily on the laws of the constitution of musical sound so beautifully worked out by Helmholtz, but very diverse, very artificial, and very capricious.

ALEXANDER J. ELLIS[1]

In the first chapter, it was suggested that music is an art deeply rooted in human nature but not closely connected with the external world. As a consequence, different cultures create different musics, just as they create different languages. Although an ethnomusicologist may painstakingly learn to understand and appreciate the music of another culture, it is probably more difficult to do this than thoroughly to master a foreign language. Even within Europe, we cannot be sure that we appreciate music of a few centuries ago in the way that a contemporary listener apprehended it or that the composer intended it.

As our concert programmes demonstrate, the majority of Western listeners appreciate only a narrow range of music, perhaps from the middle of the seventeenth century to the middle of the twentieth century. To promote a concert consisting only of contemporary art music is usually to court financial disaster. Music composed before the seventeenth century has gained considerable popularity in the last fifty years, but remains a specialist taste. Although these limitations may be deplorable, one can hardly blame the ordinary listener for being so unadventurous. So much good music was composed during those three hundred years that there is a virtually inexhaustible treasure trove for the conventionally-minded listener to explore.

J. S. Bach is said to have composed five annual cycles of cantatas for every Sunday and feast day; that is, about 300 in all. Some two-fifths of them have disappeared, but 199 survive. In addition, there are a considerable number of secular cantatas. Although Bach's popularity has continued to grow since Mendelssohn's famous performance of the *St Matthew Passion* in 1829 began his rehabilitation, there can be very few enthusiasts who know all the sacred cantatas intimately. These cantatas alone might be thought a life's work for any composer; but, as every listener knows, this is only one aspect of Bach's achievement. There are the works for solo keyboard, keyboard concertos, orchestral suites and concertos, organ music, the *Mass in B minor*, the great Passions – the list is almost endless. Many scholars have devoted their lives to studying the works of this one composer.

The same considerations apply to Haydn. Hans Keller tells us that 45 of Haydn's string quartets are masterpieces,[2] and there are many more which are certainly worth hearing. There are 104 symphonies, over 30 piano trios, and a mountain of other music of the highest quality. No one, with the possible exception of H. C. Robbins Landon, knows it all.

Mozart, had he lived as long as Haydn, might have left as much music behind him. As it is, there is such a quantity that very few scholars could claim familiarity with everything which Mozart composed. Why venture into unknown territory when so much that is nearer home remains unmapped?

I am not defending the musical conservatism of the average listener, but simply attempting to explain it. Appreciating music other than that with which one has been familiar from childhood is more difficult and more demanding than many professional musicians admit.

Although music is sometimes referred to as a universal language, this is an entirely misleading description. The difficulty of appreciating music from different periods of history or from different cultures is a powerful argument in favour of the view that the various types of music are predominantly cultural artefacts rather than based on natural phenomena. It is true that the present dominance of Western culture has led to Chinese, Japanese, and Korean performers becoming expert in the music of the West; but how many Western musicians can perform Chinese, Japanese, or Korean music or even claim to understand such music as listeners?

I wish music could become a universal language, as the composer Percy Grainger hoped. Musical education which includes music from other cultures can do something to break down our insularity. John Blacking, who admits that it took him years to understand the music of the Venda, nevertheless ends his book 'A Commonsense View of All Music' by writing:

> Grainger's 'universalist outlook' on music and his idea of music as a universal language of the future are possible because human beings have the mental equipment to feel beyond the cultural trappings of the different worlds of music to the common humanity which inspired the music. Thus music can become a universal language when individuals are acquainted with all forms of artistic musical expression, and through the transformation of individuals it becomes a 'vehicle for world peace and the unification of mankind'. [3]

This seems to me to be a Utopian phantasy which can never be realized. It is difficult enough for anyone to claim understanding of the huge range of different varieties of music available in his own culture, let alone appreciate all forms of artistic musical expression. Blacking, as those who knew him realize, was possessed by that archetypal vision of universal brotherly love which has inspired so many political movements, but which, so far, has always failed. His experience with the Venda convinced him that Western individualistic society was one based on alienation rather than upon co-operation.

But we must return to the question of whether there are musical universals. If music is species-specific, there must be some shared human basis for its creation, just as there is for language. It is the level of this mutuality which is in question, and, more particularly, whether music is a human artefact or whether, as some claim, its roots lie deeper than language and are derivatives of the natural world.

I shall argue that music originates from the human brain rather than from the natural world. Since a number of very distinguished musicians think otherwise, I have had to use a few technical terms and arguments to support my case. The reader who finds these tiresome can skip to the conclusion at the end of the chapter.

A number of eminent writers on music, including Leonard Bernstein, Heinrich Schenker, Paul Hindemith, and Deryck Cooke, have not only affirmed that there are musical universals, but have gone much further in asserting that the Western tonal system, based on the diatonic* scale and the major triad, is directly derived from acoustic principles which can be mathematically demonstrated and which are not man-made. The sources of these principles are alleged to be the discoveries of Pythagoras and the natural harmonic series. This claim that a particular Western musical system, which was only predominant for less than three centuries, is based on universals is both insular and questionable.

The octave is the first interval to be defined in any musical system. When a bass voice sings c below middle c', a tenor sings middle c', and a soprano sings c'' above middle c', they are recognizably singing 'the same note' although the three pitches are widely separated. In fact, the frequencies of the three Cs are mathematically related by simply doubling the frequency in each case: the ratio being 2:1. This acoustic fact is said to have been discovered by Pythagoras in the sixth century BC, who found that, if a stretched string was 'stopped' at its mid-point and the half string then plucked, the note sounded would be one octave above that sounded by the unstopped string vibrating as a whole. The Pythagorean principle that the octave essentially comprised within itself all sounds used in music so far as their musical relations were concerned became established.

The octave is an acoustic fact, expressible mathematically, which is not created by man. The composition of music requires that the octave be taken as the most basic relationship, 'the same note' referred to above. It is when subdivisions of the octave are undertaken that we begin to stray both from mathematics and from nature.

Pythagoras then divided the string into three. Plucking two-thirds of the string gives the fifth: ratio 3:2. The fifth was the first

*The basic scale of Western art music. The word 'diatonic' means 'at intervals of a tone'.

subdivision of the octave to be established as a fixed interval. Dividing the string into four equal parts gives the fourth: ratio 4:3.

Hindemith points out that the octave is produced with so little difficulty that untrained voices sing it believing that they are singing in unison. He goes on to say that the fifth and fourth are the intervals most easily and naturally produced by the singing voice.

It was further discovered that the degree of difficulty in singing an interval is in direct proportion to its numerical ratio, in the sense that the more easily an interval is produced, the smaller are the numbers in the ratio that produces it.[4]

As William Pole wrote:

These three intervals, as settled by Pythagoras, have been ever since the most important intervals in music.[5]

Helmholtz alleged that unpractised singers who find that a particular piece does not fit the compass of their voice often take the fifth instinctively. Dr Pole claimed to have heard a strolling party of singers performing in this way in London at Christmas 1885. Whilst a male baritone sang the melody of 'When shepherds watched their flocks by night' in approximately the key of G, a woman and three children accompanied him singing a fifth above. It appears convincing to claim that the fifth is a 'natural' division of the octave.

The fifth reckoned upward from c' is the same note as the fourth reckoned downward from c'' and vice versa. An octave is composed of a fifth plus a fourth. So far, the division of the octave seems rooted in mathematical fact rather than appearing to be a human construct, even though the division is irregular. The perfect fifth and fourth are found in many different scales. Since these divisions of the octave are directly derived from the acoustic ratios of the fourth and fifth discovered by Pythagoras, the claim that the origin of our diatonic major scale is both ancient and also rooted in a natural phenomenon appears to deserve support.

However, the complete diatonic major scale is notably different from the scale as constructed mathematically. Dr Pole wrote:

The diatonic scale is a conventional and artificial series of notes, and not, as many people suppose, one dictated by any imperative natural, physical, or physiological laws. If it had been so it might have been expected to be perfect, whereas it is essentially imperfect by its very nature and construction.[6]

Moreover, such relation as the major diatonic scale has with the Pythagorean division is not shared by the various forms of diatonic minor scale, natural minor, harmonic minor and melodic minor, which have been passed down to us and which, at this point, need not be further differentiated.

In reality, all scales are arbitrary inventions governed by the necessity of defining musical relations within the octave. The adoption of equal temperament tuning in which the octave is artificially divided into twelve equal semitones has distanced Western tonal music still further from nature. This system of tuning was invented by Marin Mersenne in 1636, but took about two centuries to come into general use. The result is that, because the intervals between semitones have been equalized, the relationship to the Pythagorean scale and therefore to mathematically accurate ratios has been destroyed. Our ears have become accustomed to a scale which bears little relationship to nature. The claim that the diatonic scale is derived from natural law cannot be sustained.

Equal temperament also diminished the individual qualities of the different keys which were perceived by mediaeval musicians. As Busoni pointed out,

We teach four-and-twenty keys, twelve times the two Series of Seven; but, in point of fact, we have at our command only two, the major key and the minor key. *The rest are merely transpositions* . . . But when we recognize that major and minor form one Whole with a double meaning, and that the 'four-and-twenty keys' are simply an elevenfold transposition of the original twain, we arrive unconstrainedly at a perception of the UNITY *of our system of keys* [tonality]. The conceptions of 'related' and 'foreign' keys vanish, and with them the entire intricate theory of degrees and relations. *We possess one single key.* But it is of most meagre sort.[7]

Scales are highly artificial, and the laws of acoustics may be quite unconnected with their construction. The number of possible scales is incalculable: provided that a scale forms a basis for viable music, there is no reason to claim that any one scale, like our diatonic scale, is superior. As Dr Pole wrote:

> Many people, and among them some thoughtful musicians, are disposed to believe that the succession of notes in our present diatonic scale is suggested directly by the laws of nature. It comes natural to them to sing the scale, and they imagine that this is the result of some *natural instinct* which prompts them to adopt this exact succession of notes as peculiarly pleasing and satisfactory to the ear.
>
> This, however, is entirely a delusion. The impulse to sing the scale only arises from education and habit; it has been impressed upon us ever since we began to learn music, and everything we have heard or performed in our lives has conduced to keep up the idea.[8]

Many varieties of scale have been used in different parts of the world and at different periods of history. A pentatonic scale, which only uses five notes within the octave (for example, the black notes of the piano) is the basic scale of music in many non-Western cultures throughout the world, as well as being the basis of Celtic folk music. The whole-tone scale, used extensively by Debussy, consists of six notes within the octave, each a tone apart from the next. Hindu music uses scales in which the octave is divided into intervals less than a semitone. Javanese music uses two different systems: *slendro*, which divides the octave into five nearly equal intervals, and *pelog*, which divides the octave into seven, using a mixture of small and large intervals.

The diatonic scale is one pillar of the Western tonal system; the major triad is the other. When in the key of C major, the major triad consists of C, E, and G: the tonic, third and fifth. For the majority of Western listeners, the major triad constitutes 'home'. It is the place from which we depart and to which we return in a piece of classical music.

> A tonal work must begin by implying the central position of the tonic, and it must end with it; therefore everything that follows the opening and precedes the final tonic may be conceived as dissonant in relation to the tonic triad, the only perfect consonance.[9]

However, it was not until the sixteenth century that the final chord of a composition commonly included the third.

The third was certainly not included when polyphony first began. Parallel *organum* consisted of two or four voices. The *vox principalis* chanted the melody; the *vox organalis* moved for the most part in parallel fourths with the melody, although the fifth and the octave were also employed. This is a natural enough development from monophony; partly because the Pythagorean fourth and fifth were recognized as pure intervals depending upon simple ratios, and partly because the normal ranges of the bass, tenor, alto and soprano voices are roughly a fourth or fifth apart. In early mediaeval times, the fourth, fifth, and octave were regarded as the only intervals which were fully concordant or 'perfect'. Other intervals might be used; but only as intermediate or contrasting steps on the way 'home' to a perfect concord, *which was not the major triad of later diatonic music.*

As Charles Rosen writes:

A dissonance is any musical sound that must be resolved, i.e. followed by a consonance: a consonance is a musical sound that needs no resolution, that can act as the final note, that rounds off a cadence. Which sounds are to be consonances is determined at a given historical moment by the prevailing musical style, and consonances have varied radically according to the musical system developed in each culture. Thirds and sixths have been consonances since the fourteenth century; before that they were considered unequivocally dissonant. Fourths, on the other hand, used to be as consonant as fifths: in music from the Renaissance until the twentieth century, they are dissonances. By the fifteenth century, fourths had become an object of theoretical distress: the harmonic system – defined above all by the relation of consonance to dissonance – was changing, and the ancient, traditional classification of fourths as consonances could no longer be maintained. It is not, therefore the human ear or nervous system that decides what is a dissonance, unless we are to assume a physiological change between the thirteenth and fifteenth century. [10]

And Stravinsky affirms:

The superannuated system of classical tonality, which has served as the basis for musical construction of compelling interest, has had the authority of law among musicians for only a short period of time – a period much shorter than is usually imagined, extending only from the middle of the seventeenth century to the middle of the nineteenth.[11]

These considerations refute the supposition that the diatonic scale of Western tonal music has anything to do with universals, and also go some way to explaining why it is that the preferences of the majority of concert-goers seem so restricted.

Various other attempts have been made to claim that Western tonality is founded on a law of nature and is therefore a kind of universal. This is primarily based on a supposed correspondence between the tonal system and the natural 'harmonic series'. For example, Deryck Cooke writes:

> Let us be content to say that it is most unlikely that the close correspondences between the natural harmonic system and the tonal system can be pure coincidence.[12]

Leonard Bernstein, at the end of his Charles Eliot Norton lectures, given at Harvard in 1973, professes faith in the tonal system in the following incantatory phrases.

> I believe that from that Earth emerges a musical poetry which is by the nature of its sources tonal.
> I believe that these sources cause to exist a phonology of music, which evolves from the universal known as the harmonic series.
> And that there is an equally universal musical syntax, which can be codified and structured in terms of symmetry and repetition.[13]

Both distinguished musicians are claiming a special fundamental significance for the Western tonal system, on the grounds that it is rooted in a natural order of things, the harmonic series. How far is this claim actually justified?

The harmonic series itself is certainly a universal, since it is based on invariant acoustic phenomena which can be mathematically described and measured. What exactly is it?

Most people know that when a string is plucked, or when a column of air is made to vibrate, the note thus produced is not a single, pure tone, but is accompanied by 'overtones' or 'harmonics'. For example, using a standard pitch which defines middle c' as 256 vibrations per second, if the note C below the bass staff (C, 64Hz, the fundamental, conventionally numbered 1) is struck when the dampers are lifted, a series of strings above this fundamental note will vibrate in sympathy. The first to do so is the octave (c below middle c', 128Hz, No. 2). The next is the fifth (G below middle c', 192Hz, No. 3). The next note above is again the octave (middle c', 256Hz, No. 4); and the next above that is the third (E above middle c', 320Hz, No. 5). Following this the fifth again vibrates (G above middle c', 384Hz, No. 6).

The next harmonic above this cannot be represented in conventional notation (448Hz, No. 7), or heard as a vibrating piano string, since it is intermediate between the B flat and A above middle c'. The series is infinite; but, in practice, the higher ranges cannot be identified by the unaided ear, although they can be detected by suitable resonators. Indeed, when the low C on the piano is struck, it is difficult to hear any harmonic above No. 5; the E above middle c'.

The reason that these harmonics sound is that when the C string is struck by the hammer it not only vibrates as a whole, but also vibrates as two halves, as thirds, as quarters, and so on. It is the rising series of notes thus produced which constitutes the harmonic series.

Instruments vary in the number of harmonics they produce. In general, tones with few accompanying harmonics, like those produced by a tuning-fork, are rather dull and monotonous. Instruments with reeds, like the oboe, produce many overtones; and it is this series of overtones which causes the particular timbre of the instrument. Altering the shape of a wind instrument, or modifying the way in which the sound is produced, alters the way in which overtones are enhanced or suppressed, and so changes the timbre of the instrument.

The conical tubes of the oboe and bassoon emphasize one set of harmonics, whilst the cylindrical tube of the clarinet strengthens others. The single reed in the clarinet mouthpiece and the contrasting double reeds of the oboe and bassoon produce similar changes of emphasis. Harmonics are a vital part of our experience of music.

As already indicated, if we take the fundamental note C as 1, harmonic 2 is the octave, harmonic 3 is the fifth, harmonic 4 is the octave, harmonic 5 is the third.

Deryck Cooke's attempt to show that the third in the major triad of Western classical tonality is derived from the harmonic series is doubtful on two counts. First, as we have seen, the triad's importance is confined to a very limited period of Western music. Second, the interval of the major third to which we have become accustomed is sharp compared with the pure third. However, a contemporary musician tells me that

> in certain circumstances it [the 5th harmonic] can force its way into the harmony and persuade us to hear a non-existent major triad. In final (third-less) chords, such as those which end several movements of Mozart's *Requiem*, one sometimes distinctly hears a major third overtone.[14]

The derivation of the major triad from the harmonic series must be regarded as an open question. Cooke admits that not all modern theorists agree with his contention that the harmonic series is the unconscious basis of Western European harmony and the tonal system; but it suits him to make this claim because of his wish to establish the natural supremacy of Western music. Cooke is so convinced of this that he writes:

> Wherever Western European civilization has penetrated another culture, and set the people's thoughts along the road to material happiness, the tonal music of Western Europe has begun to oust the music of that culture from the people's affections.[15]

This may bear witness to the bulldozing effect of Western dominance, which tends to destroy every indigenous aspect of the cultures with which it comes into contact, but it is not a good argument for the superiority of European music. American popular music has swept the world; but few musicians consider it better than the varieties of music which it has displaced.

Bernstein's claims for the harmonic series are still wider, but not by any means convincing. He said, for example, that research demonstrates that children all over the world use the same notes in calling one another: a repetitive, descending minor third, often extended by a fourth in singing games; such as G, E, and A. 'Bye baby bunting' can be represented as G,E,A,G,E. The E above middle c' is the 5th harmonic; the G is the 6th harmonic; but the A, in fact, is the 7th harmonic which, as we have already observed, cannot be represented in conventional notation, which is why Bernstein referred to it as 'sort-of-A'.

Bernstein argued that these three notes are directly derived from the harmonic series, and that they constitute 'a real musico-linguistic universal'.

> Those three universal notes are handed to us by Nature on a silver platter. But why are they in this different order – G, E, and sort-of-A? Because that is the order in which they appear in the harmonic series: G, E, and sort-of-A. Q.E.D.[16]

The next harmonic above the equivocal 7th is again the octave: c'' above middle c': 512Hz, adopting the modern way of indicating frequencies. The 9th harmonic is D, 576Hz. Bernstein points out that, if D is added to the series C, E, G, and sort-of-A, two possible pentatonic scales are created, according to whether sort-of-A is construed as B flat or A.

> Let's opt for the second of these, the lower one, which is by far the more common of the two. This is humanity's favorite pentatonic scale . . . In fact, the universality of this scale is so well-known that I'm sure you could give *me* examples of it, from all corners of the earth . . . now *that* is a true musico-linguistic universal.[17]

Bernstein believed that all mankind possess the musical competence to 'construe those naturally serialized overtones', even though we may not be able consciously to identify them. In his eagerness to find a musical analogy to Chomsky's universal transformational grammar, he stated:

> But the overriding fact that emerges from all this is that *all* music – whether folk, pop, symphonic, modal, tonal, atonal, polytonal, microtonal, well-tempered or ill-tempered, music from the distant

past or the imminent future – all of it has a common origin in the universal phenomenon of the harmonic series. And that is our case for musical monogenesis, to say nothing of innateness.[18]

However, Bernstein did not demonstrate that harmonics are encoded in the central nervous system, or that most people can naturally identify them in their higher ranges. The sheer inaudibility of the higher ranges of the harmonic series without the use of special techniques to demonstrate them makes it unlikely that most people can construe overtones in the way that Bernstein suggested.

Other musicians are dubious about Bernstein's claims. For example, Brian Trowell, Heather Professor of Music at the University of Oxford, accepts that Bernstein's three-note call is a kind of constant in children's singing, but goes on to argue:

It seems most unlikely to me that it could be learned from the overtone series. While these notes are indeed prominent in 'overtone singing' (a kind of forced emphasis of the upper harmonics practised in one or two Eastern cultures), they are not the only overtones used; nor are instruments that use overtones restricted to these harmonics, and they use them discretely, unlike the overtone singers, who (at least the ones I've heard) pass conjunctly up and down the higher harmonics.

If it is learned, it will be from mothers crooning. An untrained voice has a small compass (and a child's compass is smaller still at first). The pitches seem to me the smallest cell of the pentatonic scale, which is I believe universally known, and which fits perfectly into the major sixth which is the natural compass of the untrained voice: CDEGA.[19]

Concerning the children's call, Jeremy Montagu, Curator of the Bate Collection of Historical Instruments in the Faculty of Music at Oxford, writes:

I must say that I'm dubious. For one thing he is fairly high up in the harmonic series, talking of harmonics 6 to 5, and then adding the 7th. This I'm even more dubious about; if he postulates A–G, the seventh harmonic is well above A and is really a slightly flat B flat . . .

By referring to the 7th harmonic as sort-of-A, Bernstein is implying that it is nearer to A than to B flat, which fits in with his choice of the lower of the two possible pentatonic scales ending in B flat or A. Since the scale ending in A is much more commonly found than the one ending in B flat, and is named by Bernstein as a musico-linguistic universal, it suits his purpose to ignore the fact that the 7th harmonic is actually nearer B flat. This looks suspiciously like special pleading.

Montagu continues:

> Bernstein then goes on to add the 9th harmonic to complete his 'universal' pentatonic scale. It's not as universal as he'd like to make out. For one thing, pentatonic scales vary; not all are anhemitonic* by any means. Even those that are anhemitonic are by no means all made up of our whole tones and minor thirds . . . What puzzles me about the influence of Pythagoras etc. is how small a part of the world's population produces music which is recognisably related to the harmonic series. We do in Europe today in our art music (a lot of folk music doesn't), and so they do in India, and that's about it. Even the African areas which use the musical bow (and therefore use harmonics in that music) use different intervals when singing. Even the ancient Greeks used some very odd intervals indeed in their music.[20]

Although there is some evidence that some forms of music are connected with acoustic universals, this is certainly not true of all types of music. Roger Sessions puts it clearly.

> A great deal of musical theory has been formulated by attempting to codify laws governing musical sound and musical rhythm, and from these to deduce musical principles. Sometimes these principles are even deduced from what we know of the physical nature of sound, and as a result are given what seems to me an essentially specious validity. I say 'essentially specious' because while the physical facts are clear enough, there are always gaps, incomplete or unconvincing transitions, left between the realm of physics and the realm of musical experience, even if we leave 'art' out of account . . . Such

---

*Anhemitonic indicates a scale without semitones: either a whole-tone scale, or else one of the pentatonic scales.

speculations have been in many cases the product of brilliant minds, of indisputable musical authority, and I do not wish to minimize this fact. Yet it would be quite easy to point out that each author, in a manner quite consistent with his musical stature, found in the overtone series a tool he could adapt to his individual and peculiar purpose. Above all it seems to me clear that physics and music are different spheres, and that, though they certainly touch at moments, the connection between them is an occasional and circumstantial, not an essential, one.[21]

I think, therefore, that it is right to conclude that there is no one type of music which is more rooted in the nature of things than any other. No one can learn to appreciate all the possible varieties of music which have been invented; but, if we can clear our minds of the belief that the Western tonal system in which most Europeans were raised is superior because it is derived from nature, we may more easily be able to accept other musical systems as equally valid and thus enlarge our musical experience.

This conclusion will disappoint or fail to convince people who want to believe the opposite. Why should it matter that music is not a universal language, or that our Western tonal system has only tenuous links with natural phenomena?

It is understandable that those for whom music is vitally important should want to explain or justify their subjective feeling by finding an objective basis for it in the natural world. The words 'natural' and 'nature' have inescapable associations of 'better' which are widely exploited by advertisers. 'Natural' foods and drinks are all the rage, irrespective of the reality that those who live on them in the Third World die prematurely from diseases directly attributable to what they eat and drink. The life of 'natural' man is 'nasty, brutish and short', as Thomas Hobbes perceived; but we still idealize it.

For those who believe that nature is both fundamental and good, it is gratifying to persuade oneself that the musical system in which one has been brought up and which has provided such rich experience is more closely derived from nature than any other. This is elevating nature to the status of a deity. It is as if a believing Christian not only found a convincing proof of God's existence, but could also point to evidence which demonstrated that the Christian view of God is the only right one. Bernstein's incantatory phrases already quoted sound like the Creed because they are his Creed. 'I believe that from that Earth emerges a musical poetry . . .' From the Earth emerges tetanus and gas gangrene as well as beauty. Bernstein was a religiously inclined romantic as well as a great musician.

As I shall hope to show in later chapters, music can best be understood as a system of relationships between tones, just as language is a system of relationships between words. There are many varieties of music, just as there are many languages. W not need to relate music to some feature of the external world in an effort to demonstrate its fundamental importance. It is not surprising that Bernstein's conversion to Chomsky makes him look for universals which substruct every variety of music; but strange that he chooses the harmonic series.

What we need to consider is not nature, but human nature. Chomsky's examination of language leads him to conclude that the human brain must contain innate structures facilitating language learning, language understanding, and language use. He does not look *outside* the brain to support his theory of a universal grammar. Language does not emanate from the Earth, but from the human brain. So does music. The universality of music depends upon basic characteristics of the human mind; especially upon the need to impose order upon our experience. Different cultures produce different musical systems just as they produce different languages and different political systems. Languages are ways of ordering words; political systems are ways of ordering society; musical systems are ways of ordering sounds. What is universal is the human propensity to create order out of chaos.

CHAPTER IV

SONGS WITHOUT WORDS

> People usually complain that music is so ambiguous, that it leaves them in such doubt as to what they are supposed to think, whereas words can be understood by everyone. But to me it seems exactly the opposite.
>
> FELIX MENDELSSOHN[1]

Today, if I ask a new acquaintance whether he or she is interested in classical music, it will probably be assumed that I am thinking primarily of instrumental music: of symphonies, concertos, chamber music, and sonatas of the kind which fill our concert halls every evening. Music accompanying words, as in opera, oratorio, *lieder*, or church music may also be implied, but will not usually be foremost in the mind. Indeed, even amongst the other varieties of music associated with words, opera continues to be in a special category: one which sometimes rouses enthusiasm in people who are not interested in, or moved by, any of the other kinds of music just listed. We may justly suppose that such people are more interested in drama or in vocal display than in music.

This predominance of instrumental music is a recent phenomenon. As we observed in Chapter Two, the modern concert did not become established until late in music's history. According to Michael Hurd, a building with a specially designed music room, York Buildings in Villiers Street, London, was erected in about 1678. It may well have been the first public concert hall in Europe.[2] It certainly long predated the Holywell Music Room in Oxford, built in 1742–8, and claimed by Nikolaus Pevsner to be the first building in England designed for the sole purpose of musical performance.[3] But the Holywell Music Room is still in use as a concert hall, whilst York Buildings is not.

Early musical instruments were melodic imitators of the human voice; and it took centuries to establish music as a series of sounds unrelated to the voice and detached from any verbal association.

> It was the greatest of all the imaginative flights which music has achieved, and it is now so integral a part of our experience that we cannot easily realize how fundamental was the change. We still enjoy music without instruments, but our forefathers who learnt to appreciate music without voices were the real discoverers, opening up new artistic fields of which we cannot yet gauge the limits.[4]

Charles Rosen claims that the final emancipation of music from verbal association did not become fully established until much later in its history than most people realize.

> Before the middle of the eighteenth century, public music was, with few exceptions, vocal music tied to the expression of words (at least in theory and most often in fact as well) both religious and operatic. For centuries, of course, there had been pure instrumental music played in public but it consisted either of arrangements of vocal music, introductions to vocal music (preludes or overtures to church services or operas), interludes between the acts of operas and oratorios, or dance music, which had no prestige whatever (naturally, this did not prevent the creation of masterpieces in that genre). Only religious settings and opera had the prestige of truly public music.[5]

We take it for granted that instrumental music without the voice can express every variety of human emotion, even if it cannot exactly define a particular emotion; but this is a comparatively modern idea, as a passage from the memoirs of Samuel Wesley (1766–1837) demonstrates.

> Haydn's Allegros are generally characterized by a Cheerfulness which always enlivens the Hearer: and his Adagios are so pathetic and tender that although performed by inarticulate Instruments, their effect is irresistibly pathetic and affecting.[6]

Today, we are more likely to refer to instruments as eloquent rather than inarticulate, but, even as late as the early years of the nineteenth century, Wesley was clearly surprised that instruments could equal the voice in expressive power.

Although concerts are public occasions, their inception also established the listener as a separate entity from the participant. There are always particularly skilled performers and composers of music in any culture, but when music is used as an accompaniment to rituals, dances, and celebrations, the emphasis is on collective participation. When music is performed by professionals, listeners are not expected to join in, and so the musical experience becomes more individualized and less predictable.

One consequence of the separation of music from words is to render the meaning of music equivocal. Because words define its content, we know what we are intended to feel when we hear a song in a language with which we are familiar; but we cannot be as sure when we hear a symphony. Disputes about the meaning of music, which are still heated, are centred around 'absolute' music: that is, they concern instrumental music which does not refer to anything outside itself. When music accompanies words, or is closely associated with public events such as triumphs or funerals, questions of its meaning hardly arise. We know what we are expected to feel, and we usually feel it. As we saw in Chapter Two, music adds significance to ceremonies and to words because it induces arousal and structures that arousal in a way that ensures collective participation.

Although listeners to a concert may experience a degree of arousal in common, the way in which the music is presented makes possible a greater range of individual reactions than can be expected if everyone is taking part in music which is familiar to them. I have already quoted research indicating that there is some measure of agreement between listeners about the emotional significance of particular musical works; but this agreement only applies to the most general features of the work in question. Even on the most public occasions, I cannot be entirely sure that my neighbour is feeling *exactly* what I feel. It is possible, though unlikely, that he is laughing at funerals, sneering at coronations, feeling malice at weddings. At the end of an orchestral concert of music which has no external reference it is more difficult to be sure of what other members of the audience are feeling. We may all applaud enthusiastically, but I cannot be certain that we are sharing the same experience.

Moreover, unfamiliar music may induce different intellectual and emotional reactions on a first hearing from those experienced subsequently. Twentieth-century music exhibits a wide variety of styles, and even sophisticated musicians may need repeated hearings of a new piece before they can fully appreciate it. It is also the case that an unfamiliar performance of a familiar work may throw new light on it and deepen or alter one's perception of it. Music is inescapably dependent on performance. A poor performance can make a great work sound incoherent or trivial; and, in contrast, a great conductor like Beecham, or a great soloist like Kreisler, can temporarily persuade us that a trivial work is more significant than it is.

A particular concert may provoke varying reactions even in highly trained listeners. Music critics are renowned for giving contradictory accounts of the same concert in different newspapers; but one must remember that, because of the conservatism of the general public, such criticisms are more often concerned with how familiar music has been performed than with the assessment of new music.

Reviewing new compositions is a difficult undertaking. An analytical, critical stance toward a piece of music partly precludes emotional involvement with it, as we saw in Chapter Two. Both attitudes are required in musical appreciation, but they cannot usually function simultaneously. Critics of new music are probably attempting an impossible task. If they stand back and write about its form and structural coherence, they may miss its expressive significance; if they allow themselves to experience the music's emotional impact, detached, intellectual assessment becomes more difficult. Now that recordings are so easily available, I think we should refrain from expecting our critics to give a reasoned appraisal of new, and possibly important, works of music after only one hearing.

The same individual may find that the same piece of music arouses different emotions on different occasions, even though he knows the work thoroughly. If a person's mood is one of depression, the intensity of his response, even to familiar music, is likely to be less than when his mood is one of elation. It is also true that music may alter his mood from one condition to the other. People occasionally report that music has increased depression; but, unless someone is so depressed as to be unresponsive to any external stimulus, music is more likely to raise his spirits or at least relieve the sterility of being unable to care about anything or anybody which is so characteristic of depression. It is better to feel that life is tragic than to be indifferent to it.

The writer William Styron provides a striking example. For months, he had been suffering from severe, deep depression. Realizing that he could not get through the following day, he made preparations for suicide.

> My wife had gone to bed, and I had forced myself to watch the tape of a movie in which a young actress, who had been in a play of mine, was cast in a small part. At one point in the film, which was set in late-nineteenth-century Boston, the characters moved down the hallway of a music conservatory, beyond the walls of which, from unseen musicians, came a contralto voice, a sudden soaring passage from the Brahms *Alto Rhapsody*.
>
> This sound, which like all music – indeed, like all pleasure – I had been numbly unresponsive to for months, pierced my heart like a dagger, and in a flood of swift recollection I thought of all the joys the house had known: the children who had rushed through its rooms, the festivals, the love and work . . .[7]

The music's sudden impact made him realize that he could not injure those close to him by committing suicide. Next day, he had himself admitted to a psychiatric hospital.

There is a psychological test, named after its inventor, Hermann Rorschach, which consists in presenting a subject with ten standardized, symmetrical inkblots. Since there is 'nothing in' inkblots, even though standardized, it is rightly supposed that any content which a subject describes is a product of his own psyche rather than pertaining to the inkblot. So, if he sees outlines of mysterious strangers, demons, and ghosts, some of his internal unease is made manifest. If he sees nothing but islands of love and serenity, his report reveals his own inner harmony. The Rorschach test is the ancestor of many other 'projective techniques'; that is, devices by which a subject is induced to ascribe his own thoughts and attitudes to something or someone outside himself. Leonardo da Vinci employed the same technique in advising students of painting to stimulate their imaginations by looking at damp-stained walls and unevenly coloured stones. These, he said, would enable them to see and 'reduce to their complete and proper forms' all manner of landscapes and human figures in action.[8]

It can be argued that music acts in similar fashion. To some extent, a listener's response to a particular piece of music is governed by his subjective state of mind at the time; and some part of his experience is likely to be derived from the projection of his own emotions rather than being solely a direct consequence of the music.

If a piece of music has no verbal association or frame of reference but is simply performed for its own sake, it is not surprising that there are sometimes different responses to it. What is more interesting is the degree of consensus. In spite of the difficulties outlined earlier, we can be fairly confident that listeners to great music which is familiar to them are usually sharing a closely similar experience.

Some writers suggest that music conveys the same meaning to different listeners more accurately than a verbal message; that music is *less* likely to be misinterpreted or variously interpreted than words. The epigraph to this chapter is an extract from a letter by Mendelssohn in which he continues:

> a word does not mean the same thing to one person as to another; only the tune says the same thing, awakens the same feeling, in both – though that feeling may not be expressed in the same words.[9]

Proust speculates along similar lines. During the interval of a concert, various members of the audience chat to him.

> But what were their words, which like every human and external word left me so indifferent, compared with the heavenly phrase of music with which I had just been communing? I was truly like an angel, who, fallen from the inebriating bliss of paradise, subsides

into the most humdrum reality. And, just as certain creatures are the last surviving testimony to a form of life which nature has discarded, I wondered whether music might not be the unique example of what might have been – if the invention of language, the formation of words, the analysis of ideas had not intervened – the means of communication between souls. It is like a possibility that has come to nothing; humanity has developed along other lines, those of spoken and written language.[10]

It is clear that both Proust and Mendelssohn are referring to music within a particular Western tradition. Communication between souls is only possible if both share the same culture and hence the same kind of music.

However, in a different context, sounds without words can be accurately interpreted. If two people conduct a 'conversation' by humming, without parting their lips or using words, a good deal of information can be conveyed, such as 'I am weary'; 'I am pleased'; or even 'I love you'. The prosodic elements of speech can operate without the syntactic, even between adults from different cultures, because the sounds made reflect basic human emotions and have not been elaborated into different varieties of music. Some composers have been particularly aware of the prosodic aspects of language. Janáček systematically recorded the melodic curves of speech; and what he called 'speech melodies' remained central to his method of composition.[11]

It must always be remembered that emotional arousal is partly non-specific; that emotions overlap and can change from one feeling to another quite easily. Critics may agree that a particular work of art is 'significant' because they find themselves moved and interested; and are likely to agree in general terms about whether a work is tragic, humorous, profound or superficial. But detailed, specific descriptions of their subjective reactions may differ considerably.

There is a good example in Bernstein's Harvard lectures. He takes the opening bars of Beethoven's Piano Sonata in E flat, Op. 31, No. 3, and asks whether we listeners are hearing what Beethoven supposedly felt when he wrote them. Bernstein then verbalizes what Beethoven's music makes him feel in terms of pleading question and equivocal answer.

Please, Please . . . I implore you . . . I'll do anything if . . . Yes; but only on certain conditions.

Bernstein then asks:

But, did Beethoven feel all that, or anything like it? Did I just make up these feelings, out of the blue, or are they to some degree related to Beethoven's feelings transferred to me through his notes? We'll never know, we can't phone him up: but the probability is that *both* are true. And if so, we have just discovered a major ambiguity – a beautiful new semantic ambiguity to add to our fast-growing list.[12]

Bernstein's projections tell us more about Bernstein than about Beethoven. If I had to put words to Beethoven's phrases, I should choose different ones. But that is unimportant. We certainly share the perception that the initial contrasting phrases of this sonata are cast in terms of question and answer, and recognize that Beethoven uses this pattern elsewhere. For example, Beethoven himself annotates the opening phrases of the finale of his last string quartet (Op. 135 in F major) by writing 'Muss es sein? Es muss sein! Es muss sein!'

Question followed by answer is so habitual a pattern in human existence that we hardly recognize it as such. In these two musical works, Beethoven is distilling the essence of question and answer in music without words. Although I disagree with some of what Schopenhauer writes about music, I can appreciate his reference to music as expressing 'the inner nature, the in-itself, of every phenomenon'.

In *The Jewish Bride*, Rembrandt represents the deepest essential features of human love without one needing to know anything personal about the individuals portrayed. In similar fashion, Beethoven is abstracting the general features of human questioning and answering from the particular. That is why Bernstein's interpretation in terms of a pleading interchange between individuals causes momentary unease, as he would have been the first to appreciate. Beethoven's masterly generalization should not be interpreted in terms of purely personal needs. We are bound to bring our prejudices and feelings with us when we approach a musical work; but it is the extent to which a work *transcends* the personal which makes it great.

Deryck Cooke, in *The Language of Music*, attempted to show that within the Western tradition there is a consensus between composers as to which musical devices are used to represent particular emotions. For example, the interval of the major third commonly expresses joy; whilst the minor third is generally associated with grief. The augmented fourth, called by mediaeval theorists *diabolus in musica* because of its 'flawed' sound, is often used by composers to depict demons, hell, or other horrors. Cooke's examples of its use include works by Mozart, Wagner, Liszt, Berlioz, Gounod, Busoni, and many others. I don't think that anyone reading Cooke's book could fail to be convinced that there is a good deal in what he says; but there are also so many exceptions that his views have been sharply criticized. Moreover, Cooke explicitly confines his discussion to European art music which is tonal.

The emotional effects of music are more dependent upon context, less upon purely musical devices, than Cooke allowed. Eduard Hanslick, the famous Austrian critic whom Wagner pilloried as Beckmesser in *Die Meistersinger*, pointed out that the melody of Gluck's 'Che faro senza Euridice' might be thought rather jolly if we did not know that the aria is reflecting poignant loss. The French carol 'Quelle est cette odeur agréable, Bergers qui ravit tous nos sens' appears as a beautifully tender melody when sung as a carol; but the same tune serves as a rumbustious drinking song, 'Fill every glass', in *The Beggar's Opera*. There is a point in the 'Offertorio' of Verdi's *Requiem* at which the tenor, pleading to be granted eternal life, sings something suspiciously like 'Au près de ma blonde'.

Most experienced listeners agree that Mozart's String Quintet in G minor, K. 516, is a predominantly tragic masterpiece. But some people feel that the last movement expresses joy because, after its adagio introduction, the key changes to G major and the time signature to 6/8. However, the Mozart scholar, Alfred Einstein, refers to this last movement as being in 'the disconsolate major that Mozart utilizes in so many of his last works',[13] thus indicating that, for him at any rate, the change to the major key continues the tragedy rather than lightening it.

Deryck Cooke defined music as 'the supreme expression of universal emotions, in an entirely personal way, by the great composers'.[14] However, it is not a direct evocation of those emotions within himself which moves the listener but rather the way in which a great composer transforms universal emotions into art.

So many musicians and critics have wrestled with the problem of the meaning of music, that some have abandoned any attempt at linking absolute music with human feelings. The 'formalists' or 'non-referentialists' consider that music is an entirely autonomous art; that works of music have no meaning outside themselves; and that the experience induced by hearing a work of music is entirely the consequence of the listener's appreciation of its structure. Hanslick attempted to maintain this position. He wrote:

> Reading so many books on musical aesthetics, all of which defined the nature of music in terms of the 'feelings' it arouses, and which ascribed to music a definite expressive capability, had long excited in me both doubt and opposition. The nature of music is even harder to fix within philosophical categories than painting, since in music the decisive concepts of 'form' and 'content' are impossible of independence and separation. If one wishes to attribute a definite content to purely instrumental music – in vocal music content derives from the poem, not from the music – then one must discard the precious pearls of the musical art, in which no one can demonstrate a 'content' distinct from the 'form', nor even deduce it. On the other hand, I readily agree that it is idle to speak of absolute lack of content in instrumental music, which my opponents accuse me of having done in my treatise. How is one to distinguish scientifically in music between inspired form and empty form? I had the former in mind; my opponents accused me of the latter.[15]

By admitting the notion of inspired form versus empty form Hanslick is, I think, partially retreating from the strictly formalist position, especially with his use of the word 'empty'. If form has to contain something, what it contains must surely have some emotional significance.

Stravinsky found himself in rather the same position when, in his conversations with Robert Craft, he was discussing his famous remark 'Music is powerless to express anything at all.' Stravinsky strongly objected to the notion that a piece of music is a transcendental idea expressed in terms of music or that there was any exact correspondence between the composer's feelings and what he set down in notes. Stravinsky did admit that 'a composer's work *is* the embodiment of his feelings', but emphasized that, for him, the important fact about a composition was that it was something new, '*beyond* what can be called the composer's feelings'. He said that 'A new piece of music *is* a new reality'; and that 'music expresses itself'. Of the composer he claimed: 'All he knows or cares about is the apprehension of the contour of the form, for the form is everything. He can say nothing whatever about meanings.'[16]

It is possible to appreciate Stravinsky's point of view without total agreement. A great deal of gushing nonsense has been written about the meaning of music; but when Stravinsky expresses his dislike of the music of Richard Strauss by calling it 'treacly' he is not referring to its form but to its expression of sentiment.[17]

Hindemith agrees with Stravinsky in so far as he writes:

Music cannot express the composer's feelings . . . Here is what he really does: he knows by experience that certain patterns of tone-setting correspond with certain emotional reactions on the listener's part. Writing the patterns frequently and finding his observations confirmed, in anticipating the listener's reaction he believes himself to be in the same mental situation.[18]

Hindemith does not deny that music induces emotion in the audience, but he regards the composer as a skilled manipulator who 'believes that he feels what he believes the listener feels'.[19]

He continues:

A composer can never be absolutely sure of the emotional effect of his music on the listener when using complex material, but by experience and clever distribution of this material, moreover with frequent references to those musical progressions that evoke the uncomplicated feeling-images of sadness or gaiety in an unambiguous form, he can reach a fairly close approximation to unanimity of all listeners' reactions.[20]

In asserting that certain musical patterns correspond with certain emotional reactions, Hindemith appears to be anticipating Deryck Cooke's position. But they soon part company. For Hindemith, there is no question of the composer expressing either universal or personal emotions and conveying them to the audience. Moreover, Hindemith believes that

> The reactions music evokes are not feelings, but they are the images, memories of feelings . . . Dreams, memories, musical reactions – all three are made of the same stuff.[21]

As we shall see in a later chapter, Schopenhauer singled out music as being more directly expressive of the true, inner nature of reality than the other arts. Hindemith's view of music is exactly the opposite. Hindemith believes that the visual arts and poetry arouse emotions directly, whereas the emotions released by music are 'not real emotions'.

> Paintings, poems, sculptures, works of architecture . . . do not – contrary to music – release images of feelings; instead they speak to the real, untransformed, and unmodified feelings.[22]

Hindemith's account suggests that composers are confidence tricksters who skilfully manipulate audiences into experiencing false emotions, rather as Hitler did with his oratory. It is true that mass audiences are easily deceived; but I doubt whether this applies to a sophisticated listener who has the opportunity of hearing a work repeatedly. Hindemith claims that music can only recall feelings which the listener has experienced before in the course of 'real life'.

Susanne K. Langer, on the other hand, considered that music can not only put us in touch with emotions which we have felt previously, but can also

> present emotions and moods we have not felt, passions we did not know before. Its subject–matter is the same as that of 'self-

expression,' and its symbols may even be borrowed, upon occasion, from the realm of expressive symptoms; yet the borrowed suggestive elements are *formalized*, and the subject-matter 'distanced' in an artistic perspective.[23]

Some musicians go further than Stravinsky and Hanslick in discounting the expressive aspect of music. They claim that aesthetic judgement should be confined to questions of form and structure, expressed in technical terms, without reference to any emotions engendered by the music, which they consider irrelevant. Donald Tovey's description of the second main subject of the first movement of Haydn's 'Military' Symphony as 'one of the gayest themes in the world', or his reference to a section of Brahms's Fourth Symphony as rising 'through heroism to radiant happiness' would certainly cause raised eyebrows and exclamations of disapproval in such purists.[24] In their view, writing about music ought to be confined to describing the composer's techniques: his use of dissonance, consonance, modulation from one key to another, changes of tempo, orchestration, and every other device. But such descriptions actually exclude the listener's experience. As Frances Berenson points out, this type of technical analysis can be made by examining the score. The critic who employs it need never hear a single note of the music.[25]

Although Joseph Kerman appreciates the necessity and value of musical analysis, he refers to the analysts who concentrate on musical form alone as 'myopic'.

> Their dogged concentration on internal relationships within the single work of art is ultimately subversive as far as any reasonably complete view of music is concerned. Music's autonomous structure is only one of many elements that contributes to its import.[26]

I am the last person to dispute that technical analysis is important and valuable. Any insights which we gain into how a composer obtains his effects are helpful; although the technical language used to express such insights is more likely to be useful to embryo composers and conductors than it is to listeners. Many listeners appreciate musical forms and structures without being able to clothe their insights in technical language. If they did not, I claim that music would not continue to be important to them. Appreciating musical form and structure is not a technical matter which only the trained musician is equipped to undertake. It is true that describing musical form in words requires study and that the ability to do so implies a more complete appreciation of the work involved than that available to the ordinary listener. But an untrained listener who loves music does not simply immerse himself in a sea of treacle, although some nineteenth-century music comes close to providing that experience. He is also acutely aware of repetition, change of key, and resolution, to put it at its minimum. The pleasures of the unexpected are not confined to musical theorists. For example, the listener does not have to be a trained musician to recognize that Haydn is a master of surprise.

I think we do need a new type of language to describe music. Although Tovey was unrivalled in his knowledge of the music of the classical tradition, his language is old-fashioned and possibly not technical enough for today's listeners, who are often well-informed. But it is manifestly absurd to restrict the way we talk and write about music to language which deliberately excludes any reference to what makes a musical work expressive and capable of causing arousal. To do so is reminiscent of structuralists who write about 'the text' as if literature had nothing to do with human beings, either as readers or as authors.

The formalist analysts are trying to make the appreciation of music purely cerebral, whereas music is rooted in bodily rhythms and movement. The expressive aspect of music is difficult to discuss for the reasons outlined earlier, but that should not prevent us from making the attempt. I think it is possible to do justice to the views of both formalists and expressionists without distorting either.

When music was still directly tied to words, and to underlining or accompanying public ritual, there could be little argument of this kind. Disputes between formalists and expressionists only begin to be important with the rise of 'absolute' music. Music was bound to take on a life of its own when it became emancipated from other forms of expression. The rise of romantic music inevitably follows the separation of music from verbal and other associations. Music itself increasingly incorporated within its own structure the human, emotional meanings which had previously belonged to the words or public occasions which the music accompanied and enhanced. To maintain that absolute music parted company with human emotions because it began to exist in its own right is clearly untenable. The opposite would be more accurate.

Music is a temporal art. Its patterns exist in time and require duration for their development and completion. Although painting and architecture and sculpture make statements about relationships between space, objects, and colours, these relationships are static. Music more aptly represents human emotional processes because music, like life, appears to be in constant motion. The fact that musical movement is more apparent than real will be discussed later.

It can be argued that 'programme' music retains references to the external world and cannot therefore be the self-contained, isolated, and more or less perfect structure which formalists admire. But a great deal of 'programme' music is simply music for which some event, story, sound, or picture has been the trigger. Beethoven's Sixth Symphony (Op. 68 in F major) is the obvious example. If Beethoven had not headed his movements with titles, which, incidentally, he adapted from the titles given to the movements of an entirely different symphony by Knecht, we should accept the 'Pastoral' Symphony as a piece of absolute music, without worrying whether Beethoven is depicting 'By the brook side' or 'Merry gathering of country folk'. The same consideration applies to Mendelssohn's overture *The Hebrides*. It is interesting to know that Mendelssohn jotted down the main theme whilst in the Hebrides (Tovey alleges, probably inaccurately, that he was actually in Fingal's cave); but the piece stands on its own as a magnificent work of orchestral music which needs no title. As Jacques Barzun points out, it is not the case that when titles are used 'something alien has got into the pure stream of sound.'[27]

Rimsky-Korsakov's popular orchestral suite *Scheherazade* is overtly programmatic. Every listener recognizes that the sinuous solo for violin which links the movements represents the voice of Scheherazade herself telling the stories of the thousand and one nights to the Sultan. But how many listeners can recall the titles which the composer attached to each movement: 'The Sea and Sinbad's Ship'; 'The Story of the Kalender Prince'; 'The Young Prince and the Young Princess'; 'The Festival of Baghdad'; 'The Sea' – 'The Ship goes to pieces on a Rock surmounted by a Bronze Warrior'? Rimsky-Korsakov himself later discarded the titles; and the ballet derived from the suite which Diaghilev, Bakst, Fokine, and Nijinsky made famous is based on an entirely different story. The music stands by itself, requiring no verbal explanations at all.

Liszt, who wrote twelve symphonic poems and two symphonies to which he gave titles, himself used the term 'programme music'. But, as his biographer Alan Walker points out,

> The essential point is that these pieces are not 'representational' in the strict sense of being about specific things or events. For Liszt, the music is always more important than the literary or pictorial ideas behind it, and it will always unfold according to its own laws. By giving his works these titles, he is really disclosing the source of his inspiration, which we may accept or lay aside.[28]

Liszt's provision of titles for his music was partly designed to prevent his admirers applying inappropriate titles invented by themselves, a fate suffered by many composers from Bach onward. The nickname 'Moonlight' which became ineradicably attached to Beethoven's Piano Sonata Op. 27, No. 2 is a case in point. It originates from a review written by the poet Ludwig Rellstab, author of the words of Schubert's famous 'Ständchen', from his song–cycle *Schwanengesang*. For some reason Rellstab found that the first movement reminded him of moonlight on a lake; but most other listeners seem not to have shared his perception, and may unjustly feel that they are missing something because of the implications of the title.

Barzun claims

> (1) that all music is programmatic, explicitly or implicitly, and in more than one way; (2) that keeping out all extraneous ideas or perceptions while composing, hearing, or analysing music is impossible and unnecessary; and (3) that musical people who call literary the elements or the influence they deprecate in music do not fully understand what literature is.[29]

Barzun is reinforcing Alan Walker's point about Liszt's symphonic poems. Even absolute music may have originally been inspired by some external stimulus; but, if the music is good enough, we do not need to know what that stimulus was.

When actual sounds from the external world are reproduced in music, they often stand out inappropriately. We wait for the cuckoo in Delius's *On Hearing the First Cuckoo in Spring*, and detach the familiar call from the musical texture in which it is embedded, perhaps to the detriment of our appreciation of the piece as a whole. Programme music is less programmatic than the titles applied to it suggest; and if we feel that we really need a title, the probability is that the music is not compelling enough to stand on its own.

Charles Rosen makes the illuminating suggestion that it was the rise of sonata form which encouraged the development of orchestral concerts in which music was entirely unrelated to words. For sonata form provided 'an equivalent for dramatic action': a story in sound which had a definable beginning, middle and end comparable with the form of a saga, novel, or short story. The dance forms which preceded the development of sonata form relied chiefly on symmetry; on the satisfaction which we experience when repetition provides a framework, rather akin to the pleasure we gain from contemplating the regularities of classical architecture, or recurrence in poetry. Dramatic development has no part to play. Since a work of music exists in time, we cannot examine and re-examine it in the same way that we can re-examine a picture, a work of architecture, or other static objects. This is why repetition, both of themes and rhythms, has usually been found essential in defining the structure of a musical work, although some twentieth-century composers have attempted to dispense with it. But symmetry is an even more essential feature of music based on dance forms than it is of works based on sonata form. The minuet and trio, so characteristic of eighteenth-century symphonies and quartets, is an obvious example. The first minuet is succeeded by a second, often scored for fewer instruments – perhaps only three wind instruments, hence the name 'trio'. The original minuet is then repeated, giving an A–B–A structure to the movement as a whole.

Bach's third Brandenburg Concerto, which is known to every listener, is an exhilarating piece of rhythmical pattern-making, in which contrast is maintained by alternating groups of three string players with nine; but it does not *develop* in the sense of combining new themes together, or in progressing to an expected or unexpected goal. The first movement is based on one main idea; the third on another. Bach's extraordinary skill maintains our interest; but it is an interest based on elaboration, symmetry, and rhythmic pulse, rather than upon progress.

Although rather few compositions adhere rigidly to textbook descriptions of sonata form, the framework itself is interesting. The *exposition* presents, and often repeats, a *first subject* or group of subjects in the home key or tonic. Next, a transitional or *bridge passage* modulates to the dominant or to some other closely-related key, in which the *second subject* or group of subjects is stated. Second subjects are traditionally more lyrical than first subjects, and are often referred to as 'feminine'. The next section is the *development*, in which the two main subjects are combined, fragmented, juxtaposed, or re-stated in different keys. This is followed by the *recapitulation*: a return of the initial first subject as in the exposition, followed again by a bridge passage and the second subject. But this time, the bridge passage is altered in such a way that the second subject is re-stated in the tonic key, thus uniting first and second subjects, and bringing the movement home to a satisfying conclusion.

This scheme can be seen as outlining a story. Indeed, Tovey refers to a Haydn movement 'setting out on adventures'.[30] Hero myths typically involve the protagonist leaving home, setting out on adventures, slaying a dragon or accomplishing other feats, winning a bride, and then returning home in triumph. Sonata form also celebrates a journey toward a new union between elements which were originally contrasted. The end of the piece is usually indicated by a return 'home' to the tonic; most commonly to the major triad, less commonly to the minor.

A hero myth is an archetypal pattern, deeply embedded in the psyche, because it reflects the experience of nearly all of us. We all have to 'leave home' by severing some of the ties which bind us to it, so that we can make our own way in the world and achieve a new home of our own. This may not sound a heroic enterprise; but initiation rites would not exist if it were not realized that embarking on independent adult life is an adventure involving risk. This is because the slow pace of human development from childhood to adulthood requires a long period of dependency from which it is difficult to escape. We are all heroes when we become autonomous and self-supporting.

The pattern is so conventionally banal that it seems dreadful to apply it to some of the greatest masterpieces of Western music; but a similar pattern underlies many novels. The pattern of contrast, conflict, and final resolution so characteristic of sonata form applies not only to relations between the sexes but to many other dualities. Alex Aronson gives a number of instances of critics appraising novels as sonatas in words, including Virginia Woolf's *Mrs Dalloway*, E. M. Forster's *A Passage to India*, James Joyce's *Ulysses*, Thomas Mann's novella *Tonio Kröger*, and Hermann Hesse's *Steppenwolf*. Aronson writes that these books

are each one of them in its own way, studies in human polarity employing a traditional musical form in order to illustrate opposing layers of consciousness which eluded the writers of fiction in less introspective periods of literary history . . . The novelist's increasing awareness of polarity in the life of the individual and the social antagonism with which he is faced appeared most forcefully reflected in the sonata form with its play upon contradictory emotional pressures and tensions, its tendency towards introspective self-analysis and its striving for resolution.[31]

It is not trivializing either literature or music to point out that conventional forms in both arts are based on archetypal patterns of a simple kind which are probably encoded in the brain. Symmetry is one such pattern; stories are another. Rowell suggests a third.

Variation, . . . one of the most pervasive processes in music at all times and in all places, playing upon one of the most basic musical values – the sense of *identity* . . . I venture to suggest that the popularity of variation in world music is due to its psychic symbolism; the preservation, development of, and reinstatement of identity of the Self during the passage through life.[32]

The forms chosen by composers to shape and order their ideas – sonata form, rondo, and many others – originate outside music, and equally apply to quite different human activities. Effective oratory conventionally uses an A–B–A form, a simplified exposition, development, and recapitulation. 'Say what you are going to say, then say it, then tell them what you have said.' It is surely no coincidence that when music finally emancipated itself from words composers increasingly employed forms which can be related to human stories as well as continuing to use repetition, elaboration of pattern, contrapuntal techniques, and symmetry as defining structure.

One of the best known theories linking music with human emotional patterns is that of Leonard Meyer. He suggests that

> Music activates tendencies, inhibits them, and provides meaningful and relevant resolutions. [33]

This formulation can be related to the underlying pattern of a story discussed earlier. It is more obviously applicable to music in sonata form than to dance forms; but is so general that it can be applied to both.

The theory of emotion based on the work of John Dewey and others which Meyer adopts claims that emotions are aroused when a tendency to respond is prevented or inhibited. Within a cultural tradition, we learn certain expectations; for instance, that the chord of the dominant seventh *must* be followed by the tonic for satisfying resolution. Meyer claims that the great composers arouse our emotions because they are expert at heightening expectation and postponing resolution.

A telling example is found in Beethoven's String Quartet in C sharp minor, Op. 131, in Beethoven's own opinion, the greatest of all his sixteen string quartets. Meyer analyses the fifth movement, drawing our attention to the way in which Beethoven arouses our expectations without fulfilling them by destroying the rhythmic, harmonic, and melodic patterns which have been established. At last

> the little figure which opens the movement and the first phrase raises our hopes and redirects our expectations of completion and return. Now we are certain as to what is coming. [34]

Meyer applies information theory to music, affirming that musical meaning arises when the listener's expectation of that which follows what he has already heard is contradicted. Information and meaning march hand in hand. In ordinary life, habit governs much of our daily behaviour. We go up and down a flight of stairs confident that the height of the next tread will be the same as those which preceded it. If one tread is suddenly twice the height of its predecessors, we are suddenly jerked into awareness. We have been given a new and unexpected piece of meaningful information which may have painful consequences. And, although we may register exactly where the anomalous stair is situated, its incongruity will continue to impress us.

Meyer's description shares certain features with the theory of music advanced by Hans Keller, in that both musicians link compositional skill with the listener's expectations, and therefore postulate an experienced listener who is able to make judgements and comparisons within a particular stylistic context.

Keller claims that musical logic depends on unpredictability. He contrasts what he calls 'background' and 'foreground' in musical works. (The terms are also employed by Schenker, but used in a different sense by Keller.)

> The background of a composition is both the sum total of the expectations a composer raises in the course of a piece without fulfilling them, and the sum total of those unborn fulfilments. The foreground is, simply, what he does instead – what is actually in the score . . . The background boils down to form, which many pieces have in common, and which can be found in the textbooks; the foreground is the individual structure, which happens instead of the form, unless the music is a bore and fulfils all expectations – in which case you can write it yourself after the first few bars: you don't need a composer for it.[35]

This view chimes with the idea that many musical compositions depend upon a substructural pattern or background which may be simple or even banal. It is the foreground which supplies the value and individuality of the work, whilst the background pattern is conventional. What the composer does with it is what counts. The same is true of novels.

Keller believes that musical meaning depends for its existence on the conflict between background and foreground: that is, between the expectations aroused and implied by the background and the unexpected fulfilments provided by the really original composer.

> It is this tension, varying in intensity according to the junction a composition has reached, between what the composer does and what he makes you feel that he was expected to do that constitutes musical logic. The clearer the tension, the more logical the music – and the clearest tension is that which combines a maximum of contradiction with a maximum of unity between the contrasting elements.[36]

Both Keller's theory and Meyer's depend upon the composer's ability to confound expectations. Both theories combine some degree of structural analysis with consideration of emotional effects.

At the time when Keller summarized his theory of music in *The Listener*, I raised the obvious objection that after a piece of music had become familiar, expectation could no longer be contradicted, since the listener knew what was coming. Keller's response was that such knowledge was intellectual, leaving the listener's *emotional* expectations unchanged.

> The dominant seventh produces the inevitable emotional expectation of the tonic, whether you intellectually realise or not that it isn't going to happen in a given instance – that the submediant, an 'interrupted cadence', is going to ensue instead. In fact, paradoxically if none the less demonstrably, the experience of contradicted emotional expectation becomes deeper once the feeling of surprise is itself expected.[37]

The same may be true of the anomalous tread in a staircase. That which was unexpected remains unusual or original however often it is encountered.

In Meyer's view, delaying closure is one way in which composers contradict the listener's expectations and increase his degree of arousal. If the ability to postpone resolution was the only defining characteristic of greatness in a composer, Wagner would undoubtedly deserve the title of the greatest composer who ever lived, a title still accorded him by some of his admirers. The Prelude to *Tristan und Isolde* is a famous example of chromatic postponement in which the chord of the dominant seventh 'suddenly appears, no longer as pointing toward the goal, but as the goal itself!'[38] Indeed, the whole opera can be regarded in a rather similar light; the final resolution being postponed for over four hours of music. Since most compositions are considerably shorter than *Tristan*, it follows that the skills employed in raising and prolonging the listener's expectations cannot be the only important ones pertaining to musical composition.

Although Meyer has defined a significant pattern in musical works, it could be argued that this part of his contribution to theory does not really distinguish between music and a Hitchcock film, which also arouses expectations, heightens suspense, postpones resolution, and finally makes all well. But maybe he does not need to make such a distinction. Archetypal patterns substruct the trivial as well as the profound.

A more important objection to Meyer's theory is given by Peter Kivy. Although affect can certainly be increased by inhibiting immediate response, there are surely cases in which our response to music is instantaneously joyful.

Frustration is no more the sole cause of emotion in music (if it is a cause at all) than it is the sole cause of emotion in our ordinary lives.[39]

It is extraordinary that there should be any continuing dispute between formalists and expressionists. It seems obvious that appreciation of *both* form *and* emotional significance enter into the experience of every listener and cannot be separated. I suggested earlier that the mental set required for the intellectual appreciation of the structure of a musical work might be difficult to combine with appreciating its expressive qualities. This chiefly applies to new music rather than to music already absorbed. When a particular piece of music has become embedded in memory, when the listener knows what is coming next, he has already grasped something of its structure.

Jean-Jacques Nattiez draws attention to a passage in Proust which illustrates how the Narrator gradually improves his appreciation of form each time a piece of music new to him is repeated.

> Then, to change the course of my thoughts, rather than begin a game of cards or draughts with Albertine, I would ask her to give me a little music. I remained in bed, and she would go and sit down at the end of the room before the pianola, between the two bookcases. She chose pieces which were either quite new or which she had played to me only once or twice, for, beginning to know me better, she was aware that I liked to fix my thoughts only upon what was still obscure to me, and to be able, in the course of these successive renderings, thanks to the increasing but, alas, distorting and alien light of my intellect, to link one with another the fragmentary and interrupted lines of the structure which at first had almost been hidden in mist. She knew and, I think, understood the joy that my mind derived, at these first hearings, from this task of modelling a still shapeless nebula.[40]

How refreshing to read that Proust experienced joy in appreciating structure! Formalists often write about music as if understanding form was only an intellectual exercise. In fact, the form of a musical work can give us the same acute pleasure that we get from the balanced symmetry of architecture, especially when allied with the unexpected structural irregularity or decorative detail which serves to dispel monotony and reveals the individual hand of a master. If a listener comes to know a work of music well, he is responding to it as a whole. Form and content in music and body and soul in human beings are equally indivisible if either are to live.

CHAPTER V

ESCAPE FROM REALITY?

Musick, the greatest good that mortals know,
And all of heav'n we have below.

JOSEPH ADDISON[1]

Appreciation of music and the other arts is an activity somewhat removed from our ordinary life of getting and spending. We set aside particular periods of time for it; and we often go to special places like concert halls and art galleries to find what we are looking for. In pre-literate cultures, the arts are more closely integrated with ordinary life. In Western societies, the arts tend to occupy a special niche of their own, as if they might be a luxury rather than a vital part of human life. This has made it possible for the unenlightened to argue that music and the other arts are some kind of substitute for, or escape from, 'real' life. It is a conclusion with which I profoundly disagree; but, since some influential psychoanalysts have put forward notions of this kind, it is worth examining their ideas, if only to refute them.

Freud himself was an extraordinarily well-read individual with a lively appreciation of literature. At school, where he was top of the class for six years running, he became familiar with the Latin and Greek classics. He learned Hebrew, English and French, and also taught himself some Italian and Spanish. Shakespeare and Goethe remained his favourite authors; but he considered Dostoevsky not far behind Shakespeare, and believed *The Brothers Karamazov* the greatest novel ever written. Freud himself was recognized as a literary stylist, and was given the Goethe prize for literature. He was also moved by sculpture, and to a lesser extent by painting. It is true that, in the introduction to his paper 'The Moses of Michelangelo', Freud acknowledged that he was almost incapable of obtaining any pleasure from music. His nephew Harry wrote:

> He despised music and considered it solely as an intrusion! For that matter the whole Freud family was very unmusical.[2]

In spite of this blind spot, Freud was a widely cultured man who greatly admired the artists and writers who appealed to him. At first sight, it seems surprising that his references to artists often seem disparaging, until one realizes that this is an inescapable consequence of psychoanalytic theory.

One of Freud's fundamental ideas was that the organism is continually seeking to rid itself of disturbing stimuli. As noted in Chapter Two, he thought that the nervous system was an apparatus for getting rid of both external and internal stimuli as soon as possible. If this is true, it follows that the ideal state must be one of tensionless tranquillity.

According to Freud, the prototype of this state is that of the satisfied infant. Interaction between mothers and infants includes stimulation and arousal as well as blissful union; but psychoanalysis has emphasized union whilst usually neglecting arousal. In infancy, Nirvana is attained at the breast; in adult life, it follows (or should ideally follow) sexual orgasm; the 'little death', precursor of that final tranquillity only to be found in the grave.

> No one who has seen a baby sinking back satiated from the breast and falling asleep with flushed cheeks and a blissful smile can escape the reflection that this picture persists as a prototype of the expression of sexual satisfaction in later life.[3]

Freud continued to regard sexual fulfilment as the prime source of satisfaction for both men and women, although he recognized that complete discharge of sexual tensions was difficult to attain. Civilization itself is oppressive, since it imposes restraints upon instinctual expression which human beings find hard to tolerate. A degree of sublimation, of the conversion of sexual impulses into non-sexual forms, is obligatory for everyone who attempts to comply with civilized standards; but it is nevertheless a defence mechanism or second best to sexual fulfilment itself.

Neurotics are particularly precluded from obtaining complete sexual satisfaction because of the persistence of remnants of infantile sexuality which prevent their reaching sexual maturity. These remnants manifest themselves in neurotic symptoms, in dreams, and in a retreat into phantasy.

> Neurotics turn away from reality because they find it unbearable – either the whole or parts of it.[4]

Freud believed that phantasy was derived from play. Since play and phantasy involve turning away from, or denying, reality, both are childish activities which ought, ideally, to be outgrown. As all forms of art depend upon the exercise of phantasy, of the artist's imagination, it is unsurprising that Freud considered that artists are closer to being neurotic than the average person.

> An artist is once more in rudiments an introvert, not far removed from neurosis. He is oppressed by excessively powerful instinctual needs. He desires to win honour, power, wealth, fame and the love of women; but he lacks the means for achieving these satisfactions. Consequently, like any other unsatisfied man, he turns away from reality and transfers all his interest, and his libido too, to the wishful constructions of his life of phantasy, whence the path might lead to neurosis.[5]

In Freud's view, all forms of art and literature are sublimations of unsatisfied libido.

> An artist is originally a man who turns away from reality because he cannot come to terms with the renunciation of instinctual satisfaction which it at first demands, and who allows his erotic and ambitious wishes full play in the life of phantasy.[6]

Artists are burdened with the same elements of arrested sexual development as neurotics, but, because of their gifts, are able to sublimate their impulses in their creations. Because Freud's theory of human nature was based upon the assumption of only two drives, sexuality and the death instinct, he rated creativity in both art and science as a secondary phenomenon.

> A satisfaction of this kind, such as an artist's joy in creating, in giving his phantasies body, or a scientist's in solving problems or discovering truths, has a special quality which we shall certainly one day be able to characterize in metapsychological terms. At present, we can only say figuratively that such satisfactions seem 'finer and higher'. But their intensity is mild as compared with that derived from the sating of crude and primary instinctual impulses; it does not convulse our physical being.[7]

The oddest consequence of Freud's theory is its implication that, if total sexual fulfilment were possible by means of complete adaptation to reality, the arts, including music, would become otiose. I have discussed the unsatisfactory nature of this conclusion elsewhere.[8]

References to music in Freud's own writings are meagre and unimportant; but many of Freud's followers have not shared his lack of response, and a number have ventured upon psychoanalytic interpretations of music.

Psychoanalysis is based on Freud's theories of infantile development: it includes the idea that no one, however mature, entirely outgrows his or her infantile past. For example, the earliest 'oral' stage of libidinal development continues to manifest itself in adults in such forms of behaviour as smoking, sucking pencils, or in various types of eating disorders. Psychoanalytic theory proposes that human beings regress to earlier stages of emotional development whenever they are fatigued, physically ill, neurotically disabled, or prevented from finding mature instinctual satisfaction. The assumption is that the infantile past exerts a constant seductive pull upon the adult present and that it is easy to yield to its enticements. Although psychoanalysis recognizes that no human being reaches complete emotional maturity, the implication is that regression to infantile modes of satisfaction and communication is to be deplored: at best, it is a respite from the burden of being an adult; at worst, a permanent failure to grow up.

Some psychoanalysts have attempted to explain the emotional effects of music in terms of regression. If music originated from the expressive vocal sounds which are important in maintaining the intimate relationship between the infant and its mother, the psycho-analytic theory that music represents a non-verbal or pre-verbal form of communication related to earliest infancy becomes compre-hensible, though unconvincing. Kohut, for example, writes:

> Music, however, as an extraverbal mode of mental functioning, permits a specific, subtle regression to preverbal, i.e., to truly primitive forms of mental experience while at the same time remaining socially and aesthetically acceptable.[9]

Other psychoanalysts refer to regression to a stage of narcissism, or to an early period in which the ego was not yet differentiated from external objects. Pinchas Noy records that several of his patients admitted a recurrent pressing need to hear music. 'Some time later all these patients vividly recalled early memories of their long-dead mothers.'[10] The same psychoanalyst alludes to 'longings for the lost paradise of oral infancy', and to music as taking a person back to the primary period when the maternal voice conveyed loving reassurance. He also observes that some of his patients had become 'addicted' to music, and felt deprived and unhappy if they had no access to it. This special need for music was not necessarily linked with musical ability, although interest in music and an aptitude for it are generally correlated to some extent. Pinchas Noy suggests that addiction to music is found in patients who have an especially strong desire to regress to the earliest type of emotional communication, that between mother and infant; whereas musical ability is rooted in an unusual sensitivity to sound. Such statements are unconvincing anecdotes rather than evidence.

There are many objections to these theories. For example, the psychoanalytic assumption that pre-verbal communication is necessarily infantile cannot be sustained. Communication between mother and infant is the earliest manifestation of prosody: cooing may develop into music, babbling into clear articulation, but it does not follow that the prosodic elements of speech are infantile or primitive. Words alone are never enough to convey meaning: prosody is an essential feature of *adult* verbal exchanges. Consider the exclamation 'Really!' It can imply surprise, disbelief, disapproval, enthusiasm, disdain, and perhaps many other meanings, each of which must be conveyed by intonation rather than by the word itself.

In Chapter Two, we observed that children with damage to the right hemisphere of the brain were unable to communicate their feelings because their speech was monotonous. The same is true of adults who are autistic, or suffering from some types of schizophrenia. Their speech is abnormal because it precisely lacks those prosodic features which psychoanalysis calls infantile. Flat, unemotional speech indicates brain damage or mental illness, not intellectual sophistication or being grown-up.

Computers can now programme synthesizers to imitate the human voice. However,

> Musically experienced listeners typically noted that these performances sounded like a singer who was gifted with a good voice but who unfortunately lacked the desire to communicate anything particular in his singing.[11]

What human performers actually add chiefly derives from the prosodic elements of speech patterns.

As indicated earlier, Freud believed that in adult life a period of tensionless satisfaction followed sexual orgasm. It is obviously possible, though not fruitful, to compare musical experience with sexual experience. Music can cause intense emotional arousal accompanied by a desire for physical movement and all the physiological changes already described. When the music is over, feelings of peace, tranquillity, and satisfaction may supervene. But exactly the same sequence of events may take place in enthusiasts watching championship tennis. It does not follow that either experience is a substitute for, or even remotely related to, sexuality. The pattern of arousal followed by relaxation is ubiquitous – an inescapable aspect of both human and animal life.

> Sleep after toyle, port after stormie seas,
> Ease after warre, death after life does greatly please.[12]

Some psychoanalysts, noticing that music can trigger feelings akin to the 'oceanic', have applied Freud's interpretation of this experience to music, supposing that music represents feelings of blissful union between mother and infant at a stage before the infant has become aware of itself as a separate entity. This interpretation is wrong on two counts. First, although music can trigger the oceanic experience, this is rare and does not usually occur during the actual performance of music. Second, the oceanic experience is not comparable with either orgasm or with union with another person.

The term 'oceanic' originates from a letter which Freud received from his friend Romain Rolland. After reading Freud's attack on religion, *The Future of an Illusion*, Rolland complained that Freud did not understand the true source of religious sentiments, which, so Rolland alleged, originated from 'a sensation of "eternity", a feeling as of something limitless, unbounded – as it were, "oceanic"'.[13]

The oceanic feeling is usually compared with the states of mind described by the mystics in which the subject feels at one with the world and with him or her self. It is almost invariably a solitary experience; and the feelings of unity or wholeness which occur refer to the universe or God, and not to merging with another human being. In my book *Solitude*, I referred to descriptions of oceanic experiences by Wordsworth, Walt Whitman, Edmund Gosse, A. L. Rowse, Arthur Koestler, Bernard Berenson, C. S. Lewis, and Admiral Byrd.

Freud describes the oceanic feeling as 'a feeling of an indissoluble bond, of being one with the external world as a whole'.[14] He compares this with the height of being in love, a state in which 'the boundary between ego and object threatens to melt away'. Freud interprets this temporary adult abolition of boundary lines as a regression to the period of infancy when the infant at the breast has not yet differentiated itself from the external world. The oceanic experience, in Freud's view, represents a return to a total merger with the mother.

I think it important to distinguish between the experience of high arousal and the oceanic state which may occasionally *follow* an intense emotional experience. Both high arousal and the oceanic state are sometimes loosely miscalled 'ecstatic', but excitement is not the same as the oceanic experience, which is usually deemed tranquil. As noted above, music can cause intense emotional arousal followed by feelings of relaxation and satisfaction; but this common response to being moved by musical performance is far removed from the uncommon oceanic state.

Musicans sometimes describe feelings of being 'taken over' or 'possessed' during a performance; a type of ecstasy which may or may not be enhanced by drugs. There may be an experience of being so much at one with the music that it seems to be playing itself. This is certainly being 'taken out of oneself', and thus has something in common with the oceanic experience; but it is qualitatively different, because it lacks the sense of utter tranquillity which is so characteristic of the latter.

Marghanita Laski's book *Ecstasy* reveals that respondents to her questionnaire who named one or other of the arts as triggers of the ecstatic experience more often quoted music than any other art.

> In both the questionnaire and the literary groups music was the most frequently named art-trigger (there were no art-triggers in the religious group). I believe that of all the more common triggers to ecstasy, music would be the most rewarding to study in any attempt to find a relation between the qualities of triggers and the effects produced.[15]

I know someone who described such feelings in association with Mozart's famous duet from *Don Giovanni*, 'Là ci darem la mano'. Although he already knew the piece well, it suddenly took hold of him, ran in his head, and transformed his existence for part of the day. He described what he felt as a tranquil state of ecstasy in which he was at one with mankind, the world, and himself. In a lifetime of listening to music, this was the only occasion on which he could recall music acting as a trigger for the oceanic experience. He clearly distinguished this type of ecstasy from the spine-tingling, intense physical arousal which occasionally occurred whilst listening to a superb performance of music.

Perhaps the oceanic experience more often occurs to composers of music than it does to listeners. Alexander Goehr describes the early stages of embarking upon a new composition as intensely troubling, coloured with disappointment, frustration, and inner rage. Then, when at last the notes begin to come,

> the music writes itself . . . There is no longer a composer who pushes the material about, but only its servant, carrying out what the notes themselves imply. This is the exact experience I seek and which justifies all else. For me such experience exceeds all other satisfactions that I know or can imagine . . . For, at this moment, I find myself overcome by an oceanic sensation of oneness with all around me.[16]

At an earlier point in this chapter, we commented that the pattern of arousal followed by relaxation was a common feature of a great many different human experiences, including sexuality. In this context, it is worth noting that in Marghanita Laski's enquiry even those who claimed that sex occasionally acted as a trigger for ecstasy sharply distinguished between the two. The most rewarding sexual experience does not necessarily provoke ecstasy; and ecstasy is entirely different from the relaxation which follows orgasm.

It is certainly true that a great performance of great music can temporarily uplift us, remove us from all our anxieties, and enable us to escape 'entirely from all our affliction', as Schopenhauer described this experience. This can perhaps be compared with the peaceful sense of relaxation which follows sexual release, but is not necessarily accompanied by the marvellous sense of tranquillity and unity which we call 'oceanic'.

Manic-depressives, when in the manic phase of their illness, sometimes describe the feeling of unity with God or with all creation which occurs in states of ecstasy. In mania, however, this experience is usually, though not invariably, followed by more sinister manifestations: uncontrollable excitement, racing thoughts, irritability, and grandiose delusions. Such symptoms are never part of the ecstasies of normal people, who usually look back on their experience with delight, feeling that their mental organization has been improved rather than disrupted.

But there may be another parallel with manic-depressive illness in that some people who report ecstatic states, who are not necessarily diagnosed or diagnosable as manic-depressive, also experience periods of anguish, emptiness, and hopelessness which are the very opposite of ecstasy. The religious call this state 'the dark night of the soul', a description more evocative of its actual nature than the psychiatric diagnosis 'depressive illness'. Marghanita Laski found that, against her will, she was compelled to include a chapter on desolation in her book *Ecstasy*, since both states were so often found in the same person.

As we shall see later, some philosophers have thought that music enabled a listener to escape the pains of existence by temporarily entering a realm of peace. This hypothesis fails to account for the state of arousal which music usually induces. Nevertheless, some music is undoubtedly concerned with 'other worlds' into which the listener can imagine being transported.

When this is in question, it usually has to be spelled out in words; either in a poem of which the music is a setting, or else by the composer verbally citing the source of his inspiration. I am thinking, for example, of Duparc's marvellous setting of Baudelaire's poem 'L'Invitation au Voyage', and of Rachmaninov's symphonic poem *The Isle of the Dead*, which is surely his most convincing orchestral achievement. Baudelaire's journey ends in that wonderful country we all imagine but never enter.

> Là, tout n'est qu'ordre et beauté,
> Luxe, calme et volupté.

Rachmaninov's *Isle of the Dead* was inspired by a picture by the Swiss artist Arnold Böcklin of an uninhabited island where the dead lie undisturbed: a more realistic idea of Nirvana than Baudelaire's, though described by the artist himself as a dream picture. Its appeal to Rachmaninov must surely have been connected with the composer's liability to depression; perhaps with a belief that only in the peace of death is man relieved of sorrow. If Freud had been musical, this music would surely have appealed to him also.

Freud's pejorative view of phantasy is incomplete rather than wholly wrong. Day-dreams are sometimes escapist as Freud suggests; but they can also be precursors of creative discovery and thus of new ways of adapting to reality. Like the other arts, music can provide a temporary retreat from the pains of existence; but this is only one of its functions, and by no means the most important. Music can also aid our adaptation to life in a variety of ways hinted at in earlier chapters, but not yet fully explored.

Composers, like writers, have often been inspired by countries of the imagination. When in 1903 Debussy wrote 'Soirée dans Grenade', the second movement of his suite for piano *Estampes*, his knowledge of Spain was limited to one day spent in San Sebastian. The Spain which inspired him was the Spain of his imagination; it continued to do so, as is evident from the three sections of *Ibéria*, the second part of the orchestral suite *Images*, which were composed between 1906 and 1909.

The same lack of actual knowledge of Spain was true of Ravel, whose orchestral *Rapsodie Espagnole*, opera *L'Heure Espagnole*, and piano piece *Alborada del Gracioso*, date from the same period.* Although Ravel's mother spoke fluent Spanish, and had spent some of her youth in Madrid, the composer himself had never crossed the border. Those who share Keats's belief in 'the truth of imagination' will rejoice that Manuel de Falla paid glowing tribute to the subtlety and authenticity with which both composers had evoked the spirit of his country, in spite of hardly knowing it.

Ravel provides another example of an imaginary land giving inspiration, this time with words as an intermediary. His beautiful song-cycle *Shéhérazade* is a setting of three poems written by Léon Leclère, using the Wagnerian pseudonym Tristan Klingsor. The *Asie* depicted is as remote from the realities of Persia, India, and China as it is possible to get.

An anecdote told by Hélène Jourdan-Morhange illustrates Ravel's recognition that reality's power to provide inspiration is severely limited.

At Fez, M. Boris Masslow, the Director of Fine Arts, was showing Ravel round the Embassy and its wonderful gardens.

'*Cher maître*,' he said, 'what a setting to inspire you to write something Arabian!'

To which Ravel replied briskly,

*This last-named work, originally part of *Miroirs*, is probably better known in its orchestral version. The title, meaning 'The Jester's Serenade', refers to the Galician practice of including a jester in a nobleman's household.

'If I wrote something Arabian, it would be much more Arabian than all this!'[17]

Walter de la Mare's well-known poem 'Arabia' is also a romantic phantasy celebrating a country which bears no resemblance to its real counterpart. He writes of dark-haired musicians, green banks and gliding streams without any reference to the desert.[18] Vaughan Williams's Seventh Symphony, which was given the title *Sinfonia Antartica*, was inspired by Captain Scott's last expedition to the Antarctic; but now that nearly all the world is mapped, explored, and trampled over, writers and composers can no longer spin phantasies round actual countries, which is why they turn their attention to science fiction or, like Holst, to the music of the spheres.

However, because a writer or composer takes as his theme Utopia, the Isles of the Blessed, the Orient, or another place unknown to him, it does not follow that the listener is transported into some never-never land. This may be the case when the composer is setting poems, as in *Shéhérazade*, but it does not hold for absolute music, even when titled. Imaginary countries are, for the composer, Rorschach inkblots, or triggers of inspiration. What comes out of such inspiration is a work of music, not a looking-glass through which one can walk into an escapist limbo.

As Stravinsky said, once a composition is finished, it exists as something in its own right. This is why music is not a direct communication of the composer's feelings to his audience, but rather a communication about how he makes sense of his feelings, gives them structure, transforms them from raw emotions into art.

The psychoanalytic interpretations of music so far discussed have not been illuminating, since escape from the troubles of life is only a minor part of musical experience, but there is another which is more interesting. In Chapter Two, we noted that the condition of arousal could be exciting or distressing according to its intensity. Some psychoanalysts speculate that hypersensitivity to noise may play a part in the development of musical ability. The argument is as follows.

Everyone reacts to unexpected or loud noise by physical movement of some kind. We may turn toward the noise in the hope of identifying it; or we may react with a sudden start in an attempt to avoid it. Whereas we can blot out an unpleasant sight by closing our eyes or turning our back on it, it is harder to avoid a piercing sound. We cannot dispel it by turning round. Tracing its source may be impossible; and, even if we succeed in this, there is no guarantee that we can stop it. Blocking one's ears is more difficult than shutting one's eyes and less effective. The sound of a pneumatic drill or the screech of a police-car siren are noises hard to avoid. Unwanted noise can be a threat, an experience one must abolish or control. In South Africa's brutal prisons, special tapes of human screams, breaking glass, barking dogs, and roaring lions have been relayed continuously at high volume to prisoners in solitary confinement. The effects are devastating.

The British psychoanalyst Donald Winnicott was once asked by a distracted mother what she should do about her two-year-old son who reacted to every loud noise with startle and distress. Winnicott suggested giving the child a tin tray and a spoon so that he could make a loud noise back. This is one technique for abolishing a feeling of helplessness in the face of threat and restoring a sense of competence. The physical movement involved in banging a tray is as important as the noise produced. When auditory sensory input is so unpleasant or so loud that it constitutes a threat, violent physical movement is a natural response. As Robin Maconie points out, we learn to control what we hear by manipulating the auditory environment.

> This manipulation of the auditory field is expressed in two main strategies: (1) physical movement which changes the intensity and positional relationships of events in the perceptual field, and (2) vocalization or other sound production (including music) which introduces a controllable and dominating element into an otherwise uncontrolled auditory environment. We like to dance and we like to sing and play.[19]

We do not know if Winnicott's patient later became a composer; but his hypersensitivity to sound might well have made it particularly important for him to develop techniques of ordering and organizing sounds into acceptable patterns, which is exactly what composers do.

Noise can be threatening to normal people. If someone is hypersensitive to noise, and unable to filter out what is irrelevant from all the different noises which constantly impinge upon him, he may be specially inclined to deal with it by trying to impose a new order on it, make sense out of it, and thus turn what was threatening into something manageable. Maconie puts it succinctly:

> If there is an underlying truth in the exclamation 'this noise is driving me mad', there may be an equivalent truth in its comic inversion, 'this music is driving me sane'. The form of words suggests a dynamic relationship between sensory input and perceptual response.[20]

I have noticed that there are considerable differences between individuals in response to auditory input. Some people cannot bear trying to conduct a conversation through background music; others apparently do not notice it, or can cut it out of their perceptual field. Many people seem to have their television sets switched on all day, irrespective of whether any conversation is going on in the same room or not. A few individuals become acutely distressed if, whilst listening to a talk on the radio, someone in the room addresses them with a comment. Such people complain that they cannot listen to two things at once, and miss the sense of what both the broadcaster and the interrupter are saying. For a moment, they are threatened with chaos.

Auditory discrimination depends on being able to filter out extraneous sounds and identify what is significant. A mother will often respond to the cry of her own infant when no one else in the room has heard it. I remember sitting at breakfast with Konrad Lorenz who suddenly rose from the table saying 'I hear the cry of a goose-baby': a sound which no one else had noticed. Sure enough, a tiny gosling was in trouble and had to be rescued.

Pinchas Noy suggests that the child who is hypersensitive to auditory stimuli may find it particularly difficult to eliminate or ignore more than a few of the incoming sounds to which he is exposed, and must therefore adopt a different strategy.

> The only way out of this dilemma is an effort toward orientation in and mastery of the auditory perceptual field. The infant will have to

develop an ability to concentrate his attention to directing and mastering twenty different, simultaneously recurring sound stimuli.

An extreme example of such an accomplishment is presented in the person of the prominent conductor of an orchestra, who has the extraordinary gift of simultaneously listening to the orchestra as one body and to each of the instruments separately, distinguishing each by its playing as if he concentrated on it alone.[21]

The author admits that this hypothesis lacks experimental confirmation, but it chimes well with the idea that those who are especially threatened by disorder are those most strongly motivated to discover order.

We know that sufferers from schizophrenia are hypersensitive in that they need protection from relatives who are intrusive, smothering, or critical. They feel threatened by such negative input, and are more likely to relapse than if they find themselves surrounded by tolerant acceptance. In Chapter Two, reference was made to experiments with dichotic listening, which demonstrated that, in normal subjects, language was better perceived by the left hemisphere, music by the right. Research suggests that in people suffering from mental illness, both schizophrenia and the various forms of affective disorder, the functions of the two hemispheres are not so clearly differentiated as they are in normal people.[22]

Since specialization of hemispheric function has developed partly to facilitate the efficient processing of incoming auditory information, whether this be speech or music, it is not surprising that some mentally ill people are hypersensitive to such information and may feel threatened by it. Modern theories of information processing postulate that, in the normal person, incoming information is rapidly scanned so that stimuli which are unwanted, inappropriate, or irrelevant are excluded from consciousness. Schizophrenics sometimes complain of being overwhelmed by stimuli, as if this filtering process was absent or inefficient.

A number of writers have suggested that creative people are hypersensitive in metaphorically lacking a sufficiently thick protective skin to shield them from the impact of the external world. There is a link between mental illness and creativity, in that the ability to think creatively, to make new links between concepts, is more often found in families which include a member who is diagnosable as mentally ill. I am not suggesting that all creative people are mentally ill, although some of the greatest have been so, but only that unconventional thought processes of a similar kind can be demonstrated in both the mentally ill and the creative. From what has already been noted, it appears likely that the mentally ill and the creative may share a difficulty in dealing with sensory input from the external world, whether this takes the form of speech, non-verbal sounds, or emotional pressure. The mentally ill are overwhelmed by the threat of confusion and disorder. The creative meet the challenge by creating a new order in their works and thus master the threat. Robert Schumann and Hugo Wolf are examples of composers who suffered from manic-depressive illness. Although ultimately defeated by the severity of their mental disturbances, there is no doubt that their creativity was partly a product of their instability. Rachmaninov also experienced severe depression. This condition can be so extreme that it prevents production altogether, but *liability* to depression and the threat of its recurrence can act as a spur to creativity. Berlioz, when suffering tormenting depression and anxiety, told his father that without music he could not go on living.[23] Tchaikovsky, who also endured severe bouts of depression, wrote 'Truly, there would be reason to go mad if it were not for *music*.' His biographer, John Warrack, thinks that he was stating nothing but the sober truth.[24]

The creative process depends on both conscious and unconscious mental functions. We are still so influenced by Freud that many people believe that anything emanating from the unconscious must be emotional, irrational, unacceptable, and probably disreputable. In reality, this is not the case. Unconscious processes are just as much concerned with pattern and structure as they are with emotional expression.

Even the irrationality of dreams is more apparent than real. Dreams certainly exhibit incongruities, impossibilities, temporal confusion, and many other features unacceptable to the rational mind. But most dreams are stories. The scanning process which goes on in sleep matches recent events with past events and links together mental contents which share a similar feeling but which may not be related in any other way. The dream attempts to make sense out of this hotchpotch by trying to impose the order of a story-line.

As I have argued elsewhere, the human species is compelled to theorize and strive to make sense of both life and the universe. Because human behaviour is not principally governed by the in-built 'instinctive' patterns of response to stimuli which direct the behaviour of animals lower in the evolutionary order, human beings are forced to become inventive. They are compelled to try to understand the world and themselves, and, in so doing, can reach new and better adaptations. The processes by which this is achieved are both unconscious and conscious. We cannot avoid making some attempt to find coherence in the world and within ourselves; but the originally unconscious impulse which makes us do this is reinforced, refined, and given rationality by conscious reasoning.

I am sure that one of the reasons why music affects us deeply is its power to structure our auditory experience and thus to make sense out of it. Although I have been at pains to dispel the psychoanalytic view that music is an escape from reality or a regression to an infantile state, there is no doubt that music provides one path of temporary withdrawal from the hurly-burly of the external world. This is refreshing, because it permits the same kind of scanning, sorting, and rearrangement of mental contents which takes place in reverie or in sleep. There are many others ways of achieving this, from going for a solitary walk in the country to practising transcendental meditation. When we take part in music, or listen to an absorbing performance, we are temporarily protected from the input of other external stimuli. We enter a special, secluded world in which order prevails and from which the incongruous is excluded. This in itself is beneficial. It is not a regressive manoeuvre, but *reculer pour mieux sauter*; a temporary retreat which promotes a re-ordering process within the mind, and thus aids our adaptation to the external world rather than providing an escape from it.

If music and the other arts were more closely interwoven with our daily activities, we might not need this temporary retreat so much. People of other cultures sometimes cannot understand why Europeans seem so tense. When Jung visited New Mexico he talked with an Indian chief who said:

See how cruel the whites look. Their lips are thin, their noses sharp, their faces furrowed and distorted by folds. Their eyes have a staring expression; they are always seeking something. What are they seeking? The whites always want something; they are always uneasy and restless. We do not know what they want. We do not understand them. We think that they are mad.[25]

If there appears to be an escapist element in musical participation, it is because our culture is so concerned with achievement and the pursuit of conventional success that it makes ordinary life into a tense and anxious business from which the arts are absent. Music can and should be a life-enhancing part of our day-to-day existence.

Music plays a special role in aiding the scanning and sorting process which goes on when we are asleep or simply day-dreaming. Stravinsky refers to the pleasure we gain from unorganized natural sounds, which may be considerable, but which lacks the further dimension provided by music.

But over and above this passive enjoyment, we shall discover music, music that will make us participate actively in the working of a mind that orders, gives life, and creates.[26]

Psychoanalysts refer to this participation as 'projective identification': the process by which a person imagines himself to be inside some object external to himself. Imitation is not only the sincerest form of flattery, but a way of learning. By identifying ourselves with those more gifted, we can actually improve our own capacities. Teachers of music know that 'do it the way I do' is often a more effective way of teaching than theoretical instruction.

Music not only brings order to muscular movement, but also promotes order within the mind. This is why John Blacking, writing in his book 'A Commonsense View of All Music' under the heading 'The Power of Music', is able to say:

The development of the senses and the education of the emotions through the arts are not merely desirable options. They are essential both for balanced action and the effective use of the intellect.[27]

Instead of being threatened by an overload of incoherent auditory stimuli, we learn by means of music to impose our will upon this input, to exclude the irrelevant, to pay attention to what is important, and thus to create or discover some order in the world. This is comparable with the pleasure we get from the explanatory hypotheses of science.

Because a scientific theory makes the world more comprehensible, we feel less at the world's mercy, and more able to control events. Of course, we cannot control everything. However detailed our scientific knowledge of geology, we are still vulnerable to earthquakes. We may become auditorily sophisticated, but an unexpected, loud noise will still alarm us. However, being able to make some sense out of the world gives us confidence. Music is important in a number of different ways. This is one which is insufficiently appreciated.

Music can enable brain-damaged people to accomplish tasks which they could not master without its aid. It can also make life liveable for people who are emotionally disturbed or mentally ill. Because music is not so obviously necessary to most of us, we tend to underestimate its significance in the lives of normal people. Yet it is difficult to imagine a world without it. Even if playing music were forbidden, and every device for reproducing music destroyed, we should still have tunes running in our heads, still be using music to order our actions and make structured sense out of the world around us.

CHAPTER VI

THE SOLITARY LISTENER

Human music is the harmony which may be
known by any person who turns to contemplation
of himself.

GIOSEFFO ZARLINO[1]

The solitary listener to music is a modern phenomenon. Music's
original functions of underlining the significance of public events
and promoting social solidarity continue to this day. In the home,
music can also play some part in enhancing personal relations.
Domestic music-making has declined in recent years; but those
who still engage in it know that making music together is an
irreplaceable way of achieving closeness. The members of a string
quartet sometimes develop a special intimacy which they claim is
unmatched by any other relationship.

It is true that solo instrumentalists have always existed, and no
doubt they find that their daily practice brings them many rewards.
But the solitary *listener* to music depends upon modern technology
and is therefore historically a newcomer.

Has music's function changed because it is no longer necessarily
shared? Or does the possibility of experiencing music in solitude
simply clarify and underline its effects upon the individual listener?

It can be argued that even at a public concert each member of the
audience is isolated. As outlined earlier, the establishment of
concerts of instrumental music emphasized the distinction between
performer and listener and also made different individual responses
to particular pieces of music more likely. But this is not equivalent
to being alone. At a public concert, a listener may wish to be
separated as much as possible from his neighbours. He may shut his
eyes to their reactions; remain unwilling to share his appreciation

with others; stay cocooned within his individual seat. But he cannot totally deny the reality that he is attending a public occasion, or abolish the inductive effects of crowd responses.

Very few people are rich enough to emulate Proust, who used to pay a string quartet to play for himself alone; but those who prefer to experience music without the company of other people have access to another resource, established so recently that its impact on musical composition and performance is still in progress and cannot yet be finally assessed. Modern inventions have made it possible for the listener to enjoy music in complete isolation, unaffected by the responses of others, perhaps temporarily unaware of his surroundings, concentrating only on the music that he himself has selected.

Music's significance for the isolated listener has been greatly increased by modern methods of recording music. No one need go to concerts in order to hear superb performances. Although some musicians deplore the development of high-fidelity reproduction and claim that listening to live performance is the only genuine way to experience music, there is no reason to believe that the radio, the cassette, and the compact disc have diminished the number of live concerts or performances of opera which take place. In the West, the reverse is true. Although it is regrettable that concerts do not contain more contemporary music, the audience for live, classical music has continued to expand throughout the twentieth century.

Critics of recorded music are right to point out that repeated hearings of a particular performance may cause the listener to think that the interpretation to which he has become accustomed is the only possible one. Moreover, modern recording techniques, which often, though not invariably, involve repeated 'takes' of short sections of a work in order to eliminate minor slips, may also eliminate spontaneity. Great music demands an emotional commitment from performers which cannot easily be combined with an obsessional insistence on perfection. But the advantages of being able to listen to recorded music easily outweigh the undoubted disadvantages.

The Canadian pianist Glenn Gould retired from the concert platform at the age of thirty-one. He believed that personal display was corrupting, deplored applause at concerts, and thought that the concert hall would disappear by the year 2000 because of progress in the technology of recording. He claimed that the listener to recordings at home, by adjusting controls to his or her personal taste, could come closer to an ideal performance and reach a depth of musical experience unattainable at a live concert.

Gould's dislike of audiences was rooted in his own peculiar temperament. He was predominantly solitary, preferring telephone conversations to face-to-face encounters. Some of his performances reflect his eccentricities, whilst others, especially of J. S. Bach, are unsurpassed. But his ideas should not be dismissed because of his personal oddities. Music can and does affect the listener without having to be experienced live or in the company of others.

Modern technology makes it possible for individuals to listen to whatever music they want whenever it is convenient to them. At no previous period has such a huge variety of music been so easily available. Contemporary catalogues of compact discs include recordings of works by obscure composers who were formerly unknown to anyone other than specialists. Recordings also make it possible to hear music by great composers which has been forgotten or is seldom played. As Robbins Landon points out,

> Anyone can now listen to almost the complete major works of Haydn, something that no one except the composer was in any position to do hitherto . . . Hence we are for the first time in a position to view that mighty procession of works, the sum total of which is staggering and far beyond that of any other known composer.[2]

Modern recordings have proved an invaluable resource for students and historians. They have also enabled listeners to come to terms with difficult music through repeated hearings. Those who find that reading what is being played in the printed score enriches their listening usually discover that it is more convenient to do this at home. People who like to respond to music with physical movement can do so without disturbing others. Listening to recorded music has advantages as well as disadvantages. Professional musicians who dismiss such listening as inauthentic are not only misguided but also snobbish.

However, we must consider whether solitary listening to music is in any way peculiar or neurotic. I have already disputed the psychoanalytic idea that music is an escape from life or a regression to infancy. I am sure some psychoanalysts also believe that listening to music or playing an instrument when alone are substitutes for personal relationships. This is an entirely inadequate interpretation, but one which cannot be totally dismissed.

It is true that music is sometimes a source of comfort for people who find themselves alone without wanting to be so. In another book, I emphasized the distinction between solitude and loneliness, and drew attention to the benefits which solitude can bring.[3] Many people turn on the radio or the record-player whenever they find themselves without human company. By doing so, they reduce their capacity to enjoy being alone, and deprive themselves of the opportunities which solitude affords for the exercise of the imagination. A perpetual background of good music to which little serious attention is paid diminishes both the music and the listener. Although some intellectuals claim that their capacity for study is enhanced by background music, there is evidence that music interferes with intense concentration. As Zuckerkandl points out, chess contests are never accompanied by music; and, whilst persons peeling potatoes may sing at their work, scholars and scientists seldom do so.[4]

But even those who do appreciate solitude and make good use of it are lonely at times, and there is no doubt that music can alleviate loneliness, although this is a very minor one of its functions. Perhaps the listener demanding comfort of this kind should be content with Erik Satie's *musique d'ameublement*, which was composed especially with comfort in mind. When it was performed during the entr'actes of a play, whilst the audience were also looking at pictures, Satie specifically requested that no one should listen to it, and was annoyed when they stopped talking to do so.[5]

The fact that music can temporarily alleviate loneliness combined with the observation that it can affect relationships between both performers and listeners, raises an interesting question which goes far beyond the limitations of psychoanalytic interpretations of music as a substitute. Are our encounters with music in any way comparable with encountering persons?

Music is generally regarded as the most abstract of the arts, but there is a sense, albeit a limited one, in which getting to know a composer's music is also getting to know him or her as a person. The theory that composers embody their own feelings in a composition which then transmits those feelings direct to the listener was earlier dismissed as incomplete and unconvincing. But the ways in which great composers present universal emotions are, as Deryck Cooke put it, 'entirely personal'; and I think that our preferences and prejudices in music are partly related to the way in which the personal characteristics of different composers are embodied in their music.

Stravinsky's ideal was to create works in which the personal dimension is eliminated, which is why Constant Lambert condemned his neoclassical work as inhuman and mechanical. But, however successful a composer is in achieving elimination of the obviously subjective, an irreducible minimum of his own personality is bound to come through, making his works identifiably his. I suggest that it is this element which sometimes determines whether or not we can 'get on with' a particular composer.

This may not be a deeply important aspect of appreciating music, but it is a fascinating one. In the last chapter, I shall concur with Stravinsky in affirming that the form and structure of a musical work are more important than any personal feelings which it embodies. But, if we can come to terms with our own prejudices and learn to discount them, we may be able to understand the music of composers whom we do not take to at first, and thus widen our experience.

I earlier referred to Worringer's dichotomy of abstraction and empathy, and related it to two different, but equally valid, ways of appreciating music. We can approach music intellectually, and talk to each other about its structure in technical terms if we have learned the language. This is a justified way of discussing music which is essential to scholarship, history, and formal description. Detachment and cool judgement is needed in research and other scholarly activities, whether scientific, historical, literary, or musical. Such an attitude can become exaggerated. Musical scholars, who may spend their time studying scores in the same way that scholars in other subjects study verbal texts, sometimes complain that their research is so absorbing and so time-consuming that they no longer play music or listen to it. For them, music has become a scholastic endeavour devoid of emotional significance.

On the other hand, we can also involve ourselves with a musical work by means of empathy, identifying with its expressive aspects, allowing ourselves to be aroused emotionally, without paying much attention to its formal characteristics. This approach can also be exaggerated, leading to a loss of self-identity and a suspension of critical judgement. As already observed, it is difficult to combine both attitudes in a balanced fashion, especially when encountering music with which one is not already familiar.

The same considerations govern our encounters with other human beings. Experimental psychologists need to employ a strictly objective approach to other human beings which excludes their own feelings when they are conducting research. But social life demands a degree of empathy. We are not programmed to understand our fellow human beings scientifically, as if they were experimental subjects in a laboratory, and social intercourse would be impossible if we adopted such an attitude. Our ordinary understanding of other people depends upon an assumption of similarity. We need to believe that they possess an inner life of thoughts, feelings, desires, and choices which, though differing in detail, is not unlike our own. On the other hand, we can identify so closely with another person that we can no longer regard him or her objectively.

Encountering a new piece of music is not unlike making a new acquaintance. In both instances, increased familiarity will bring greater understanding. 'X is much nicer and more interesting than at first appears' may apply equally to a difficult person and to a difficult piece of music. Getting to know a difficult piece of music is comparable with getting to know a person who does not immediately reveal him- or herself, or who may appear to erect barriers against intimacy. As Frances Berenson writes:

> Personal knowledge of a work is an important aspect of one's engagement with it, an engagement which has the character of a relationship which is akin to friendship . . . Music has essentially human characteristics.[6]

The greatest compositions are highly individual and usually identifiable as the work of a particular composer. Of course there is room for error. Styles can be copied; and even experienced professional musicians make mistakes when asked to identify a piece of music which they have not heard for years, or when invited to name the composer of a work unknown to them. Because particular styles flourish at particular periods, it is sometimes easier to guess the date of an unknown composition than to identify its composer. This is often the case with minor composers whose music lacks the individual stamp of genius. The early works of a great composer may be similarly difficult to place because they were composed before he had discovered his own authentic, individual style.

But these cases are exceptional. What is more remarkable is the consistency of a great composer's style, even when attempting pastiche. A composer's style is at least as individual as a writer's use of language.

> When music is not making use of ready-made formulas, and sometimes even then, it is expressing. Through that expressiveness we come to learn the composer's style, to read his mind, and thus to share his meaning.[7]

I have quoted from Jerrold Northrop Moore's introduction to his biography of Elgar in another book but what he writes is so apposite that I do not apologize for repeating the quotation here.

> The artist, like the rest of us, is torn by various desires competing within himself. But, unlike the rest of us, he makes each of those desires into an element for use in his art. Then he seeks to synthesize his elements all together to form a style. The sign of a successful synthesis is a unified and unique style plain for all to recognize. So it is that a successful style can seem to its audience full of indefinably familiar things – and at the same time invested with godlike power of 'understanding' that is far indeed from the daily round. The process by which a man has forged such a unity is the most profound and most exalted of human stories.[8]

Nietzsche would have agreed with this. He referred to giving style to one's character as 'a great and rare art'.

Every creative artist is to some degree constrained by the *Zeitgeist*. Originality can only be recognized as such by comparison with the past or with prevalent contemporary modes of composition. We are all creatures of our age, influenced both by history and by our contemporaries. Yet genius, as Bernard Berenson defined it, is 'the capacity for productive reaction against one's training'.[9] The greatest composers, even when using the conventional forms of the age in which they lived, confound our expectations. In doing so, they affirm their individuality. We feel we 'know' Beethoven because we know his compositions, just as we 'know' Montaigne because we have read his essays. Our encounters with such masters are not face-to-face, but, through knowledge of their works, we feel we know them more intimately than many of our acquaintances.

Approaching a musical work as one approaches a person has another aspect. As we become more familiar with a new acquaintance, our opinion of that person will change; usually for the better, occasionally for the worse. The same change occurs as we get to know a composer's music. We need both empathy and abstraction: the capacity to feel our way into a composer's mind and the capacity to stand back and judge the music objectively. Haydn and Wagner are two great composers whose personalities are reflected in their works and who were also entirely dissimilar. Let them serve as illustrations.

Haydn is sometimes called 'a connoisseur's composer' or a 'musician's musician', as if only professionals could appreciate his skill, originality, and inexhaustible power of invention. This modern assessment is contradicted by history: in the eighteenth century, Haydn was in fact widely acclaimed throughout Europe. No other great composer has achieved such popularity during his own lifetime.

Haydn was both modest and deeply religious. He was well aware of his exceptional talent; but he treated it as a gift from God. When a visitor asked him how he managed to compose such a quantity of excellent music he replied:

Well, you see. I get up early, and as soon as I have dressed I go down on my knees and pray God and the Blessed Virgin that I may have another successful day. Then when I've had some breakfast I sit down at the clavier and begin my search. If I hit on an idea quickly, it goes ahead easily and without much trouble. But if I can't get on, I know that I must have forfeited God's grace by some fault of mine, and then I pray once more for grace till I feel I'm forgiven.[10]

He completed *The Creation* in 1801, at the age of sixty-nine. Griesinger reports him as saying:

Only when I reached the half-way mark in my composition did I perceive that it was succeeding, and I was never so devout as during the time that I was working on *The Creation*. Every day I fell to my knees and prayed God to grant me the strength for a happy completion of this work.[11]

Haydn displayed obsessional traits of character, as did Stravinsky and Rossini. He was preoccupied with cleanliness and order. He rose early, worked regularly, and kept to the same timetable of activity for most of his life.

Love of order seemed as inborn in him as industry. The former was to be observed, as also his love of cleanliness, in his person and in his entire household. He never received visits, for instance, if he were not first fully clothed. If he were surprised by a friend, he tried to get at least enough time to put on his wig.[12]

Both the contemporaries from whom I have quoted comment on Haydn's sense of humour.

A harmless roguery, or what the British call *humour*, was one of Haydn's outstanding characteristics. He easily and by preference discovered the comic side of anything, and anyone who had spent even an hour with him must have noticed that the very spirit of Austrian cheerfulness breathed in him.[13]

In contrast with Beethoven, who was briefly his pupil, Haydn always paid tribute to those who had taught him, and to composers who had influenced him; especially C. P. E. Bach, Gluck, and Handel. Original artists are prone to decry the work of their contemporaries. It is rare for an artist to acknowledge that a younger person working in the same field is his superior. Yet Haydn's modesty and generosity recognized Mozart's genius as greater than his own. The two composers were close friends; learned from each other, and played in string quartets and quintets together. When Mozart died, Haydn called his loss 'irreparable', and wept as he recalled his friend's clavier playing.

I don't think anyone who knows Haydn's music can fail to recognize that some of the characteristics of his personality are embedded in it. The listener does not even have to be able to read music to recognize Haydn's robustness and humour, combined with his capacity for deep feeling. A greater degree of musical sophistication may be needed to understand the scope of Haydn's inventiveness, ingenuity, intelligence, and originality. But no other composer, to my mind, has a greater capacity to dispel irritation or banish a mood of depression. There is an objectivity about his music which shames self-absorption and makes personal pre-occupations look petty. I believe that this is connected with his religious faith; with what Nietzsche referred to as the artist's need for 'protracted obedience' to 'something transfiguring, refined, mad and divine'.

Toward the end of his life Haydn wrote:

Often when I was wrestling with obstacles of every kind, when my physical and mental strength alike were running low and it was hard for me to persevere in the path on which I had set my feet, a secret feeling within me whispered: 'There are so few happy and contented people here below, sorrow and anxiety pursue them everywhere; perhaps your work may, some day, become a spring from which the careworn may draw a few moments' rest and refreshment.'[14]

It is not only the careworn who owe a debt to Haydn. His reinstatement as a great composer has been long delayed, but is now secure.

Occasionally, getting to know someone better results in dislike rather than in greater appreciation. This is relevant to the case of Wagner, whose music has evoked greater extremes of adoration and hatred than that of any other composer. According to Bryan Magee, it is because Wagner's music has the power to plumb new depths and uncover passions never before consciously experienced, that it and Wagner himself have been and still are the subjects of bitter controversy.

Magee's explanation is Freudian. *Tristan und Isolde* presents the most overtly erotic music ever composed. Oedipal themes can be discerned in both *Siegfried* and *Parsifal*. *Die Walküre* has incest between brother and sister, Siegmund and Sieglinde, as one of its main themes. Siegfried's beloved Brünnhilde was fathered by Wotan, his own grandfather, and is thus his aunt as well as his mistress. Magee suggests that some listeners dislike Wagner's music because it arouses or puts them in touch with unconscious desires which they cannot accept and are compelled to repudiate.

The philosopher Susanne K. Langer believed that music can present us with emotions and moods which have never before been felt and with passions hitherto unknown. She is not the only writer to recognize that music touches the unplumbed depths of our being. Proust wrote:

> Music, very different in this respect from Albertine's society, helped me to descend into myself, to discover new things: the variety that I had sought in vain in life, in travel, but a longing for which was none the less renewed in me by this sonorous tide whose sunlit waves now came to expire at my feet. [15]

This is true of widely different types of music; but, in this context, Proust was thinking of Wagner. Proust agreed that Wagner's music has a particularly penetrating quality, but suggested that this may not always be pleasant.

> I was struck by how much reality there is in the work of Wagner as I contemplated once more those insistent, fleeting themes which visit an act, recede only to return again and again, and, sometimes distant, drowsy, almost detached, are at other moments, while remaining vague, so pressing and so close, so internal, so organic, so visceral, that they seem like the reprise not so much of a musical motif as of an attack of neuralgia. [16]

Although I agree that music can present moods and passions which we have not yet encountered, I think it unlikely that

Wagner's music upsets some listeners because it is related to incest or to other repressed contents of the Freudian unconscious. There are other possible reasons. The intense dislike which some people feel for Wagner's music may be related to his personality as expressed in his music rather than to his capacity to stir Freudian depths. Adoration of Wagner followed by repulsion is not confined to Nietzsche. Cecil Gray, the composer, critic, and historian of music went through exactly the same process. In adolescence, he cared little for any music other than that of Wagner. He describes it as being like a fever in his blood, and himself as going through a 'phase of absolute self-immolation to the wizard of Bayreuth'.[17] Then, other kinds of music, especially Russian, French, and Italian, displaced Wagner in his affections. As we shall see later, the parallel with Nietzsche is exact.

Thomas Mann wrote:

> A passion for Wagner's enchanted *oeuvre* has been a part of my life ever since I first became aware of it and set out to make it my own, to invest it with understanding. What it has given me in terms of enjoyment and instruction I can never forget, nor the hours of deep and solitary happiness amidst the theatre throng, hours filled with frissons and delights for the nerves and the intellect alike, with sudden glimpses into things of profound and moving significance, such as only this art can afford.[18]

Yet Mann displayed ambivalence toward Wagner from the beginning. In a letter to the stage designer Emil Preetorius, he wrote:

> The man had so much ability, talent and interpretative skill – more than words can say. Yet so much affectation with it, such lordly pretension, self-aggrandizement and mystagogical self-dramatiza-tion – again, more than words can say or patience can bear.[19]

The first quotation comes from a lecture requested by the Goethe Society in Munich. Although the content of the lecture is pre-dominantly adulatory, Mann's reservations about Wagner incensed the Nazis and led to his exile from Germany, which lasted until his death.

Wagner's personality was charismatic, and so is his music. Both are predominantly Dionysian. Apollonian serenity and control are not what one looks for in Wagner. Nor are many of the pleasures associated with structure, form, and symmetry, although Wagner's use of the leitmotif is characteristic. I do not mean to suggest that Wagner did not understand such things. He was one of the most accomplished musicians to have ever lived, and could employ any compositional device which appealed to him, including sonata form. But this is not what he was aiming at.

Charismatic individuals, such as Wagner, open the doors of our perceptions, transcend our limitations, and reveal mysteries unknown to us. Eventually, they often disappoint us, because their narcissism and self-absorption preclude engagement with them as human beings of the same order as oneself. Composers who are as gifted as Mozart and Haydn are, of course, far superior to the ordinary person; but they retain their humanity and we can relate to them as human beings. Wagner is in a different category. His contemporary admirers treated him as a god. The modern listener succumbs and becomes a disciple, or else becomes disillusioned and escapes. 'How well he understands the soul! He rules over us with the arts of a demagogue!' Nietzsche's ambivalence toward Wagner is faithfully reflected in this remark from an imaginary conversation in 'Daybreak'.[20]

Wagner's music either overwhelms or repels because his style faithfully reflects his personality. The immense length of his later operas illustrates his disregard for the listener. He does not wish to communicate; only to convert. It need not prevent one from recognizing, and being intensely moved by, his music; but it is understandable that some listeners resent the feeling of being taken over rather than charmed or persuaded.

I think that people who are repelled by Wagner's music might well come to appreciate its power and beauty if they realized more clearly what was disturbing them. I believe that listeners to Wagner have to allow themselves to be temporarily overwhelmed if they are fully to appreciate the music. But many people are fearful of 'letting go' to this extent, and consequently shy away from the intense emotional experience which Wagner offers us.

In applying personal considerations to music, I want to

emphasize that the music always comes first. I call this chapter 'The Solitary Listener' because I am interested in the increase in purely private appreciation of music which has taken place in recent years. Solitary people who are interested in music listen to music more often than was possible before the advent of modern technology; but I am not arguing that listening to music is, or ever could be, a substitute for personal relationships. Some aspects of a composer's personality inevitably manifest themselves in his music; but the object of listening is to get to know the music, not to get to know the composer.

Great music transcends the individual who created it. My purpose in comparing getting to know a piece of music with getting to know a person was to point out the inadequacy of approaching music *only* as if it were a mathematical construction, not to deny that music has an impersonal dimension.

The examples of Haydn and Wagner are deliberately chosen as extremes. Although music inevitably reflects the personality of the composer to some degree, Stravinsky was surely right when he referred to a composition as being beyond the composer's feelings. Listening to music does bring us into indirect contact with the composer, but this meeting of minds is not closely comparable with encountering another human being or listening to a person speaking. Elements of both are present; but they do not account for the most important effects of music upon the listener.

As suggested in the last chapter, urban civilization cuts us off from our own inner lives. We have to be watchful, or we shall get run over. We are assailed by many varieties of noise, most of which are unpleasant. We cannot escape from other people, from the telephone, from having demands made upon us. We easily lose touch with the wellsprings of creative phantasy which make life worth living. Life for the ordinary man and woman must have been very different when it was predominantly rural and agricultural: when bird-song, rather than the noise of machinery, filled the ears; when the farmer could observe the changing seasons and enjoy the passage of the clouds; and when, however exhausting the toil, solitude allowed the exercise of the imagination.

Many sophisticated pursuits require intellectual concentration and detachment which would be contaminated if aesthetic considerations intruded. Conceptual thought requires the separation of thinking from feeling, of object from subject, of mind from body. We have already observed the divergence between song and speech, and the development of language as the vehicle of rational thinking as distinct from emotional expression. Human beings require this division if they are to function efficiently as objective thinkers; but they also need to bridge the Cartesian gulf between mind and body if they are to live life as creatures enjoying a full complement of human feelings. A great deal of what is generally considered to be 'real life' is woefully one-sided. But listening to or participating in music can restore a person to himself, as the epigraph to this chapter suggests. People need to recapture what has been excluded during working hours: their subjectivity.

Music began as a way of enhancing and co-ordinating group feelings. Today, it is often a means of recovering personal feelings from which we have become alienated. William Styron's account, quoted earlier, of how music suddenly reawakened his appreciation of his home and family, applies not only to sufferers from mental illness, but to each and every individual who, for whatever reason, is cut off from the life of the body and from the capacity to feel which ultimately makes life colourful, interesting, and exciting.

Music can certainly alter a person's mood, as many sufferers from recurrent depression have realized. We have noted some of the ways in which music has been used therapeutically in the treatment of the physically disabled, the mentally handicapped, and the mentally ill. Its therapeutic effects on the ordinary listener require further research, but there is no doubt that these effects occur whether or not the listener is alone. Listening to music by oneself restores, refreshes, and heals.

When we get to know a particular piece of music after repeated hearings, it is incorporated as a schema. The music becomes stored in the long-term memory as a whole – both form and content. It is therefore subject to voluntary recall. If I want to recapture the opening of Beethoven's first Razumovsky Quartet or the third movement of Brahms's Fourth Symphony, I can do so without difficulty, although I might not be able to remember the whole of either movement accurately. This is evidence that music can become part of our mental furniture. Because of this, I believe that music not only has a positive function in organizing our muscular actions but also, less obviously, our thoughts and the words in which we express them. The balanced sentences of a prose stylist like Edward Gibbon are probably derived from the antiphonal singing of psalms. Music informs and structures day-to-day actions to a much greater extent than most people realize.

This statement is confirmed experimentally by an interesting investigation into the capacities of ordinary people to create tunes. The study confirmed the authors' hypothesis that 'any person, whether musician or not is capable of composing music such as a song verse, using the musical patterns and structures provided by his/her daily musical environment (radio, TV, singing, etc.)'.[21]

Furthermore, the authors found that they had attained a new and different understanding of the part played by music in the daily lives of the people they studied, who varied from peasants to university students.

> In a part of our experiment not included in this study we dealt in greater detail with inner musical activity; we found that most people produce music by themselves for one or two hours a day, mainly by varying what they know or by combining the known tunes according to their tastes. In addition, if we also take into account music we just hear each day as background, it becomes evident music is practically a permanent part of most people's everyday mental activity.[22]

These findings confirm the suggestion that music plays a more important part in adaptation to life than is generally realized. They also imply that early exposure to all kinds of music should play a part in every child's education. Indeed, a study of New York children aged between two and six who had played in Alexander Blackman's Orchestra claimed that all the children who had had this opportunity were well ahead of their classmates when they entered school.[23]

If we do not provide adequate opportunities for our children to learn and participate in music, we are depriving them of something priceless. It is important that such provision should be made as early as possible. I am entirely in favour of recent methods of teaching children to play stringed instruments from an early age. Not all of them will turn into competent violinists, viola players, 'cellists, or double-bass players; but those who do will taste the delight of playing chamber music, than which there is no greater pleasure.

Let my own case serve as an example. Music has been a vital part of my life since early childhood. Although I am not gifted as a performer, playing the piano and the viola has been very rewarding to me, if not to others. I was lucky in being sent to a school where music was taken seriously. Since my voice declined tactfully rather than 'breaking', I had the pleasure of singing treble, alto, tenor, and bass successively, both in the Chapel choir and in the choral society, which performed at least two major choral works a year. I hated school; but, entirely because the musical opportunities were so great, my existence was made tolerable. Playing in an orchestra and singing in a choir are exhilarating experiences; but playing in a string quartet is better still.

I find it unsurprising that musical education has a good effect upon studying other subjects; but this is not generally appreciated by educational planners and politicians. My guess is that future research will disclose that those who have been lucky enough to receive an adequate musical education in early life are better integrated in every way when they reach maturity; and are therefore likely to be both happier and more effective. I agree with Plato's statement that music is 'a heaven-sent ally in reducing to order and harmony any disharmony in the revolutions within us'.[24]

Music which I voluntary summon is not the only music which I hear internally, without external stimulus. Whenever my attention is not fully engaged, music 'runs in my head' involuntarily. Sometimes it is music which I have heard recently, but often it is not. It can be annoying. I do not understand why some music is so persistent that it is hard to rid oneself of it. For me, one such piece is a theme from Berlioz's overture *Les Francs-juges*, the same theme which was used as introductory music to John Freeman's series of interviews on television, *Face to Face*. Even writing about it is enough to ensure that it will run in my head for an hour or two.

Another reason for annoyance is being unable to identify the music. I once spent a considerable period of time vainly searching through the scores of Haydn's quartets, convinced that the tune which was preoccupying me was the slow movement of one of them. It turned out to be from his 88th Symphony, which I had not heard for a long time.

What purpose is served by music running in the head unsummoned and perhaps unwanted? What follows is subjective speculation, but it is unlikely that my experience is unique. If I am engaged in any occupation not requiring intense concentration, the music which comes unbidden to my mind usually has physical and emotional effects of a positive kind. It alleviates boredom, makes my movements more rhythmical, and reduces fatigue. A routine trudge can be transformed into enjoyable exercise by the march 'Non più andrai' from *The Marriage of Figaro*. Music drawn from memory has many of the same effects as real music coming from the external world.

But I do not institute the process of recall. I do not determine that at that particular moment I need music, or choose what music shall come to the surface. It just happens. It is as if a beneficent deity was determined to ensure that I should not be bored and that my muscular movements should be efficiently and pleasurably co-ordinated. I conclude that music in the head is biologically adaptive.

Music running in the head may also have other functions. I have noticed – and again I would like confirmation from other sources – that when I am puzzled by the fact that one particular piece of music rather than another has spontaneously come to mind, prolonged consideration often, though not invariably, reveals the music's connection with other preoccupations. Jung once said that if one thought long enough about a dream, something almost always comes of it. The same applies to music which manifests itself out of the blue. The associations may be trivial. If I find myself humming Brahms's *Wiegenlied* it may be because I have been visiting a grandchild. On the other hand, identifying a tune which I cannot at first account for sometimes leads me to discover that I am more interested in, or worried by, some problem which I have been consciously neglecting.

Edward Cone of Princeton University confirms the supposition that music running in the head is evidence that music, for many of us, has become an integral part of our inner mental life, and therefore of living itself.

We can let it have its way, or we can direct it to our will; we can force it into new paths, or we can rehearse familiar works; we can listen to it, or we can relegate it to our subconscious; but we can never get rid of it. For one so endowed – or so burdened – to live is to live music.[25]

If music becomes a permanent part of our mental furniture, it must exert an influence on our lives. Educationalists and parents expect that exposure to great literature will influence their children. Spanning the centuries, we may say that reading Montaigne, Samuel Johnson, and Tolstoy enriches our understanding of reality, and therefore enlarges our capacity to enjoy life and enhances our adaptation to it. Shakespeare, Keats, and the other great poets reveal the inner nature of the world and sharpen our sensibilities because their perceptions and their gift for metaphor make it possible for us to transcend our own limited vision by sharing theirs. We take it for granted that encounters with the great minds of the past through literature are a vital part of education which may enable people to live lives which are less trivial, less circumscribed, and more imbued with meaning.

But Western society is so predominantly verbal that we fail to recognize that music has similar effects. Participating in music, whether as performer or listener, brings us into contact with greatness, and leaves traces of that greatness as permanent impressions. I share Plato's conviction that musical training is a potent instrument 'because rhythm and harmony find their way into the inward places of the soul'. I am subjectively certain that my involvement with Bach, Beethoven, Mozart, Haydn, Sibelius, Brahms, Bartók, Stravinsky, Wagner, and many other great composers has not only brought me pleasure but has deepened my appreciation of life, and I am not alone in feeling this.

The structure of autobiographies is usually determined by descriptions of places, occupations, and events which made up the author's life, together with accounts of the people who have influenced him or her, whether in person or through their writings. Only in biographies of musicians does one usually read of what music has influenced them – the first encounter with Bach, with Mozart, with Schoenberg. Yet such early experiences can be crucial in the emotional development of many people who do not become professional musicians: they are often milestones on the journey toward maturity which can be as important as the personal influence of teachers.

CHAPTER VII

THE INNERMOST NATURE
OF THE WORLD

Far from being a mere aid to poetry, music is
certainly an independent art; in fact, it is the most
powerful of all the arts, and therefore attains its
ends entirely from its own resources.

ARTHUR SCHOPENHAUER[1]

Schopenhauer is unusual amongst philosophers not only in paying
a great deal of attention to the arts in general, but also in according
music a special place amongst the arts. This is why it is important to
consider his views on music in some detail. It is worth recalling that
two great composers recorded their indebtedness to Schopenhauer.
Wagner first encountered *The World as Will and Representation* at the
age of forty-one, and from then on read and re-read Schopenhauer
continually. The indexes to the two massive volumes of Cosima
Wagner's diaries give 197 references to Schopenhauer. Mahler,
according to his wife, thought that Schopenhauer's account of
music was the most profound ever likely to be written. He gave a
complete edition of Schopenhauer's works to Bruno Walter as a
Christmas present.[2]

In order to understand what Schopenhauer had to say about
music, a brief, partial, and necessarily inadequate outline of some of
his philosophical ideas is required. Following Kant, Schopenhauer
thought that human beings are pre-programmed in that they are
bound to perceive objects in the external world as existing in space
and time, and as being governed by causal relations. We are
compelled to experience the world in this way; we cannot avoid
doing so. But, since these ways of experiencing the world are
rooted in the construction of the human perceptual apparatus and

the human brain, the way we see objects and the relations between them may not correspond to the way those objects actually are.

We all know that there are sounds which our ears cannot hear, and colours which our eyes cannot see, but which can be perceived by other species or by special instruments. Dogs can respond to tones of very high frequency which the human ear cannot hear; infra-red cameras can 'see' objects which the human eye cannot. The limitations of our perceptual apparatus restrict our apperception of the world; the limitations of our cerebral apparatus restrict the ways in which we can think about it. The world may not only be stranger than we think it is, but stranger than we can possibly imagine.

But Schopenhauer goes further than this. Even if our ingenuity enlarges our perceptual grasp, by inventing special techniques which enable us to incorporate the sounds we cannot hear and the sights we cannot see into our incomplete picture of external reality, we can never transcend the limitations imposed by our concepts of space, time, and causality. Schopenhauer therefore concluded that we could never perceive objects as noumena or 'things-in-themselves', as Kant called them. All we can do is register the ways in which they appear to us; that is, their 'representations' as phenomena in the external world.

But, if this is true, it must follow, as a correlative concept, that 'things-in-themselves' exist, and that they have their being in an underlying reality to which our categories of space, time and causality do not apply. For it makes no sense to say that our perceptions are subjective or partial unless there is a reality which is supposedly objective and complete, even if we have no access to it.

However, the underlying reality postulated must be one in which objects are not differentiated: in other words, a unity. For abolishing the categories of space, time and causality necessarily makes it impossible to distinguish one object from another. Hence Schopenhauer's vision is that ultimate reality is a unity – the *unus mundus* of mediaeval philosophy, which is both beyond our human categories of space, time and causality and also beyond the Cartesian division into physical and mental.

Both Kant and Schopenhauer thought that this underlying reality was inaccessible. However, according to Schopenhauer, one type of experience brings us closer to the underlying noumenon than any other. He suggested that we have a direct knowledge from inside our own bodies which is unlike the perception we have of anything else. Of course, our bodies, like other objects in the material world, are perceived by others, and can be partly perceived by ourselves in the same way as we perceive other objects, with all the limitations which this implies. A man can look at his own right hand exactly as he looks at anyone else's right hand. But, in addition, Schopenhauer claims that we have this private, subjective, knowledge of our own physical being and its movements. The distinguished British philosopher, David Pears, writes,

> At the basis of Schopenhauer's system there is a thesis in speculative metaphysics: we do have a resource which allows us to discern the nature of the reality behind the phenomenal world; we have our experience of our own agency. According to Schopenhauer, when we act, our knowledge of our own agency is neither scientific nor the result of any other kind of discursive operation of the intellect. It is direct, intuitive, inside knowledge of our own strivings, and he believed that it gives us our only glimpse of the true nature of reality.[3]

In Schopenhauer's scheme of things, this inner knowledge is the nearest we get to perception of the Will, the driving force or energy underlying everything of which individuals are but manifestations. For, in his view, bodily movements are the phenomenal expression of that irrational, inexplicable, underlying striving toward existence which he called the Will, but which he might equally well have called Energy or Force. Nietzsche's Will to Power is a derivative of Schopenhauer's notion. It is important to realize that Schopenhauer's Will (and Nietzsche's) include the impersonal as well as the personal; that is, the Will refers to cosmic energy, the force that moves the planets or forms the stars, as well as to the energy which activates human beings. Schopenhauer himself referred to Will as 'endless striving', and also as 'the *thing-in-itself* proper'.[4] Schopenhauer regarded the Will with deep pessimism, whilst Nietzsche took a neutral view of the Will to Power.

In an interesting passage, Schopenhauer states that, if we proceed along the path of objective knowledge, we shall never get beyond the representation, i.e., the phenomenon. We shall therefore remain at the outside of things; we shall never be able to penetrate into their inner nature, and investigate what they are in themselves, in other words, what they may be by themselves. So far I agree with Kant. But now, as the counterpoise to this truth, I have stressed that other truth that we are not merely the *knowing subject*, but that *we ourselves* are also among those realities or entities we require to know, that *we ourselves are the thing-in-itself*. Consequently, a way *from within* stands open to us to that real inner nature of things to which we cannot penetrate *from without*. It is, so to speak, a subterranean passage, a secret alliance, which, as if by treachery, places us all at once in the fortress that could not be taken by attack from without. [5]

It is fair to say that Schopenhauer qualifies this statement by affirming that even this inner knowledge and approach to 'the thing-in-itself' is necessarily incomplete. Schopenhauer is not saying that the special knowledge which comes to us from awareness of our bodies from inside is direct knowledge of the Will itself; for all knowledge must itself exist in the phenomenal world. The very concept of knowledge requires a dichotomy between the thing which is known and the knower; and such dichotomies, as we have seen, cannot exist in the underlying unity, in which all opposites have disappeared.

But he is claiming that this special, inside knowledge of the inner strivings which manifest themselves in our physical movements, together with our vaguer intuitions of the unconscious drives which motivate us, give us pointers or hints about the nature of the underlying reality to which we have no direct access. This is the point at which the phenomenon is closest to the noumenon.

In his exposition of Schopenhauer's doctrine, Patrick Gardiner writes:

What I am aware of in self-consciousness is not, it is true, something separate from what I am aware of when I look at my body and observe its movements, if by this it is implied that I have to do with two different entities or with two different sets of occurrences. The point is, however, that when I am conscious of myself as will I am not conscious of myself *as an object*; I am only conscious of myself under the latter aspect when I perceive myself at the same time as a body, for my body is the 'objectification' of my will.[6]

For example, I see, but my eye cannot see itself, unless I am looking in a mirror. This is Will in action. Schopenhauer states that 'the action of the body is nothing but the act of will objectified . . . Every true, genuine, immediate act of the will is also at once and directly a manifest act of the body . . .'[7]

We are not usually *conscious* of our inner sense of striving as manifested in bodily movements except under special circumstances when we plan some action which is not habitual, as when we are learning to ride a bicycle or play a musical instrument. In the ordinary way, we just move in accordance with some prior intention which may or may not be consciously perceived, and then evaluate the move we have executed according to its results. If this was not the case, we might find ourselves in rather the same quandary as the centipede who found himself immobilized because he had been asked to indicate which leg followed which when he was walking. The Will may be operative in physical actions, as Schopenhauer alleges, but, whenever we become conscious of the body's operation, we are regarding it in the same way that we regard other objects. However, it is certainly true that my own body occupies a special niche in my experience of the world, even if I am only intermittently aware of its operations.

Schopenhauer thought that men's actions were far less governed by premeditation and deliberate planning than they believed. Very commonly, men act in accordance with their inner strivings without realizing what those strivings are, and then attempt to justify them afterwards. Anticipating Freud, Schopenhauer noted that we are frequently unaware of our true motives, and may only become conscious of what we were aiming at (or what the Will was aiming at) after we have acted and noted the results of our actions.

Jung, who read Schopenhauer in adolescence and who admitted being deeply influenced by him, begins his autobiography by writing, 'My life is a story of the self-realisation of the unconscious.'[8] This initial sentence expresses Schopenhauer's idea in different words. The individual is one possible manifestation of an underlying force which is always seeking to realize itself in the world of phenomena, but which is antecedent to all phenomena. Each bloom on a rose tree may be slightly different; but each is an expression of whatever inner force makes rose trees grow, flourish, and put forth blooms. Neither Schopenhauer's term, the Will, nor Jung's term, the Unconscious, are satisfactory; but it is hard to think of anything better. Like Nietzsche, Jung believed that there was only one fundamental striving: the striving after one's own being.

In his visionary *Septem Sermones ad Mortuos*, written in 1916, when he was going through a period of personal turmoil, Jung refers to the underlying reality as the *pleroma*, a term which he borrowed from the Gnostics. The *pleroma* cannot be described, because it has no qualities. In the *pleroma*, there are no opposites, like good and evil, time and space, or force and matter, since all these opposites are created by human thought.

Jung also believed that we have partial, occasional access to this underlying reality outside space and time; but his subterranean passage was not by way of bodily action but through 'synchronicity': that is, meaningful coincidence in time which is outside our habitual categories of space and causality. Jung gives as an example Swedenborg's vision of a fire which arose in his mind at the same time as an actual fire was raging in Stockholm. Jung comments:

> We must assume that there was a lowering of the threshold of consciousness which gave him access to 'absolute knowledge.' The fire in Stockholm, was, in a sense, burning in him too. For the unconscious psyche space and time seem to be relative; that is to say, knowledge finds itself in a space-time continuum in which space is no longer space, nor time time.[9]

Those who are inclined to dismiss such ideas as nonsense may find that David Peat's book *Synchronicity* persuades them otherwise. Peat understands modern physics, and is prepared to defend the idea that there is an underlying order in the universe in which causality and the division between mind and matter do not apply.[10]

Why did Schopenhauer single out music as being different in nature from the other arts? As we have already observed, music is neither propositional, nor does it usually imitate phenomena. It does not put forward theories or inform us about the world; nor, except in rare instances like Delius's *On Hearing the First Cuckoo in Spring*, or Haydn's *The Creation*, does it represent the sounds of nature. Schopenhauer explicitly rejects imitative music as being inauthentic, including Haydn's *The Seasons, The Creation*, and all battle pieces, because such music is no longer fulfilling its true function of expressing the inner nature of the Will itself.[11]

Schopenhauer considered that the other arts were not merely imitations of external reality; or, that if particular works of art were so, they were also being false to their high calling. In his view, the function of the arts is not to depict particular instances of reality, but to represent the universals which lie behind the particular. For example, a painting portrays a particular woman and child as a representation of the Madonna and Christ; but, in order to qualify as high art, the picture must convey something of the essence of maternal love itself. Innumerable paintings of the Madonna and Child exist, but only the greatest artists create an image which transcends the personal, and which seems to portray the 'divine' element in maternal tenderness. What a great painting is concerned with is an archetype: an Idea which can only be manifested in a particular, but which itself transcends particulars.

The word *Idea* in the last sentence is given a capital letter because Schopenhauer took over Plato's theory that Ideas, as ideal examples of, say, Justice, Goodness, Love, and Truth, existed as definable entities in some realm of generalities which could only be entered when men detached themselves from considering particulars in the mundane here-and-now.

> And there is an absolute beauty and an absolute good, and of other things to which the term 'many' is applied there is an absolute; for they may be brought under a single idea, which is called the essence of each.[12]

Plato thought that to understand what it is to be a good man, one must have an appreciation of Goodness as an absolute. In like fashion, if one wished to know whether a particular action or decision was just, one must have knowledge of Justice as an abstract ideal. Schopenhauer said of the Ideas, 'These are outside time, and consequently *eternal*.'[13]

Jung thought precisely the same of archetypes, which he equates with the Platonic Ideas. Archetypes are primordial images which manifest themselves particularly in creative phantasy:

> there are present in every psyche forms which are unconscious but nonetheless active – living dispositions, ideas in the Platonic sense, that preform and continually influence our thoughts and feelings and actions.[14]

Jung came to believe that reality was

> grounded on an as yet unknown substrate possessing material and at the same time psychic qualities. In view of the trend of modern theoretical physics, this assumption should arouse fewer resistances than before.[15]

Although, at first glance, one might equate an Idea with a concept, Schopenhauer repudiated this. In his view, concepts, the tools of thought and of human communication, are cerebral constructs, whereas the eternal Ideas are antecedent to human thinking. The Idea manifests itself in various forms. The concept may bring together a variety of such manifestations under one heading; but it is not antecedent to thought but a product of thought.

> The *Idea* is the unity that has fallen into plurality by virtue of the temporal and spatial form of our intuitive apprehension. The *concept*, on the other hand, is the unity once more produced out of plurality by means of abstraction through our faculty of reason; the latter can be described as *unitas post rem*, and the former as *unitas ante rem*.[16]

Concepts, in Schopenhauer's view, are essentially abstract cerebrations, which are somewhat lifeless. Artists who plan every detail of a work before embarking on it are using conceptual thought only; and hence produce dull, boring works because they have cut themselves off from the deeper sources of inspiration – the

Ideas. Schopenhauer thought that it was the function of art to represent the Ideas. Art, he wrote:

> repeats the eternal Ideas apprehended through pure contemplation, the essential and abiding element in all the phenomena of the world. According to the material in which it repeats, it is sculpture, painting, poetry, or music. Its only source is knowledge of the Ideas; its sole aim is communication of this knowledge.[17]

To appreciate art, the observer must adopt a special attitude of mind; the same attitude required by Plato, of detachment from personal concerns, so that the work of art can be appreciated in contemplative fashion uncontaminated by personal needs or preoccupations.

For example, a man can look at a beautiful painting of a nude like the *Rokeby Venus* in two ways. He can see her as an object of desire, and perhaps experience some degree of sexual arousal. Or he can see her as an archetype of Woman, the essence of the feminine. The latter way of looking, in which personal interests and aims are temporarily discarded, is, according to Schopenhauer, the only way to appreciate art, and the only way, therefore, of obtaining a glimpse of the inner nature of the world. Schopenhauer calls this the 'aesthetic way of knowing'. It is an exercise in *empathy*. Worringer expresses it thus: 'We are delivered from our individual being as long as we are absorbed into an external object, an external form, with our inner urge to experience.'[18]

When we employ the aesthetic way of knowing, we are temporarily removed from the tyranny of hopes and fears, of desire, of personal striving. And we are also abandoning the scientific way of knowing, which enquires into the nature of the object as existing in the external world, and into its relations with other objects. Thus, in the case of the *Rokeby Venus*, we might want to know when Velázquez painted the picture; how he obtained his effects; who was his model; who commissioned it, and so on. This is a perfectly legitimate way of approaching the painting; but employing it must necessarily prevent our appreciation of its inner meaning and significance during the time we are pursuing our enquiries. As noted earlier, the contrast between aesthetic and scientific knowing, between empathy and abstraction, is a particularly apt dichotomy when we consider the appreciation of music, and one which has given rise to controversy. It is a pity that Schopenhauer referred to what we now call empathy as the 'aesthetic' way of knowing, for abstraction is equally 'aesthetic'; perhaps more so, since it is more concerned with appreciation of proportion and structure.

Art was important to the pessimistic Schopenhauer because the aesthetic mode of knowing, the pure contemplation of beauty, the tranquil appreciation of the Ideas, enabled the individual to escape, for the time being, from the never-ending misery of unsatisfied desire into a Nirvana of spiritual peace.

> There always lies so near to us a realm in which we have escaped entirely from all our affliction; but who has the strength to remain in it for long? As soon as any relation to our will, to our person, even of those objects of pure contemplation, again enters consciousness, the magic is at an end. We fall back into knowledge governed by the principle of sufficient reason; we now no longer know the Idea but the individual thing, the link of a chain to which we also belong, and we are again abandoned to all our woe.[19]

Whatever we may think of Schopenhauer's philosophical explanation, we can appreciate as accurate and illuminating this description of aesthetic experience temporarily 'taking ourselves out of ourselves' before we return to the everyday world of getting and spending. But Schopenhauer's portrayal of the aesthetic mode of knowing does not include arousal. Reading his account leaves one with the impression that being taken out of oneself, forgetting oneself as an individual, as he puts it, invariably leads to a contemplative state from which all passion is absent. In fact, he describes the aesthetic attitude as an objective frame of mind, as if stepping into another world, 'where everything that moves our will, and thus violently agitates us, no longer exists'.[20]

But music can cause intense excitement. For example, hearing the fugal Finale of Beethoven's Razumovsky Quartet in C major, Op. 59, No. 3, is an exhilarating experience which is as far removed from the peace of Nirvana as one can possibly imagine. So is listening to Haydn's 'Oxford' Symphony, or to Mozart's overture to *The Marriage of Figaro*. In Chapter Two, the relation between music and arousal was discussed. Physiological arousal does not always manifest itself in exhilaration, although this state is that most obviously incompatible with the tranquillity of Nirvana. We are also deeply moved, and therefore physiologically aroused, by tragedy. Arousal also enters into our appreciation of the other arts, although less obviously. I am sure that Schopenhauer, who had a wide knowledge and appreciation of the arts, was often deeply moved by them; but he did not make it clear that being deeply moved was compatible with the aesthetic way of knowing.

Schopenhauer's aesthetic mode of knowing is a mental set in which personal desires and strivings are abolished because the subject has lost himself in the contemplation of beauty. Freud's Nirvana is reached by the satisfaction of personal desires through instinctual discharge, or by regression to a condition resembling earliest infancy. For both men, the ideal is a tensionless state rather than one of arousal or excitement. Emotions are not pleasures to be sought, but intruders to be banished.

A profound pessimism underlies these ideas. The wish to abolish willing and striving, to avoid arousal, to purge oneself of desire, is life-denying rather than life-enhancing. Most human beings feel that arousal, in one form or another, is what makes life worth living. We crave excitement, involvement, enjoyment, and love. The Nirvana sought by Schopenhauer and Freud can only finally be found in Swinburne's 'The Garden of Proserpine', where 'even the weariest river winds somewhere safe to sea'. It is not surprising that Freud postulated a death instinct; an inner striving toward return to the inorganic state.

> If we are to take it as a truth that knows no exception that everything living dies for *internal* reasons – becomes inorganic once again – then we shall be compelled to say that '*the aim of all life is death*' and, looking backwards, that '*inanimate things existed before living ones*'.[21]

Wagner died in 1883, twelve years before Freud published his first psychoanalytic papers. Had he lived to appreciate Freud's later work, I feel sure that he would have embraced it with the same enthusiasm with which he welcomed the writings of Schopenhauer. For Wagner, the highest bliss was 'the bliss of quitting life, of being no more', as he himself wrote. The final scenes of *Der Fliegende Holländer*, *Götterdämmerung*, and *Tristan und Isolde* demonstrate his initial belief that love can only find its ultimate fulfilment in death. In *Parsifal* and in the characters of Wotan and Sachs in *Siegfried* and *Die Meistersinger* respectively, Schopenhauerian renunciation of the will, rather than death, is the key to redemption. *

It is also possible to believe that love finds its fulfilment in more life – in children, grandchildren, and later descendants. But this implies a genuine appreciation of the importance of others. Narcissists are bound to feel that their own death is the end of everything that really matters.

> Wagner had expressed at once the ultimate triumph, and the fallacy of humanism. He believes only in himself: his own feelings are the universe. That being so, his feelings can lead to nothing but their extinction. A yearning so fierce can be appeased only in its cessation; so the fulfilment of love is death. [22]

Schopenhauer and Freud were explicit atheists. Wagner vacillated throughout his life, at times denying Christianity, at times appearing to embrace it. Schopenhauer and Freud denied the possibility of an after-life; but all three believed in the immortality of their works. It is unsurprising that extinction of desire and striving constitutes an ideal state for each of these men of genius.

Schopenhauer put music in a special category. How does music differ from the other arts? Schopenhauer considered that poetry and drama are concerned with revealing the Idea of mankind as it manifests itself in the particular situations with which the poet or dramatist presents us. The Will, the underlying dynamic, is manifesting itself through the Idea, which is here acting as an intermediary.

> The (Platonic) Ideas are the adequate objectification of the will. To stimulate the knowledge of these by depicting individual things (for

*I am indebted to Lucy Warrack for this observation.

works of art are themselves always such) is the aim of all the other arts (and is possible with a corresponding change in the knowing subject). Hence all of them objectify the will only indirectly, in other words, by means of the Ideas.[23]

In Schopenhauer's view, music is different from all the other arts because it speaks to us direct: it bypasses the Ideas.

Therefore music is by no means like the other arts, namely a copy of the Ideas, but a *copy of the will itself*, the objectivity of which are the Ideas. For this reason, the effect of music is so very much more powerful and penetrating than is that of the other arts, for these others speak only of the shadow, but music of the essence.[24]

Because music neither represents the phenomenal world, nor makes statements about it, it bypasses both the pictorial and the verbal. When we look at a picture, the fact of the picture's existence as a tangible object in the external world acts as an intermediary between ourselves and the underlying Idea which the artist is expressing. When we read a poem, the words in which the poem is written act similarly. Since the painter must, by definition, express what he has to express in a picture, and the poet must express what he has to express in words, it may seem stupid to write of pictures and words as intermediaries. But, if we consider that paintings are representations of something which the painter wishes to convey to us, and if we also accept that language is intrinsically metaphorical, we can appreciate that the medium is not identical with the message, and may, in some sense, distort it, or present it incompletely. This, of course, is why artists are never satisfied with what they have produced, but are compelled to go on striving to find a yet more perfect way of expressing whatever it is that they want to convey.

Music, according to Schopenhauer, is understood immediately without any need to give any account of it or form any abstract conception of it. Hence, he is excluding Worringer's 'abstraction': the objective mode of perception by which we judge the structure and coherence of a musical work. What music expresses is the *inner* spirit.

This close relation that music has to the true nature of all things can also explain the fact that, when music suitable to any scene, action, event, or environment is played, it seems to disclose to us its most secret meaning, and appears to be the most accurate and distinct commentary on it . . . Accordingly, we could just as well call the world embodied music as embodied will; this is the reason why music makes every picture, indeed every scene from real life and from the world, at once appear in enhanced significance, and this is, of course, all the greater, the more analogous its melody is to the inner spirit of the given phenomenon.[25]

Busoni had closely similar views about music expressing the inner significance of events and human feelings.

The greater part of modern theatre music suffers from the mistake of seeking to repeat the scenes passing on the stage, instead of fulfilling its proper mission of interpreting the soul-states of the persons represented. When the scene presents the illusion of a thunderstorm, this is exhaustively apprehended by the eye. Nevertheless, nearly all composers strive to depict the storm in tones – which is not only a needless and feebler repetition, but likewise a failure to perform their true function. The person on the stage is either psychically in-fluenced by the thunderstorm, or his mood, being absorbed in a train of thought of stronger influence, remains unaffected. The storm is visible and audible without aid from music; it is the invisible and inaudible, the spiritual processes of the personages portrayed, which music should render intelligible.[26]

Schopenhauer claims that music expresses the Will direct as it manifests itself in the emotional life of man; that it closely corresponds to the fluctuations in emotional state which we all experience.

Now the nature of man consists in the fact that his will strives, is satisfied, strives anew, and so on and on; in fact his happiness and well-being consist only in the transition from desire to satisfaction, and from this to a fresh desire, such transition going forward rapidly. For the non-appearance of satisfaction is suffering; the empty longing for a new desire is languor, boredom. Thus, corresponding to this, the nature of melody is a constant digression and deviation from the keynote in a thousand ways, not only to the harmonious intervals, the third and dominant, but to every tone, to the dissonant seventh, and to the extreme intervals; yet there always follows a final return to the keynote. In all these ways, melody expresses the many different forms of the will's efforts, but also its satisfaction by ultimately finding again a harmonious interval, and still more the keynote.[27]

But, given Schopenhauer's belief that life predominantly consists of suffering, why should anyone want to contemplate the fluctuations of desire and satisfaction which Schopenhauer claims that music portrays, even if this portrayal is in the abstract? Would it not be preferable to concern oneself only with the impersonal: for example, with the beauties of the natural world? One might assume, from Schopenhauer's attitude, that he would only like music which predominantly portrays peace and stillness.

It therefore seems surprising that Schopenhauer singles out Rossini, whose music is so often vivacious that Tovey pejoratively described it as voluble, facile, and a rollicking rattle. Such descriptions are unfair to Rossini, but it is true that his music is usually lively rather than peaceful.

> Everywhere music expresses only the quintessence of life and its events, never these themselves, and therefore their differences do not always influence it. It is just this individuality that belongs uniquely to music, together with the most precise distinctness, that gives it that high value as the panacea of all our sorrows. Therefore, if music tries to stick too closely to the words, and to mould itself according to events, it is endeavouring to speak a language not its own. No-one has kept so free from this mistake as Rossini; hence his music speaks its *own* language so distinctly and purely that it requires no words at all, and therefore produces its full effect even when rendered by instruments alone.[28]

Since Rossini was predominantly a composer of opera, in which words and music are closely intertwined, Schopenhauer's choice seems, at first sight, inexplicably eccentric. But he believed that, although the music of an opera was composed with reference to the drama, it was so concerned with the *inner* significance of the events portrayed that it bore little direct relation to those events as particular instances. He points out that the same music might be accompanying the passions of Agamemnon and Achilles or the dissensions of an ordinary family.

> The music of an opera, as presented in the score, has a wholly independent, separate, and as it were abstract existence by itself, to which the incidents and characters of the piece are foreign, and which follows its own unchangeable rules; it can therefore be completely effective even without the text.[29]

Schopenhauer here anticipates the kind of criticisms which have been made of Deryck Cooke's *The Language of Music*, some of which we have already encountered. Music underlines and emphasizes the emotions which drama arouses in the spectator; but its capacity to portray and arouse specific emotions in the absence of drama – whether presented on stage or in real life ceremonials – is rather limited. For example, music alone cannot specifically portray jealousy; although the music used to underline a dramatic scene of jealousy might deserve to be described as both passionate and agitated.

There is a fascinating discussion of these problems in Edward Cone's book *The Composer's Voice*. Cone points out that we are usually only partly aware of the prosodic elements of our own utterances. We can raise our voices without knowing that we are doing so; we can speak in tones which display an underlying gloom without the least awareness of our self-revelation. By adding music to words, the composer can bring out and emphasize the underlying emotional meaning of those words, irrespective of the insight or lack of insight of the character portrayed.

> So when, as in song, a musical line is combined with a text, it is natural for us to accept the music as referring to a subconscious level underlying – and lying under – whatever thoughts and emotions are expressed by the words.[30]

As the quotations given above demonstrate, Schopenhauer believed that the music of an opera was, or could be, entirely independent of the text; whereas Cone is emphasizing the close link between the two. But the philosopher and the musicologist join hands in thinking that music is concerned with the inner life rather than with external reality.

It is worth remarking that Schopenhauer was writing about the Western tonal system based upon the major triad as if it was the only musical system. He even refers to music as 'an exceedingly universal language',[31] which, as already noted, it certainly is not. Schopenhauer could not, of course, anticipate the atonality of Schoenberg or the twelve-tone system. But he does not consider music based primarily on rhythmic variation rather than upon melody; or music using a pentatonic scale; or music using intervals smaller than the semitone. On the other hand, Schopenhauer's account of melody does formulate one feature of musical experience which some later authorities say is common to all varieties of music: that musical compositions are structured by setting a norm, then by deviating from that norm, and finally by returning to it. This closely resembles the theory of music advanced by Leonard B. Meyer which was discussed earlier.

Schopenhauer also anticipates the theories of Susanne K. Langer, although he is given only passing mention in her books *Philosophy in a New Key*, and *Feeling and Form*. Schopenhauer specifically stated that music does not express particular emotions directly.

> But we must never forget when referring to all these analogies I have brought forward, that music has no direct relation to them, but only an indirect one; for it never expresses the phenomenon, but only the inner nature, the in-itself, of every phenomenon, the will itself. Therefore music does not express this or that particular and definite pleasure, this or that affliction, pain, sorrow, horror, gaiety, merriment, or peace of mind, but joy, pain, sorrow, horror, gaiety, merriment, peace of mind *themselves*, to a certain extent in the abstract, their essential nature, without any accessories and so also without the motives for them. Nevertheless, we understand them perfectly in this extracted quintessence.[32]

Instead of quoting this passage from Schopenhauer, Langer quotes from Wagner, who wrote what follows years before he encountered Schopenhauer. In view of the close similarity of the two passages, it is not surprising that Wagner later became an enthusiastic adherent of Schopenhauer's philosophy. Wagner affirms:

> What music expresses, is eternal, infinite and ideal; it does not express the passion, love, or longing of such-and-such an individual on such-and-such an occasion, but passion, love or longing in itself, and this it presents in that unlimited variety of motivations, which is the exclusive and particular characteristic of music, foreign and inexpressible to any other language.[33]

This passage states, in different words, what Schopenhauer wrote in the extract given immediately above. Langer herself comments on what Wagner has to say.

> Despite the romantic phraseology, this passage states quite clearly that music is not self-expression, but *formulation and representation* of emotions, moods, mental tensions and resolutions – a 'logical picture' of sentient, responsive life, a source of insight, not a plea for sympathy.[34]

What is not clear from Schopenhauer's account is how music differs from, say, poetry, in furnishing a more direct expression of the innermost nature of man. For are not the tones which music employs comparable with the words which poetry employs? And is it not true that both poetry and music are representations of the inner life, not the inner life itself?

Schopenhauer claimed that music more directly expresses the inner life than the other arts because it does not make use of the Ideas. Music goes deeper than pictures, deeper than words. But music employs tones; and tones, as indicated in the first chapter, are seldom found in nature. Western music, with which Schopenhauer was concerned, consists of tones arranged in a variety of melodic, rhythmic, and harmonic patterns. These patterns may have little connection with the external world; but, because their construction requires considerable artifice, music can hardly be regarded as the immediate objectification and copy of the inner life or Will which Schopenhauer claimed it to be. Music, by employing sounds which are not found in nature, and which are arranged in extremely complex ways, may certainly be expressing the inner life in metaphorical fashion; but its composition requires as much conceptual thought as poetry.

Schopenhauer did not really take this into account, as evidenced by his writing

> The invention of melody, the disclosure in it of all the deepest secrets of human willing and feeling, is the work of genius, whose effect is more apparent here than anywhere else, is far removed from all reflection and conscious intention, and might be called an inspiration. Here, as everywhere in art, the concept is unproductive. The composer reveals the innermost nature of the world, and expresses the profoundest wisdom in a language that his reasoning faculty does not understand . . . .[35]

No one can deny that melodies can be the result of inspiration; but many require much revision and amendment, as Beethoven's sketchbooks repeatedly demonstrate. It is also true, as we know from accounts by poets of their own creative processes, that some lines of poetry come unbidden to the poet's mind, and are, therefore, equally 'far removed from all reflection and conscious intention'. Schopenhauer's attempt to put music in a special category for the reasons which he advances is unconvincing. However, there are other observations which support his intuition.

Michael Tippett, the composer, echoes some of what Schopenhauer writes about music portraying the inner flow of life, but adds a comment which goes some way to explaining why we want to reproduce and experience this flow, which is exactly what Schopenhauer fails to do. Tippett writes:

> Symphonic music in the hands of the great masters truly and fully embodies the otherwise unperceived, unsavoured inner flow of life. In listening to such music we are as though entire again, despite all the insecurity, incoherence, incompleteness and relativity of our everyday life. The miracle is achieved by submitting to the power of its organized flow; a submission which gives us a special pleasure and finally enriches us. The pleasure and the enrichment arise from the fact that the flow is not merely the flow of the music itself, but a significant image of the inner flow of life. Artifice of all kinds is

necessary to the musical composition in order that it shall become such an image. Yet when the perfect performance and occasion allow us a truly immediate apprehension of the inner flow 'behind' the music, the artifice is momentarily of no consequence; we are no longer aware of it. [36]

In the present context, the most important sentence from this quotation is the second one. Tippett is suggesting that listening to music makes us aware of important aspects of ourselves which we may not ordinarily perceive; and that, by putting us into touch with these aspects, music makes us whole again. This function of music was discussed in Chapter Five.

Malcolm Budd, in his compelling assault on Schopenhauer, demolishes practically everything which the philosopher has to say about music. He ends his chapter on Schopenhauer by writing

Schopenhauer is the musician's philosopher. But Schopenhauer's philosophy of music is not a fitting monument to the art. [37]

I agree with some of the criticisms which Budd makes of Schopenhauer's philosophy; indeed, after writing this chapter, I found that I had echoed many of the same criticisms from a different point of view. And, although I accept and owe a good deal to some of Jung's ideas, I part company with Jung at precisely those points at which he is closest to Schopenhauer. That is, I find it hard to believe in the *pleroma*, or to accept the notion that archetypes, or Platonic Ideas, exist as definable items in a kind of limbo beyond time and space. If there is an underlying reality consisting of things-in-themselves, I am inclined to believe that we have no access to it.

It seems to me that the primordial images which constitute archetypes or the Ideas are powerfully compelling because they refer to fundamental aspects of experience which are common to all men. Thus, the observer who detects the Idea of Love as being instantiated in Rembrandt's *The Jewish Bride* is acknowledging Rembrandt's skill in demonstrating the deepest essential features of that universal human experience. A wedding portrait photograph of Mr and Mrs Jones, however skilfully posed and lit, is unlikely to exhibit the essentials of love because it cannot be as selective as can a painting by a great master. It is generally acknowledged that the greatest works of art in any field are great because they are concerned with universals. It does not follow that these universals have some kind of ghostly existence outside space and time. This is not to deny that there are concepts and ideas which cannot be 'placed' in space. Numbers are real but not tangible; the relation between tones which constitutes music exists but cannot be portrayed.

I am not sure that Schopenhauer's distinction between the concept and the Idea is wholly convincing; but the sense of difference which he seeks to explain by this means is certainly recognizable. Most people would agree that there are musical works which seem dull and lifeless because, regardless of the ingenuity of their construction, they do not touch the heart. Although many would not agree with him, Constant Lambert thought this of some of Stravinsky's neo-classical works. He is even more critical of Hindemith, whose music seems to Lambert to reflect nothing but sterile, workman-like proficiency.[38]

But we can surely agree with Schopenhauer in thinking that some works of art are cerebral, *voulu*, and lacking inspiration, without accepting his philosophical explanations. The greatest artists are able to plumb their own depths, and bring to the surface aspects of those basic emotions which are common to all mankind. Lesser artists are seldom able to do this; and even the greatest sometimes produce work which is clearly superficial. Schopenhauer of course realizes this; it is his interpretation of the difference which alienates his critics.

Nevertheless, I would be inclined to salvage more of what Schopenhauer writes about music than Malcolm Budd is prepared to do. Schopenhauer postulates two ways in which we can gain some kind of limited, subterranean access to the true nature of reality, one being our experience of our own physical being and its movements, the other being by way of music. Although I do not agree that either gives privileged partial access or proximity to the kind of underlying reality which Schopenhauer assumes, I am interested that he links music and subjective physical awareness as both being concerned with experience in depth. I earlier quoted John Blacking's observation that 'Many, if not all, of music's essential processes can be found in the constitution of the human body and in patterns of interaction of bodies in society . . . .'[39]

Schopenhauer's idea that our experience of our own bodies gives us a pointer to an underlying reality which we can only otherwise obtain through music is surely connected with his view that music is unlike the other arts in that it is '*a copy of the will itself* '.[40] For if music is rooted in the body, and closely connected with bodily movement, even though modern listeners in the concert hall may have to inhibit such movement, then Schopenhauer's view that both our experience of the body and our experience of music possess a depth, an immediacy, and an intensity which cannot be obtained in other ways becomes comprehensible and persuasive.

We have already discussed the emergence of 'absolute' music, unconnected with words or collective ceremonies. Schopenhauer's remarks about Rossini show that, although he appreciated the function of music in enhancing the significance of words, he rated music which was *not* associated with words still more highly.

If music has a more direct, profound and immediate effect on us than the other arts, as Schopenhauer claims, we can furnish a more convincing explanation for why this should be so than he does. We can say that music is a non-verbal art which is directly linked with physiological arousal, which, as we have seen, can be measured by scientific instruments. I can well believe that some people find that their hearts beat faster when they look at a beautiful picture, building, or sunset; but I doubt if they experience the urge toward physical motion, the increase in muscle tone, and the muscular responses to rhythm which music induces. Pictures seldom make one want to dance.

I have a lurking suspicion that music may be especially important to people who are somewhat alienated from the body, because playing an instrument, singing, or simply listening to music puts them in touch with their physical being in ways unmatched by reading poetry or by looking at beautiful objects. Neither of these two latter activities makes us want to move our bodies; but music often does. Schopenhauer failed to make explicit the relation of music with physical movement, although he perceived both as more directly connected with the operations of the Will than other human activities. If he had made the connection, he might have modified his pessimistic view of art as a temporary alleviation of the miseries of life.

CHAPTER VIII

A JUSTIFICATION OF EXISTENCE

> Art and nothing but art! It is the great means of making life possible, the great seduction to life, the great stimulant of life.
>
> FRIEDRICH NIETZSCHE[1]

Another philosopher for whom music was vitally important was Friedrich Nietzsche. Nietzsche's writings make it possible for us to appreciate the way in which music and the other arts can come to occupy the supreme place in a person's hierarchy of values.

Nietzsche, born in 1844, first encountered Schopenhauer's writings when in his twenties. He became, for a time, a Schopenhauerian convert. In 1866, when he was twenty-two years old, he described solitary walks, Schumann's music, and Schopenhauer as constituting his relaxations. By 1864, Nietzsche's belief in Christianity had already faded; so Schopenhauer's atheism at first appealed to him. He also admired Schopenhauer's insistence on the importance of aesthetic, especially musical, experience. However, Nietzsche's more positive attitude to life was reflected in his treatment of music as life-enhancing rather than escapist. Schopenhauer had suggested that great music may temporarily remove us from the trials and torments of existence; but Nietzsche believed that music was one of the arts which so sharpened our sense of participation in life that it gave meaning to life and made it worth living, as the epigraph to this chapter indicates.

In the last chapter, Schopenhauer's conception of aesthetic experience as removing the individual from the never-ending affliction of unsatisfied willing and striving was compared with Freud's very similar picture of Nirvana as a regression to infancy or a temporary abolition of desire through instinctual discharge. Both thinkers treated life itself as so intrinsically unsatisfactory that fulfilment could only be found in escape from it: ultimately in death.

Although Freud was unmusical, literature and sculpture were important to him. But his scheme of things was such that it did not and could not include the arts as necessary to life. Freud considered that art and literature were produced by sublimation of unsatisfied libido. Although artists might avoid neurosis by expressing their unsatisfied impulses in their work, they were nevertheless creating a world of phantasy instead of finding satisfaction in the real world. Freud linked play, dreams, and creative phantasy as childish, wish-fulfilling techniques of compensation for an unsatisfying reality. If Freud's view is pursued to its logical conclusion, it follows that, in an ideal world in which everyone reached full sexual maturity, the arts would have no place. Since civilized life is inescapably imperfect, Freud recognized that the arts might make it more tolerable, but the idea that they could directly contribute to its meaning was entirely foreign to him. In so far as Freud needed a *Weltanschauung* he professed to find it in science; although his disdain for experiment and proof denied psychoanalysis the scientific status he claimed for it.

It is clear that Schopenhauer was more deeply involved with the arts than was Freud, and that music was especially important to him. But, in spite of his claim that music expresses the quintessence of life, Schopenhauer still considered aesthetic experience to be in a special category which delivered the subject from affliction rather than enhancing participation in life. Neither thinker perceived aesthetic experience as promoting passionate involvement or as contributing to making sense of human existence. It is significant that both men were explicit atheists from an early age.

It is fascinating to contrast Schopenhauer and Freud with Nietzsche and Jung. The latter pair were thinkers who had been raised in families in which religion was significant. Both abandoned conventional Christianity, and both were left with a hunger to replace that which they had lost. Their solutions to finding a substitute for religious belief were very different, but their thought overlaps at so many points that comparison of one with the other is illuminating.

Jung and Nietzsche were both the sons of clergymen. Discussion of religious matters was prominent in Jung's family from his earliest childhood. His father was a minister in the Swiss Reformed Church; two of his paternal uncles were also ministers; and there were six ministers in his mother's family. Jung's father was content to accept conventional Christian teaching, and refused to discuss the basis of his faith or answer the questions about it with which his son confronted him. Because of this, Jung came to suspect the genuineness of his father's faith. In his autobiography, Jung recorded dreams and visions of a religious kind, dating from childhood, which threw doubt on the Christian vision of God as a loving father, and which also convinced him that genuine religious experience had very little to do with conventional creeds.

Both Nietzsche's parents were the children of Lutheran ministers, and Nietzsche's father was himself ordained. Although his father became mentally ill and died when Nietzsche was only five, the religious background in which he was reared led him to study theology as well as classical philology. He finally abandoned theology in 1865, at the age of twenty-one. Nietzsche, who in 1881 made his famous pronouncement that God was dead, became passionately opposed to Christianity. As a result, he became concerned with the same problem of finding a meaning in life which later preoccupied Jung.

Some men and women seem content to accept life as it is without feeling any need to seek for explanations, justifications, or systems of belief. But those who have been brought up in a strongly religious atmosphere seem unable to throw off this powerful influence. The whole of Jung's later work represents an attempt to find a psychological substitute for religious faith. Nietzsche's search for meaning in terms of aesthetic experience had a similar significance. As Roger Scruton writes:

> If proof is needed of the ease with which the aesthetic may replace the religious as an object of philosophical interest, it is to be found in the thought and the personality of Nietzsche. Nietzsche's philosophy arose out of art and the thought of art; it involved an effort to perceive the world through aesthetic value, to find a way of life that would raise nobility, glory and tragic beauty to the place that had been occupied by moral goodness and by faith.[2]

Nietzsche's quest for 'How One Becomes What One Is', as he calls it in *Ecce Homo*, is closely parallel with Jung's concept of 'individuation'. Jung thought in religious terms, Nietzsche in aesthetic terms; but both considered self-realization, making manifest the essence of one's individuality, becoming what one is, as something to be achieved rather than as an hereditary datum thrust upon one. Jung wrote:

> Personality is the supreme realization of the innate idiosyncrasy of a living being. It is an act of high courage flung in the face of life, the absolute affirmation of all that constitutes the individual, the most successful adaptation to the universal conditions of existence coupled with the greatest possible freedom for self-determination.[3]

Nietzsche thought that superior individuals, by imposing order on their passions and through sublimation, gave style to their own characters in the same way that an artist manifests his personal style in the works of art which he creates. This is the meaning of Nietzsche's famous maxim: 'It is only as an aesthetic phenomenon that existence and the world are eternally justified.'[4]

Becoming what one is is a creative act comparable with creating a work of art. It is freeing oneself from the tyranny of one's upbringing; emancipating oneself from convention, from education, from class, from religious belief, from all the social constraints, prejudices, and assumptions which prevent one from realizing one's own nature in its totality.

Individuation is essentially a religious quest, although it is not associated with any recognized creed. In Jung's view, no one could achieve psychic health and wholeness unless he or she was able to acknowledge being guided by an inner integrating factor which was independent of conscious intention: the voice of 'God' manifesting itself in dreams, visions, phantasies and other derivatives of the unconscious. Jung describes the peace of mind which comes to individuals after many fruitless struggles.

> If you sum up what people tell you about their experiences, you can formulate it this way: They came to themselves, they could accept themselves, and thus were reconciled to adverse circumstances and events. This is almost like what used to be expressed by saying: He

has made his peace with God, he has sacrificed his own will, he has submitted himself to the will of God.[5]

Jung specialized in the treatment of middle-aged people for whom life had become meaningless. In such cases, as in his own case, he regarded healing as predominantly a religious problem.

Nietzsche too retained a religious attitude, in spite of his rejection of Christianity and his proclamation of the death of God. According to Walter Kaufmann, his translator, expositor, and biographer, Nietzsche 'felt that the death of God threatened human life with a complete loss of all significance'.[6]

And Jung claimed:

Nietzsche was no atheist, but his God was dead . . . The tragedy of *Zarathustra* is that, because his God died, Nietzsche himself became a god; and this happened because he was no atheist. He was of too positive a nature to tolerate the urban neurosis of atheism.[7]

Nietzsche certainly became boastful and grandiose before he finally collapsed; but grandiose delusions are a well-recognized feature of general paresis, and Jung fails to take this into account in his pejorative description of Nietzsche's state of mind.

In fact, Nietzsche was closer to Jung's point of view than the latter allowed. Jung, referring to individuation, used religious language directly. Nietzsche preferred the language of aesthetics to describe his own search for meaning. Although Jung and Nietzsche were very different human beings, their shared loss of conventional religious belief resulted in both men acknowledging a need for dependence on something other than the ego; perhaps on an inner ordering process which proceeds unconsciously. Nietzsche was not being grandiose when, in a wonderful passage in *Beyond Good and Evil*, he refers to the artist's need for spiritual discipline, for what he calls

protracted *obedience* in *one* direction: from out of that there always emerges and has always emerged in the long run something for the sake of which it is worthwhile to live on earth, for example virtue, art, music, dance, reason, spirituality – something transfiguring, refined, mad and divine.[8]

Jung shared this notion of obedience, which he described in religious terms, but for him it was to an inner voice which emanated from the unconscious. Alluding to dreams, he once said to me: 'Every night one has the chance of the Eucharist.' He actually referred to religions as psychotherapeutic systems. For Jung, religious experience was something *sui generis*; something entirely different from the experiences provided by the arts. Jung's conception of obedience and transfiguration is much narrower than Nietzsche's. Jung's lack of aesthetic appreciation is a serious limitation of his thought, as it is of Freud's. One of the few characteristics which Freud and Jung shared was an inability to appreciate music. The only reference to music in Jung's autobiography is to the singing of a kettle. This, he wrote, 'was just like polyphonic music, which in reality I cannot abide'.[9] Had he been musical, a poet, a painter, or even a better writer, I think his psychology, which contains so much of interest and value, would have been more securely based and would also have won wider acceptance. But he could not relinquish the idea that it was possible to have some kind of especial, direct line to God. God never died for Jung as He did for Nietzsche. As a consequence, Jung failed to see that his advocacy of obedience to the wisdom of the unconscious was only one instance of the much wider 'obedience' which Nietzsche perceived.

In contrast, Nietzsche, like Schopenhauer, considered the arts to be supremely important and music particularly so. For him, it was not merely a transient pleasure but one of the things which made living possible. Nietzsche's words quoted above clearly demonstrate his realization that, for many people, the concert hall and the art gallery have replaced the church as places where the 'divine' can be encountered. Nietzsche, despite his ambivalent attitude to Socrates and hence to Plato, shared the latter's conviction that music could exert powerful effects on human beings, both good and evil. In attributing such significance to music, Nietzsche was closer to the ancient Greeks than to most modern thinkers.

Music became important to Nietzsche quite early in his life. One of his school friends was a boy called Gustav Krug, whose father was a musical enthusiast and had been an acquaintance of Mendelssohn. The Krug household was a centre of musical activity. Although Nietzsche could not have met Mendelssohn as he died in 1847 when Nietzsche was only three years old, he often visited the Krug house when he was a boy and began to compose music and write poetry before reaching adolescence. He became an accomplished pianist and a composer of songs, piano pieces, and choral works. Historians of the psychoanalytic movement will like to know that amongst Nietzsche's compositions is a setting for chorus and orchestra of a poem by Lou Andreas-Salomé, 'Hymnus an das Leben'. Nietzsche met Lou Andreas-Salomé in 1882, fell in love with her, and proposed marriage, which she rejected. She became a *femme inspiratrice* for him, as she did for Rilke. In later years, she became a psychoanalyst and a close friend of Freud. A picture of her still hangs on the wall of Freud's consulting room, now part of the Freud Museum in Hampstead.

For Nietzsche, music remained a lifelong passion. Nietzsche became hopelessly insane and finally died of general paresis in 1900. But even after his capacity to handle words had disappeared, he was still able to extemporize at the piano. Music was one of his first creative activities: it remained his last.

In *The Birth of Tragedy*, Nietzsche discusses a dichotomy to which I referred in the last chapter. It comes close to one aspect of musical experience. Nietzsche derived from Bachofen* the notion of two attitudes or principles associated with the gods Apollo and Dionysus. Whereas Bachofen had identified Apollonian culture as patriarchal and Dionysian as matriarchal, Nietzsche portrayed the two principles as representing order versus inspiration.

Apollo, the deity of light, presides over the inner world of phantasy and dream. He is the god of order, measure, number, control, and the subjugation of unruly instinct. He especially manifests himself in the art of sculpture. Dionysus, in contrast, is the god of liberation, of intoxication, of unbridled licence, and of orgiastic celebration. He especially manifests himself in music.

It is likely that Freud's sharp division of mental functioning into irrational 'primary process' versus rational 'secondary process'

*Johann Jakob Bachofen (1815–87), the promulgator of the theory that ancient cultures were matriarchal.

owed something to Nietzsche's dichotomy of Dionysian and Apollonian. Although Freud denied having read Nietzsche until after his own ideas had been formulated, it is now known that when he was at university he belonged to a student reading society in which the ideas of Schopenhauer and Nietzsche were discussed. Moreover, Nietzsche preceded Freud in the use of the terms sublimation and id.* Freud owed more both to Nietzsche and to Schopenhauer than he acknowledged or perhaps admitted to himself.

In Jungian terminology, the Apollonian state is one of introversion in which the subject contemplates the dream world of eternal ideas. It is close to Schopenhauer's aesthetic way of knowing. The Dionysian state is one of extraversion, of physical participation in the external world through feeling and sensation. Jung devotes a chapter to the subject in his book *Psychological Types*.

According to Nietzsche, Greek tragedy springs from a reconciliation or union between these two opposing principles. (In his later writings, Nietzsche uses 'Dionysian' in a different sense, as passion controlled. He attacks Christianity for attempting to get rid of passion altogether, and uses Dionysus versus the Crucified rather than Dionysus versus Apollo.)

Both Schopenhauer and Nietzsche were profoundly aware of the horrors of existence. But, whereas Schopenhauer conceived art as being a refuge, a realm into which a man could temporarily escape from the dissatisfactions of life into a state of contemplation, Nietzsche viewed it as something which could reconcile us with life rather than detach us from it. Because of art, we need not negate the will. Nietzsche believed that it was the weak who followed Schopenhauer by denying life: the strong affirm it by creating beauty. This is especially relevant to the art of tragedy.

> The metaphysical comfort – with which, I am suggesting even now, every true tragedy leaves us – that life is at the bottom of things, despite all the changes of appearances, indestructibly powerful and pleasurable . . .[10]

*It is interesting that Edmund Gurney, in *The Power of Sound* (1880), refers to 'the power of Music to have become sublimated, as it were' (p. 120).

Tragedy does *not* teach 'resignation' – To represent terrible and questionable things is in itself an instinct for power and magnificence in an artist: he does not fear them – There is no such thing as pessimistic art – Art affirms . . . For a philosopher to say, 'the good and the beautiful are one' is infamy: if he goes on to add, 'also the true,' one ought to thrash him. Truth is ugly.

We possess *art* lest we *perish of the truth*.[11]

Nietzsche's view of life, in spite of his awareness of its horrors, is essentially affirmative; whereas Schopenhauer sees no hope but denial and detachment. As Walter Kaufmann puts it:

Nietzsche envisages 'the *sublime* as the artistic conquest of the horrible'; and he celebrates the Greek 'who has looked with bold eyes into the dreadful destructive turmoil of so-called world-history as well as into the cruelty of nature' and, without yielding to resignation or to 'a Buddhist negation of the will,' reaffirms life with the creation of works of art.[12]

So the creation of tragedy is both a response to the horrors of life and a way of mastering them. From tragedy, it is possible to learn to appreciate life as sublime in spite of the suffering which living entails. Nietzsche makes us understand why it is that even tragic masterpieces, like the slow movement of the 'Eroica' Symphony, or Siegfried's Funeral March from *Götterdämmerung*, are life-enhancing. We have moved beyond mere enjoyment of music to a condition in which we are saying 'Yes' to life as it actually is: tragic, ecstatic, painful, and joyful. The essential theme of *The Birth of Tragedy* is Nietzsche's perception that art makes sense of the world and justifies existence.

Nietzsche realized – no one more vividly – that the only life we know is constituted by opposites. Pleasure is inconceivable without pain; light without darkness; love without hate; good without evil. The *pleroma* may contain no opposites, but in life, heaven and hell march hand in hand; it is only in the never-never land of the after-life that they become separate entities. This is why the greatest art always includes tragedy; why it must embrace tragedy as well as triumph; why the denial of suffering is the negation of life itself.

Nietzsche believed that the creative process was stimulated by adversity; more especially, by ill-health, whether physical or mental. He would have appreciated modern views which link liability to manic-depressive illness with creativity.[13] Nietzsche regarded illness as a challenge which ought to strengthen a person's resolve. It is only by overcoming adversity that a human being can discover his true potential. Heine puts these words into the mouth of God in the last stanza of his *Schöpfungslieder*:

> Disease was the most basic ground
> Of my creative urge and stress:
> Creating, I could convalesce,
> Creating, I again grew sound.[14]

Nietzsche believed that those varieties of philosophy which promised religious or aesthetic solutions to the problems of life were especially likely to have originated from physical illness.

> The unconscious disguise of physiological needs under the cloaks of the objective, ideal, purely spiritual goes to frightening lengths – and often I have asked myself whether, taking a large view, philosophy has not been merely an interpretation of the body and a *misunderstanding of the body*.[15]

He himself suffered from headache, indigestion, insomnia and other symptoms even before the illness which killed him had made itself manifest. When still a schoolboy in 1856, he was granted absence from school because of headaches and pain in the eyes. Headache remained a recurrent problem. He had to give up his professorship at the University of Basel at the age of thirty-four because of ill-health. In spite of this, he wrote to Georg Brandes: 'My illness has been my greatest boon: it unblocked me, it gave me the courage to be myself.'[16] Illness also had the effect of partially isolating him from social life. Nietzsche called his *Thus Spoke Zarathustra* 'a dithyramb to solitude'.

Nietzsche's repudiation of Schopenhauer's resignation and negation is closely allied with his break with Wagner. Nietzsche first encountered Wagner in November 1868, when he was twenty-four years old. Although Nietzsche was more than thirty years younger than the composer, Wagner was glad of his support and, because it contained favourable references to himself and to *Tristan und Isolde*, lavished praise upon *The Birth of Tragedy*. They remained friends for ten years. But Nietzsche, who had originally been a convert to the *Weltanschauung* of Schopenhauer, gradually emancipated himself from the earlier philosopher's influence, whilst Wagner remained an enthusiast for Schopenhauer's ideas until the end of his life.

In *Siegfried*, Wagner had seemed to be concerned with the emergence of a hero figure which was not dissimilar to Nietzsche's 'superman'. Nietzsche said that in Siegfried Wagner had invented, or discovered, 'the typical revolutionary'. Siegfried begins as an optimist: the man without fear who is destined to abolish old contracts, free the world from the tyrannies of laws, moralities, and institutions, and usher in a new society. Then, Wagner's ship 'struck a reef'.

> The reef was Schopenhauer's philosophy; Wagner was stranded on a *contrary* world view. What had he transposed into music? Optimism. Wagner was ashamed. Even an optimism for which Schopenhauer had coined an evil epithet – *infamous* optimism . . . So he translated the *Ring* into Schopenhauer's terms. Everything goes wrong, everything perishes, the new world is as bad as the old; the *nothing*, the Indian Circe beckons.[17]

Wagner himself admitted that he modified the text of the *Ring* after first reading Schopenhauer toward the end of 1854; but he also claimed that Schopenhauer merely reinforced what he had previously felt intuitively.

Wagner's last opera shocked Nietzsche even more profoundly. Wagner sent him the libretto of *Parsifal* in December 1877, not recognizing that Nietzsche had already become disillusioned with him. Wagner's incorporation of Christianity into *Parsifal* appeared to Nietzsche as a betrayal of the heroic ideal in favour of renunciation and self-sacrifice. Although Schopenhauer was an atheist, Nietzsche found that Schopenhauer's philosophy and the Christian religion alike shared a negative attitude to life which he could not accept.

Nietzsche came to prefer the music of Bizet and Offenbach to that of his former idol, Wagner. In one passage on aesthetics, Nietzsche refers to 'the divine frivolity of the dancer'.[18] In another, he gives a typically playful account of his response to *Carmen*.

> Yesterday I heard – would you believe it? – Bizet's masterpiece, for the twentieth time. Again I stayed there with tender devotion; again I did not run away. This triumph over my impatience surprises me. How such a work makes one perfect! One becomes a 'masterpiece' oneself.
>
> Really, every time I heard *Carmen* I seemed to myself more of a philosopher, a better philosopher, than I generally consider myself: so patient do I become, so happy, so Indian, so settled. – To sit five hours: the first stage of holiness![19]

Those who have never read Nietzsche seldom realize that he was a humorist. He referred to the contrast between Bizet and Wagner as an 'ironic antithesis'.

Nietzsche wanted to 'Mediterraneanize' music; to get away from the portentousness of German romantic sentiment; to replace Wagner's preoccupation with redemption and death with the blue skies and sunlit sensuality of the South.

> Against German music I feel all sorts of precautions should be taken. Suppose one loves the south as I love it, as a great school of convalescence, for all the diseases of senses and spirit, as a tremendous abundance of sun and transfiguration by sun, spreading itself over an autonomous existence which believes in itself: well, such a person will learn to be somewhat on guard against German music because, by spoiling his taste again, it will also spoil his health again.[20]

Although Nietzsche ultimately rejected Wagner, he always acknowledged his debt to him. In his late work *Ecce Homo*, completed in 1888, the year before he finally collapsed into insanity, Nietzsche says that he could not have endured his youth without Wagnerian music, and that Wagner had been the great benefactor of his life.

Nietzsche's concern to merge Apollonian with Dionysian matches Schopenhauer's observation that

> In the course of life . . . head and heart grow more and more apart; men are always separating more and more their subjective feeling from their objective knowledge.[21]

Nietzsche's insistence on aesthetic experience as the only means of justifying existence is dependent on linking subjective and objective; more especially, on linking mind and body. He said: 'I have always written my works with my whole body and life.'[22] In *The Will to Power*, Nietzsche claims that art has a direct effect on bodily experience, and that this is why it is life-affirming, even when its subject-matter is tragic.

In *The Gay Science*, Nietzsche wrote:

> And so I ask myself: What is it that my whole body really expects of music? I believe, its own *ease*: as if all animal functions should be quickened by easy, bold, exuberant, self-assured rhythms; as if iron, leaden life should be gilded by good golden and tender harmonies. My melancholy wants to rest in the hiding places and abysses of *perfection*: that is why I need music.[23]

Given this view of art, it is not surprising that Nietzsche repudiated Christianity. Nothing could be further from his vision than the insipid, conventional Christian picture of a heaven in which angels perpetually praise the Almighty with harp and song, and from which sorrow, death, sin and darkness have been entirely banished. The negation of tragedy is the negation of life.

Another reason for Nietzsche's rejection of Christianity is its insistence on the superiority of soul over body, and its tendency to label sexuality as evil. He believed that superior individuals ought to learn to control, master, and sublimate their instinctual drives; but he did not think that they should try to abolish them or regard them as evil.

Nietzsche, like Freud, thought that it was dangerous to deny the body's needs; that repression of the passions leads to crime and other evils. In *Thus Spoke Zarathustra*, Nietzsche has a section titled 'Of the Despisers of the Body'.

'I am body and soul' – so speaks the child. And why should one not speak like children?

But the awakened, the enlightened man says: I am body entirely, and nothing beside; and soul is only a word for something in the body.

The body is a great intelligence, a multiplicity with one sense, a war and a peace, a herd and a herdsman.

Your little intelligence, my brother, which you call 'spirit', is also an instrument of your body, a little instrument and toy of your great intelligence.

You say 'I' and you are proud of this word. But greater than this – although you will not believe in it – is your body and its great intelligence, which does not say 'I' but performs 'I'.[24]

Nietzsche would have agreed with John Blacking's observation that music's essential processes are found in the constitution of the human body and in patterns of interaction of bodies in society. Nietzsche's description of the effects of music in *The Will to Power* echoes Blacking's account of the communally life-enhancing effect of *tshikona*, the Venda national dance.

All art exercises the power of suggestion over the muscles and senses, which in the artistic temperament are originally active: it always speaks only to artists – it speaks to this kind of a subtle flexibility of the body . . . All art works tonically, increases strength, inflames desire (i.e., the feeling of strength) . . . Every enhancement of life enhances man's power of communication, as well as his power of understanding. Empathy with the souls of others is originally nothing moral, but a physiological susceptibility to suggestion . . . Compared with music all communication by words is shameless; words dilute and brutalize; words depersonalize; words make the uncommon common.[25]

In *The Birth of Tragedy*, Nietzsche emphasized the inability of the lyric poet to express the inner spirit of music, and, at the same time, attributed to music a special significance rather similar to that given it by Schopenhauer.

Language can never adequately render the cosmic symbolism of music, because music stands in symbolic relation to the primordial contradiction and primordial pain in the heart of the primal unity, and therefore symbolizes a sphere which is beyond and prior to all phenomena. Rather, all phenomena, compared with it, are merely symbols: hence *language*, as the organ and symbol of phenomena, can never by any means disclose the innermost heart of music; language, in its attempts to imitate it, can only be in superficial contact with music; while all the eloquence of lyric poetry cannot bring the deeper significance of the latter one step nearer.[26]

Later, again in *The Will to Power*, Nietzsche wrote: 'That music may dispense with words and concepts – oh what advantage she derives from that fact.'[27]

Nietzsche's description of the inadequacy of language in this context gains support from an unexpected source. The poet Paul Valéry envied composers because the *tones* they use to create music are precisely defined, measured, and classified. In contrast, the *words* employed by poets are often ambiguous and open to misinterpretation:

Language is a common and practical element; it is thereby necessarily a coarse instrument, for everyone handles and appropriates it according to his needs and tends to deform it according to his personality. Language, no matter how personal it may be or how close the way of thinking in words may be to our spirit, is nevertheless *of statistical origin*, and has *purely practical ends*. Now the poet's problem must be *to derive from this practical instrument the means of creating a work essentially not practical* . . . How fortunate is the musician! The evolution of his art has given him an altogether privileged position for centuries . . . Ancient observations and very old experiments have made it possible to deduce, from *the universe of noises*, the system or *the universe of sounds* . . . These elements are pure or are composed of pure – that is to say, recognizable elements. They are sharply defined and – a very important point – the way has been found to produce them in a constant and identical manner by means of instruments which are, basically, true instruments of measure.[28]

I have already noted the gradual divergence between speech and music; the development of objective, abstract language designed to convey information and to communicate ideas rather than to share feelings. This must be the kind of language to which Nietzsche is referring when he says that 'words depersonalize'. The fact that conceptual thought demands the separation of thinking from feeling, of object from subject, of mind from body, suggests that music may be one way of bridging this division. Nietzsche would have appreciated Zuckerkandl's exposition in his great book *Sound and Symbol*.

> Words divide, tones unite. The unity of existence that the word constantly breaks up, dividing thing from thing, subject from object, is constantly restored in the tone. Music prevents the world from being entirely transformed into language, from becoming nothing but object, and prevents man from becoming nothing but subject . . . It is certainly no accident that the highest unfolding of the power of tones in modern instrumental music and the highest unfolding of the power of objectifying words in modern science coincided historically with the sharpest divisions ever drawn between subjectivity and objectivity.[29]

Both Nietzsche and Zuckerkandl are referring to the language of science and conceptual thought. Neither makes it clear that, whilst this kind of language has indeed underlined the division between subjective and objective, other kinds of language serve different purposes.

Rhetoric is both emotive and subjective and may persuade without informing us, as we noted when quoting one of Hitler's speeches. Poetry, even if it is as vulnerable to misinterpretation as Valéry suggests, can be entrancing and so illuminating that we see the world around us with new eyes. Prose, especially if it is 'musical' in the sense of employing rhythmically balanced phrases like those of Gibbon, or if it is notable for its clarity like that of Freud or Bertrand Russell, can so beguile us with its elegance that we fail to appreciate its content. Kant said that he had to read Rousseau's books several times because, at a first reading, 'the beauty of the style prevented him from noticing the matter.'[30] Words are not always as shameless and brutal as Nietzsche alleges.

It is clear that all works of art must be formed of both Dionysian and Apollonian elements in varying proportion, for art cannot exist without human feelings, nor without means of ordering and expressing those feelings. Nietzsche's emphasis upon the Dionysian elements in music did not blind him to the composer's need to impose order upon his musical material. In this context, it does not matter that Nietzsche thought that Wagner's pessimistic stance had robbed music of 'its world-transfiguring, affirmative character'. What does matter is that Nietzsche believed that the music of other composers could have a world-transfiguring, affirmative character.

It seems to me that what is unusual and particularly worth noting in Nietzsche's thought about music is, first, that he recognized music as an art which could not only reconcile one to life but could also enhance it. Tchaikovsky and Berlioz, when depressed, found music to be a life-saver. Nietzsche goes further. Music not only makes life possible, but also makes it exciting. He refers to music as a means by which the passions 'enjoy themselves'; not as escapist, or other-worldly; but as an art which, by exalting life as it is, transcends its essential tragedy.

Second, he recognized that music was physically and emotionally based: it was rooted in the body, and Dionysian, however much it had to be shaped and organized by Apollonian techniques. When Nietzsche discussed his own previous writings in *Ecce Homo*, he said of *The Birth of Tragedy*: 'A tremendous hope speaks out of this essay. In the end I lack all reason to renounce the hope for a Dionysian future of music.'[31]

Third, he understood that music linked the two principles of Apollo and Dionysus in the same way as tragedy. Christianity had attempted to banish Dionysus from art; but, in music, Dionysus could be born again in gaiety and joy.

In late 1871, he wrote in a letter:

If only a few hundred people of the next generation get what I get out of music, then I anticipate an utterly new culture. There are times when everything that is left over and cannot be grasped in terms of musical relations actually fills me with disgust and horror.[32]

Nietzsche's perception of music as so significant that it can make life worth living seems utterly remote from the mundane preoccupations of Western politicians and educators. Of course it is right that they should be concerned with raising standards of literacy, with increasing expertise in both sciences and crafts, with equipping men and women with the skills necessary to earn a living in a world increasingly dominated by technology. But a 'higher standard of living' does not make life itself worth living. The arts can do so; and, amongst the arts, music is profoundly significant, as Nietzsche perceived. In my view, Nietzsche understood music better than any other modern philosopher; perhaps because he himself was an accomplished pianist and composer.

CHAPTER IX

THE SIGNIFICANCE OF MUSIC

> The aim of all intellectual pursuits, including
> science, philosophy, and art, is to seek unity in the
> midst of diversity or order in the midst of com-
> plexity. Their ultimate task is to fit multifarious
> elements into some kind of compact, cohesive,
> apprehensible scheme.
>
> D. E. BERLYNE[1]

Nietzsche's claims for music may seem extravagant, but I believe
that they are justified. I think that music is the most significant
experience in life for a great many people, and that those who feel
about it in this way include ordinary listeners as well as professional
musicians. In this chapter, I want to explore some of the reasons
why music occupies this pre-eminent place in peoples' lives. How is
it that an art which promulgates no doctrine, which preaches no
gospel, which is often entirely dissociated from verbal meaning,
can yet be experienced as making sense of life?

The epigraph to this chapter is taken from *Aesthetics and
Psychobiology*, a book by a psychologist from the University of
Toronto. As Berlyne indicates, pattern-making, Gestalt perception,
is an integral part of our adaptation. Without it, we should only
experience chaos. The creating and perceiving of apprehensible
schemes goes on at every conceivable level in our mental hierarchy,
from the simplest auditory and visual perceptions to the creation of
new models of the universe, philosophies, belief systems, and great
works of art, including music.

Even apparently simple acts of perception involve the creation of
patterns of relations between the data presented. Schemata, as these
patterns are often named, link together data into new wholes. They
are the means by which we make sense out of the incoming stimuli

to which we are constantly exposed. Even the humblest being is performing a creative act when he interprets sensory input. For example, the visual perception of colour is dependent upon the brain constructing a pattern of relations. As early as 1802, Thomas Young pointed out that we are capable of perceiving so many different colours that the retina could not possibly contain enough individual receptors designed to react separately to each colour. In fact, our perception of different colours depends mainly upon three types of receptor cell in the retina, designed to respond selectively, but not exclusively, to yellow, green, and blue. When light falls on the retina, we perceive its colour because each of these specific types of 'cone' is stimulated differently. For example, the colour red is perceived when the yellow cone is highly activated, the green considerably less so, and the blue hardly at all.[2] In other words, our perception of the colour red is dependent on pattern, on the simultaneous interaction between different neuronal responses. Yet pattern is not an anatomical entity, but a relation between entities.

The same seems to be true of our perception of speech. The phonemes of speech, vowels and consonants, can be analysed into physical variables of frequency, intensity, and duration; but what we understand as speech is the *relation* between phonemes which gives it meaning. Speech can be slow or rapid; loud or soft; high or low in register. However, a sentence which is rapidly whispered by a woman in a high register or slowly growled by a man in a low register retains its meaning if the sequential pattern of phonemes is preserved.

> The effective stimuli are relational, not absolute; ratios, not quantities . . . One modern view of the phoneme in linguistic theory seems to be that it is a kind of relational entity, not an absolute. It is a cluster of contrasts between it and all the other phonemes.[3]

We are so accustomed to thinking of auditory and visual perception as perception of particulars, whether sounds or sights, that we tend to underestimate the ubiquitous importance of appreciating relational patterns. A pattern is not like a brick; it is neither tangible nor visible.

The same considerations apply to our perception of time. When separate events follow each other in close succession, we have a strong tendency to link them together into a coherent pattern. In the cinema, a series of still pictures is presented to us at the rate of 24 frames per second. By means of a special shutter on the projector, each picture is shown three times in rapid succession. We interpret what we see as continuous movement, although movement is not actually occurring.

Our perception of music is analogously determined. As many authorities remind us, music itself does not move. For movement to occur, the same object must successively be in different places. Nothing of the kind happens in music. The simplest monophonic melody consists of a series of single tones. Think, for example, of 'God Save the Queen' ('My Country 'tis of Thee') played on a solo flute. This is a succession of separate events in time, not in space. Nothing actually moves other than the lips, chest, and fingers of the flute player and the air-waves he sets in motion. The tune itself is an example of ODTAA: 'one damn tone after another', distinctly separated by intervals of time. These intervals may be very short; but, if they were not there at all, what we should hear would be a glissando-like noise, not music.

When we listen to music, what we perceive as a tune is simply a succession of separate tones; it is we who make it into a continuous melody. Science can analyse the differences between individual tones in a variety of ways: in terms of loudness, timbre, pitch, waveform, and so on. But it cannot tell us about the relation between tones which constitutes music. 'A melody is a series of tones that makes sense.'[4]

If we want to hear a series of tones as completely separate, we either have to make the time intervals between tones longer than those usually employed in musical compositions, or the frequencies of the tones very different from one another. We only perceive a series of tones as a consecutive melody if the pitches are closely related. It is possible to rewrite a tune keeping the same notes in sequence but transposing each note to a different octave. This procedure makes the tune unrecognizable: it becomes a series of tones which no longer makes sense.

The wide intervals between tones characteristic of some of the compositions of Anton Webern and other serial composers make such music difficult to grasp. There are a number of other reasons why serial music is more difficult to appreciate which have been summarized by Fred Lerdahl. Amongst them are the attempt to abolish consonance and dissonance distinctions among intervals. These distinctions are not entirely arbitrary, as serialist theorists claim, but partly objective. As Lerdahl points out: 'The sensory dissonance of a seventh remains greater than that of a sixth, regardless of the musical purposes to which these intervals are put.'[5]

Serial music is difficult to remember because it abolishes the hierarchical structure of tonal music in which it is easy to recognize 'home' as consonance following dissonance. Some serial music is also difficult to remember because, unlike classical tonal music, it tends to avoid repetition. This is why so many listeners cannot make sense of serial music. Lack of repetition is one reason – not the only reason – why it is difficult to understand and remember Boulez's famous piece Le Marteau sans Maître. Lerdahl claims that literal repetition was regarded as aesthetically inexcusable in the music of the 1950s and 1960s. But doubts about the wisdom of abolishing repetition as a means of defining structure had been expressed much earlier, by no less a figure than Anton Webern himself, who said in 1932: 'As we gradually gave up tonality, there came the idea: we don't want to repeat, something new must come all the time! It's obvious that this doesn't work, as it destroys comprehensibility.'[6]

Our strong urge toward making sense of a series of tones has been demonstrated by experiments in dichotic listening. If two series of tones consisting of wide leaps are presented to each ear separately, the brain irons out the intervals and perceives the tones as consecutive.

When we do hear a series of tones as a melody, the melody persists. A tune can be hummed, sung, played on a single instrument or on several instruments together. It can be decorated, varied, rhythmically elaborated, played monophonically or harmonized. Through all these changes, it remains recognizably the same melody. But a melody is a *relation* between tones: a pattern, a Gestalt, not a single definable entity.

Zuckerkandl writes:

We have understood the dynamic qualities of tone as the particular kind of unfulfillment peculiar to each tone, its desire for completion. No musical tone is sufficient unto itself; and as each musical tone points beyond itself, reaches, as it were, a hand to the next, so we too, as these hands reach out, listen tensely and expectantly for each new tone.[7]

Although this is too anthropomorphic a description for my taste, for tones do not point or reach out, I can see what Zuckerkandl means. Only a relation between tones constitutes music, never a tone in isolation.

The designation 'movement' for a section of a symphony, concerto, or sonata attests the indissoluble link between music and motion in our minds; and we cannot describe the simplest melody without some reference to tonal movement. St Augustine referred to music as 'ordered movement'. We talk of a melody soaring or dipping, of music passing from one key to another, or proceeding toward a close. Donald Tovey writes of Sibelius's 'special sense of movement', and Beethoven's 'mastery of movement'. Hanslick affirmed: 'The content of music is tonally moving forms.'[8] Since music itself does not move, why is it that so many eminent authorities write of music moving?

One reason may be the alliance between hearing and spatial orientation to which I referred earlier. Our description of tones of different pitches as 'higher' or 'lower' is a modern spatial metaphor. In earlier periods 'sharp' and 'blunt' were used. But we cannot avoid referring to melodies as tones 'moving'; and I think this may be connected with the fact that the auditory system originally developed from the vestibular system which is specifically designed to provide information about up, down, left, right, back and front. The function of the auditory system is partly to enable identification of the nature of an event – 'that's a lion roaring' – and partly in order to locate the direction of the event – 'it's over there on the right.' Human beings can tell within three degrees the direction from which sound is coming; owls within one degree.

Differences in pitch and rapid movement are demonstrably connected in the Doppler effect. The pitch of the whistle on an express train rises and falls as it rushes by us, because the sound-waves which it generates are successively compressed and extended. It is impossible to separate the perception of sound from the perception of space and movement.

Whether or not the link between sound and space is anything to do with the way in which the auditory apparatus has developed, it is true to say that music exists in time, but that we can think of time only in terms of space. In time, there is no right and left, up and down; there is only before and after. But, if we want to think about before and after, we have to provide a spatial analogue. We are so constituted that we cannot do otherwise.

When we listen to a melody we have the purest impression of succession we could possibly have – an impression as far removed as possible from that of simultaneity – and yet it is the very continuity of the melody and the impossibility of breaking it up which make that impression upon us. If we cut it up into distinct notes, into so many 'befores' and 'afters,' we are bringing spatial images into it and impregnating the succession with simultaneity: in space, and only in space, is there a clear distinction of parts external to one another.[9]

Our diaries show us the days of the year arranged in a spatial sequence, usually partly vertical (say, seven days to a page), and partly horizontal: and in England, left to right through the pages. It is impossible to think about next week without having some visual image of Sunday, Monday, Tuesday etc. arranged in a linear sequence. For a Japanese, it may be from right to left, or from bottom to top, but it is still bound to be spatial. Consciousness inevitably converts the diachronic into the synchronic.

A variety of authors, including the philosopher Hegel, conceive music to be an analogue of the 'inner life' of human beings which they picture as a continuously flowing stream. Hegel pointed out that the perception of unity in a musical work required a greater effort than perceiving unity in painting or sculpture because the listener was required to remember the sounds that had passed and combine them with the sounds occurring in the present. Hegel maintained that music was the first art to give us the sense of unification occurring in time rather than in space.[10]

Michael Tippett's characterization of music as a significant image of the inner flow of life was quoted earlier. The philosopher Henri

Bergson echoes this description when he refers to 'the continuous melody of our inner life – a melody which will go on, indivisible, from the beginning to the end of our conscious existence. Our personality is precisely that'.[11] The great musical theorist Heinrich Schenker writes: 'In its linear progressions and comparable tonal events, music mirrors the human soul in all its metamorphoses and moods.'[12]

Our perception of a melody as something continuous is an illusion; but so is the stream of consciousness of which music is said to be an analogue. The inner clocks of the body inform us when it is time to eat, time to sleep, and so on, thus providing us with a subliminal, intermittent awareness of time's passage: the inner flow of life referred to earlier. Momentary discomforts make us aware of digestive and excretory processes which for the most part proceed without conscious awareness. But, just as consciousness of bodily processes is intermittent, so is consciousness of mental processes. This is so clearly the case that I am not sure whether it is legitimate to speak of being aware of a mental process.

Although we may describe what goes on in our own minds as continuous, the 'stream of consciousness', we cannot actually perceive this. It is more like a stream of unconsciousness, with elements we call conscious floating like occasional twigs on the surface of the stream. When something occurs to us, a new thought, a linking of perceptions, an idea, we take pains to isolate it, to make it actual by putting it into words, writing it down, stopping the 'flow' of mental activity for the time being as we might reach out and grab one of the twigs floating past.

We like to describe the processes of thought as continuous, as a 'train of thought' inexorably proceeding by logical steps to a new conclusion. Yet, what many thinkers describe is more like floundering about in a slough of perplexity, a jumble of incoherence, relieved by occasional flashes of illumination when a new pattern suddenly emerges. Ordered, coherent progression of thought is a retrospective falsification of what actually happens.

The interesting question is why we have this incorrigible compulsion to order thoughts sequentially and retrospectively. Our thoughts go to Birmingham by way of Beachy Head; but we feel compelled to look back at the journey as if it had been a simple, uninterrupted trip from London along the M40 motorway.

I believe that we have to falsify our experience of thinking if we are to chronicle our thoughts and remember them. We are compelled to make coherent patterns out of our mental processes if we are to retain them in consciousness. Chaos cannot be accurately recalled. Meaningful sentences are more easily recalled than nonsense syllables; and music, the great promoter of order, makes words and sentences still more easily remembered.

This creation of coherent patterns need not be the consequence of conscious deliberation. It is a mental activity which is proceeding in all of us with little intermission. We link things together, combine opposites, create new wholes out of data which were previously unconnected. J. G. Herder, the eighteenth-century philosopher whose observations on songs as repositories of tribal history were quoted earlier, is equally perceptive in this context.

> That the creation of integrated wholes out of discrete data is the fundamental organizing activity of human nature, is a belief that is central to Herder's entire social and moral outlook; for him all creative activity, conscious and unconscious, generates, and is, in turn, determined by, its own unique *Gestalt*, whereby every individual and group strives to perceive, understand, act, create, live. [13]

What is it about human nature which compels this preoccupation with creating integrated wholes?

The human species is not rigidly pre-programmed with a repertoire of fixed reponses to a limited variety of stimuli as is the case with many creatures lower down the evolutionary scale. If we were so pre-programmed we might be happier, but we should be less able to respond to changes in the environment, less flexible in our behaviour, and, above all, less imaginative and less inventive. An animal whose behaviour is governed by age-old, inherited responses does not need to question, to modify its behaviour, to phantasize that things might be better, to strive to understand, to conceptualize, to create integrated wholes out of discrete data. It just behaves in the ways laid down by nature, and implanted in its constitution. It cannot do otherwise.

Such a creature may be well adapted to the present, but its rigidity inevitably makes it vulnerable. If the environment changes, the animal often cannot change its behaviour rapidly enough to survive. Natural selection takes a long time to work: climatic or other changes may wipe out a species before it can achieve a new and more appropriate adaptation.

Man's adaptation, paradoxically, is through lack of adaptation. We are not accurately and rigidly adjusted to any one set of external conditions by means of inherited patterns of behaviour; we have to invent our own. This is why human beings can adapt to environments as different as the Poles, the Equator, or even outer space. Human behaviour depends far more upon learning and upon the transmission of culture from generation to generation than it does upon in-built responses to environmental stimuli. Human babies are provided with a few automatic responses to ensure their survival; but the ways in which older children and adults adapt to life is predominantly governed by learning; by training, education, and experience.

Because our behaviour is not primarily governed by in-built, inherited patterns, the perception of connections, the making of new patterns, is a continuous mental activity which proceeds even in the absence of consciousness. We do not decide to see three dots as a triangle; we cannot avoid doing so. Even during sleep, our brains are intermittently engaged in trying to fit things together. What we remember of our dreams often suggests that we are glimpsing part of a sorting, scanning process in which recent experience is being matched with previous experience; a process which may account for the incongruities so common in dreams, in which events from the remote past are juxtaposed with the happenings of yesterday and made into a story.

Because this scanning, sorting, and making of patterns goes on continuously, both consciously and unconsciously, we usually take it for granted and are hardly aware that it is happening. But when we first discern an unexpected linkage, a new pattern, it brings us intense satisfaction. The attempt to create new wholes, to discover new connections between data hitherto unrelated, is always perceived as a 'higher' mental activity, since it involves something more than an immediate, instinctive response to impinging stimuli.

When a new schema is discovered, it often becomes intensely important to its discoverer and to all who understand and appreciate it. This is true, not only of scientific theories and other intellectual attempts to make sense out of the universe, but also of those works of art which are more than repetitious copies of their precursors. 'Eureka' is our cry of pleasure at a new Gestalt, even if it has no immediate mundane application. Bertrand Russell's account of his first encounter with geometry illustrates the point.

> At the age of eleven, I began Euclid, with my brother as my tutor. This was one of the great events of my life, as dazzling as first love. I had not imagined that there was anything so delicious in the world. [14]

It may be argued that Russell's pleasure in Euclid at such an early age is so unusual that it is a poor example of what I claim to be a widely shared characteristic of human beings. Russell's childhood was lonely. As a privately educated orphan of exceptional intelligence, he may have been more inclined than most children to be attracted by logical coherence. However, Russell is not alone in experiencing intense pleasure in the appreciation of an impersonal system. People make sense out of experience in a variety of ways, and, as I have suggested in other books, those who are particularly attracted toward the abstract are often people whose early personal relationships have been deficient. Some of the most inventive human beings have been poorly adapted to ordinary social life, and therefore more strongly impelled toward innovation. Blissful content does not foster creativity.

But both children and adults gain satisfaction from solving problems, perceiving connections, understanding structures, learning new techniques. Anything which lessens our distress at being surrounded by chaos, or promotes our shaky sense of control and mastery, gives us pleasure. *Even the most abstract intellectual patterns engage our feelings*.

If we consider 'absolute' music objectively, we can describe it as abstract patterns of tones which have no obvious relationship either with what goes on in the external world or, at first sight, with mental processes. Mathematics and music have often been represented as similar, because both are concerned with linking together abstractions, with making patterns of ideas. Wittgenstein, another philosopher to whom music was intensely important, 'spoke with great feeling about the beauty of *Principia*,* and said – what was probably the highest praise he could give it – that it was like music'.[15] Whitehead explicitly compares music and mathematics in his Lowell lectures of 1925.

> The science of Pure Mathematics, in its modern developments, may claim to be the most original creation of the human spirit. Another claimant for this position is music.[16]

Bertrand Russell wrote:

> The love of system, of interconnection, which is perhaps the inmost essence of the intellectual impulse, can find free play in mathematics as nowhere else.[17]

And G. H. Hardy proclaimed:

> A mathematician, like a painter or a poet, is a maker of patterns . . . The mathematician's patterns, like the painter's or the poet's, must be *beautiful*; the ideas, like the colours or the words, must fit together in a harmonious way. Beauty is the first test: there is no permanent place in the world for ugly mathematics.[18]

Internal evidence suggests that G. H. Hardy appreciated music as little as I appreciate mathematics. He suggests, surprisingly, that 'there are probably more people really interested in mathematics than in music.' Nevertheless, as the novelist Graham Greene remarked when reviewing *A Mathematician's Apology*, Hardy knew from the inside what it is like to be a creative artist. Hardy maintained that pure mathematics was independent of the physical world, and that the significance of a mathematical idea had nothing to do with any practical application which it might eventually have. According to Hardy, serious mathematical ideas are distinguished by generality, depth, inevitability, economy, and unexpectedness.

*Bertrand Russell's *Principia Mathematica*.

Such criteria can also be applied to music. Within a particular aesthetic tradition like that of Western art music, generality, depth, and inevitability are all qualities frequently adduced by critics in what is widely agreed to be great music. Some of these qualities are more easily defined negatively than positively. That is, music can lack generality because it is closely dependent upon a national idiom; or it can lack depth because its rhythms suggest triviality or are monotonous, like those of much popular music today. On the other hand, inevitability is a quality of all great works of art. Once completed, we can hardly imagine that they could have been differently composed.

We have already noted that unexpectedness is a feature of both Keller's and Meyer's theories of music. Paradoxically, a composer's ability to create novel patterns and provide unexpected fulfilments is closely connected with the feeling of inevitability. The more the composer treads conventional paths, the more we feel that he could have gone another way about it. The more original touches we find in a piece of music, the more we feel that it could not have been other than it is.

Economy is often prized, as in the case of Sibelius's Fourth Symphony, which the composer and musical historian Cecil Gray called a 'White Dwarf' of music, thereby comparing it to a star in which matter is highly compressed. But extreme economy makes stringent demands upon the listener's concentration, partly because the form of musical works requires repetition. If economy is carried so far that repetition is eschewed or reduced to a minimum, the listener may be unable to perceive the work's structure, as we observed earlier when discussing serial music. Perception of structure is essential to musical appreciation. Even if the listener lacks specialized training and is unable to formulate his assessment of a musical work in technical language, his perception of structure is an integral part of his musical experience.

Concision is not such an essential aspect of beauty in music as it is in mathematics. Schubert's 'heavenly length' is appreciated by people who love his music, and criticized by those who are less enthusiastic. A concise Wagner is inconceivable: the effect of his music is inseparable from its opulent duration.

On the other hand, critics frequently claim that a musical work is too long for its material. This criticism implies that form and content in music can be separately assessed: a good theme poorly developed, for example. But this dichotomy cannot easily be discerned in the greatest works of music, in which the indivisibility of form and content powerfully contributes to our feeling of inevitability.

Music and mathematics have in common the fact that the patterns of relationship with which they are concerned are predominantly non-verbal. Language is so complex, so efficient, and so characteristically human that we tend to over-value it as a means of communication and of making sense out of experience. Proust's speculation that music could have been an alternative means of communication between souls if spoken and written language had not developed illustrates the point.

Making sense out of anything depends upon relating one thing with another, upon discovering or imposing order. Mathematics represents ordering in general, not ordering in particular. As Whitehead put it: 'The certainty of mathematics depends upon its complete abstract generality.'[19] Music can also approach the icy grandeur of the impersonal, especially when we consider music springing from the last period of a composer's life. For example, Malcolm Boyd refers to Bach's *Musical Offering* and *Art of Fugue* as existing in 'a world far removed from the *musica humana* of our own, where music, mathematics and philosophy are one'.[20]

Anyone who knows this music will appreciate the accuracy of Boyd's evocative description. But is the world he postulates objective, or is he employing metaphor? Are the patterns of music and mathematics human inventions, or are they discoveries of some pre-existing order? G. H. Hardy was so militant a disbeliever in God that he refused ever to go into any College chapel, even for College elections. Yet he did believe that 'mathematical reality' exists independently of physical reality, and that mathematical theorems are not so much creations as observations or discoveries. He wrote:

317 is a prime, not because we think so, or because our minds are shaped in one way rather than another, but *because it is so*, because mathematical reality is built that way.[21]

Roger Penrose agrees with this view. He asks:

> Is mathematics invention or discovery? When mathematicians come upon their results are they just producing elaborate mental constructions which have no actual reality, but whose power and elegance is sufficient simply to fool even their inventors into believing that these mental constructions are 'real'? Or are mathematicians really uncovering truths which arc, in fact, already 'there' – truths whose existence is quite independent of the mathematicians' activities? I think that, by now, it must be clear to the reader that I am an adherent of the second, rather than the first, view . . . .[22]

Penrose does not claim that *all* mathematical structures are of the absolute variety. Some are contrived inventions which are clearly the products of human ingenuity. Others, in which much more emerges from the structure than was put into it in the first place, seem to be discoveries in which the mathematician appears to have 'stumbled upon "works of God"'. As Penrose points out, this view is 'mathematical Platonism'.

Other mathematicians are convinced that mathematics entirely consists of man–made constructions. Kroenecker made the famous remark: 'God made the integers: all else is the work of man,' thus having it both ways.

The inclination to believe that some mathematical structures are discoveries rather than inventions is reinforced by the way in which some mathematical problems are solved. Solutions of problems, new Gestalts, come to people spontaneously, however much the ground for them has been prepared by conscious effort. The inspirational quality of sudden solutions lends them a special significance which, for a believer, seem to emanate from the Deity. The mathematician Gauss, referring to a theorem which he had been struggling to prove for years, wrote:

> Finally, two days ago, I succeeded, not on account of painful efforts, but by the grace of God. Like a sudden flash of lightning, the riddle happened to be solved. I myself cannot say what was the conducting thread which connected what I previously knew with what made my success possible.[23]

Stravinsky, like Haydn, regarded his talents as God-given and regularly prayed for strength to use them. He referred to himself as having been made the custodian of musical aptitudes, and pledged himself to God to be worthy of their development. Stravinsky said that the germinal idea for *The Rite of Spring* came to him in a dream.

> Very little immediate tradition lies behind *Le Sacre du Printemps*. I had only my ear to help me. I heard and I wrote what I heard. I am the vessel through which *Le Sacre* passed.[24]

Stravinsky shared with Jung the idea that some dreams could be messages from God. Those of us who are less certain of God's existence have to make do with the idea that the unconscious part of the mind, as well as consciousness, is ceaselessly processing and sorting information. In the course of doing so, new combinations and patterns are thrown up which, if we are lucky, prove to be novel or inspirational. Since these new patterns appear spontaneously, rather than being the direct result of conscious deliberation, it is understandable that the religiously inclined describe themselves as being inspired by a deity.

The analogy between music and mathematics cannot be pressed too far. Although both are concerned with abstract relationships, the theorems of mathematics can be proved, whereas the 'truths' of music are of a different order. The progress of a musical composition toward its close may seem *aesthetically* inevitable if the work is good enough, but it cannot really be compared with the progress of a mathematical argument toward a close which is *logically* inevitable.

Mathematics and music both exemplify the fact that making coherent patterns out of abstract ideas is a deeply significant human achievement which enthrals and satisfies those who are able to understand such patterns whether or not they are directly related to life as it is ordinarily lived. Aesthetic appreciation of this kind is not simply a cold, cerebral, intellectual exercise; it touches human feelings. We delight in perceiving coherence where there was none before; we take pleasure in contemplating perfect form.

I do not believe that musical reality exists apart from the minds that create it. Music, unlike mathematics, is too dependent upon widely differing cultural traditions to be regarded as an absolute. But I do believe that it is a paradigm of the fundamental human organizing activity: the attempt to make structured sense out of chaos. And I also believe that great works of music can be distinguished from lesser works by adopting similar considerations to those suggested by Penrose for mathematics. Indeed, Penrose himself writes:

> Great works of art are indeed 'closer to God' than are lesser ones. It is a feeling not uncommon amongst artists, that in their greatest works they are revealing eternal truths which have some kind of prior etherial existence, while their lesser works might be more arbitrary, of the nature of mere mortal construction.[25]

The patterns of mathematics and the patterns of music both engage our feelings, but only music affects our emotions. Herein lies the difference in our response to each. Emotions involve the body; feelings do not.

> When hope, awe, boredom or gladness do not transfuse the body, we have only feelings, sensations, attitudes, or what you will. But we do not have emotion. As Darwin put it: 'So a man may intensely hate another, but until his bodily frame is affected he cannot be said to be enraged.'[26]

Although aesthetic appreciation of each has much in common, mathematics does not affect the body in the ways that music does. The patterns of mathematics convince us that there must be some order in the universe, and so do the patterns of music. But music promotes order within ourselves in a way which mathematics cannot because of music's physical effects.

Music is less abstract than mathematics because it causes physiological arousal and because the sounds from which it probably originated are emotional communications. It is both intellectual and emotional, restoring the links between mind and body. For this reason, music is usually felt as more personally significant than mathematics, more immediately relevant to the ebb and flow of our subjective, sentient life. But the ordering process, the concern with abstract relations, is similar. It is not surprising that the Pythagoreans believed that the harmony of the universe was both musical and mathematical.

Rhythm, melody, and harmony are all ways of ordering tones so that they interact and form relationships. These ordered sounds resonate with physical processes in ways which we do not fully understand. For example, certain sounds 'set one's teeth on edge' or send shivers up the spine. Research has demonstrated that the sound of chalk or finger-nails on slate is 'an international sound phobia'.[27] Yet no one knows why this is so. The noise is not particularly loud, nor does it signify any danger. It is just excruciating for no definable reason. Our brains may be something like those fragile glasses which shatter in response to notes of defined frequencies.

If we find that a piece of music *moves* us, we mean that it arouses us, that it affects us physically. Bodily involvement always implies some kind of movement, whether it be tensing muscles, swaying, nodding in time, weeping, or vocalizing. We have already commented on the fact that small children tend to move their hands and feet while singing, and pointed to the difficulty which some concert-goers experience in controlling their impulse to move to music. Motion and emotion are inseparably linked, both semantically and in external reality.

The composer Roger Sessions asks us to consider that:

> The basic ingredient of music is not so much sound as movement . . . I would even go a step farther, and say that music is significant for us as human beings principally because it embodies movement of a specifically human type that goes to the roots of our being and takes shape in the inner gestures which embody our deepest and most intimate responses.[28]

John Blacking considers that the impulse to compose music usually begins as a rhythmical stirring of the body, and that performers are more likely to give an authentic rendering if they can physically identify with the composer, perhaps holding their hands as Debussy held his when playing the piano, or in some other way getting beneath the composer's skin.

Music structures time; and some musicians claim that, for them, this is music's most essential function. The sense of movement through time in music varies widely from composition to composition. I have already compared sonata form to a journey, a progress toward a goal in which elements which were contrasted at the beginning of the piece are finally reconciled. Not all music is of this kind. Although any performance of music must, of course, last for a mensurable period of time, some music appears to be more concerned with structures which are not sharply contrasted nor resolved in a final union, but which are juxtaposed in ways we perceive as more nearly 'static'.

Stravinsky distinguished two varieties of time which he called 'psychological time' and 'ontological time'. By 'psychological time' he meant time which varies according to the inner dispositions of the subject: whether he is bored, excited, in pain, amused, and so on. By 'ontological time' he meant time as it actually is, time as it is measured.

> Music that is based on ontological time is generally dominated by the principle of similarity. The music that adheres to psychological time likes to proceed by contrast. To these two principles which dominate the creative process correspond the fundamental concepts of variety and unity.[29]

Stravinsky considered that music which is primarily expressive of the composer's 'emotive impulses' substitutes psychological time for ontological time. The listener, if he is caught up in the music's drama, finds that time seems to pass more rapidly than usual. On the other hand, music which is less concerned with personal feelings was, for Stravinsky, more closely attuned to the reality of ontological time.

> For myself, I have always considered that in general it is more satisfactory to proceed by similarity than by contrast. . . Contrast produces an immediate effect. Similarity satisfies us only in the long run. Contrast is an element of variety. Similarity is born of a striving for unity.[30]

In a recent article, the music critic Bayan Northcott points to Messiaen as a musician who 'views composing wholly as a matter of revealing the divine order', and links this with Messiaen's lack of concern with progression toward a goal. He also observes that Messiaen's music is precisely related to the passage of 'real' time, an observation which confirms Stravinsky's notion.[31]

Bruckner is another deeply religious composer whose somewhat static music has been compared with walking round a cathedral. His symphonies are characterized by the juxtaposition of large sections of material, not primarily by a sense of movement toward a goal. However, it would be false to attempt a generalization. Not all religious composers make statements about an eternal order already established and therefore compose music which seems revelatory. Haydn was deeply religious; but some of his music is characterized by *Sturm und Drang*, and most of his orchestral and chamber music proceeds toward a goal in sonata-like fashion, in spite of the many innovations and variants of sonata form which his ingenuity provided.

Stravinsky's conception of music as involved with eternity and the promotion of religious feelings of communion with God perhaps makes him unfair to the composer who is more concerned with the drama of personal feelings. For the latter is also in search of unity; the union between opposites expressed in the resolution of contrasting themes. Nevertheless, Stravinsky was making a valid distinction between the different perceptions of time which are part of our experience of music. Both Joseph Kerman and J. W. N. Sullivan comment on Beethoven's late quartets as having parted company with the progression toward a goal characteristic of sonata form. Sullivan refers to movements 'radiating from a central experience'.[32] But even music which approaches a kind of monumental repose, or which is perceived as relating to a still centre, requires time for its performance.

As I suggested in the chapter on Schopenhauer, great music can be distinguished from music which is cerebral and lacking in inspiration; but this does not mean that great music necessarily originates from some ethereal limbo. Access to one's own inner psychological depths is difficult enough without postulating another form of reality outside the human psyche. But when a composer does succeed in penetrating the hidden regions of the psyche, he not only encounters his deepest emotions but also ways of bringing those emotions into consciousness by converting them into those ordered structures of sound which we call music. The controversial French psychoanalyst Jacques Lacan said that the unconscious is structured like a language. It is equally true to say that the unconscious is structured like mathematics or like music. Freud's original notion that the id, the depths of the unconscious, was a seething cauldron of passions without organization or structure has been superseded. Both the conscious and the unconscious parts of the mind are concerned with creating new patterns.

Great music invariably has something beyond the personal about it because it depends upon an inner ordering process which is largely unconscious and therefore not deliberately willed by the composer. This ordering process is something to be wooed, encouraged, waited for, or prayed for. The greatest creative achievements of human beings are a product of the human brain; but this does not mean that they are entirely voluntary constructions. The brain operates in mysterious ways which are not under voluntary control: we must sometimes let it alone if it is to function at its best.

Some people find that one or other of the great religions provides them with a belief system which makes sense out of the world and their place in it. Religions order existence in that they issue prescriptions for behaviour, provide a hierarchy culminating in a deity, and give the individual, however humble, a sense that he or she is participating in a divinely-inspired plan. Religions differ widely from one another; but they all seem to be attempts of the human mind to impose some kind of order on the chaos of existence. Life itself may continue to be arbitrary, unpredictable, unjust, and disorderly; but believers find comfort in supposing that God meant there to be order, and assume that sinful human beings have frustrated his intention. There is even some explanatory comfort to be found in the opposite assumption that men are basically sensible and good-natured, but that their well-meaning efforts are frustrated by a tyrannical and capricious deity.

Although music is not a belief system, I think that its importance and its appeal also depend upon its being a way of ordering human experience. Great music both arouses our emotions and also provides a framework within which our passions 'enjoy themselves', as Nietzsche put it. Music exalts life, enhances life, and gives it meaning. Great music outlives the individual who created it. It is both personal and beyond the personal. For those who love it, it remains as a fixed point of reference in an unpredictable world. Music is a source of reconciliation, exhilaration, and hope which never fails.

Let me end by affirming that, for me, as for Nietzsche, music has been 'something for the sake of which it is worthwhile to live on earth'. Music has incomparably enriched my life. It is an irreplaceable, undeserved, transcendental blessing.

References

INTRODUCTION

1. Claude Lévi-Strauss, *The Raw and the Cooked*, translated by John and Doreen Weightman (London: Cape, 1970), p. 18.

CHAPTER I

1. Anicius Manlius Severinus Boethius, *Fundamentals of Music*, edited by Claude V. Palisca, translated by Calvin M. Bower (New Haven: Yale University Press, 1989), p. 8.
2. Herbert Read, *Icon and Idea* (London: Faber & Faber, 1955), p. 32.
3. R. Murray Schafer, *The Tuning of the World* (New York: Knopf, 1977), p. 268.
4. G. H. Hardy, *A Mathematician's Apology* (Cambridge: Cambridge University Press, 1940), p. 26.
5. Howard Gardner, *Art, Mind and Brain* (New York: Basic Books, 1982), p. 148.
6. Charles Hartshorne, *Born to Sing* (Bloomington: Indiana University Press, 1973), p. 56.
7. Ibid.
8. Géza Révész, *Introduction to the Psychology of Music*, translated by G. I. C. de Courcy (London: Longman, 1953), pp. 224–7.
9. Claud Lévi-Strauss, *The Raw and the Cooked*, translated by John and Doreen Weightman (London: Cape, 1970), p. 19, n.
10. Igor Stravinsky, *Poetics of Music*, translated by Arthur Knodel and Ingolf Dahl (New York: Vintage Books, 1947), pp. 23–4.
11. John Blacking, *How Musical Is Man?* (London: Faber & Faber, 1976), p. 7.
12. Bruce Richman, 'Rhythm and Melody in Gelada Vocal Exchanges', *Primates*, 28(2): 199–223, April 1987.
13. Howard Gardner, *Art, Mind, and Brain* (New York: Basic Books, 1982), p. 150.
14. Géza Révész, op. cit., p. 229.
15. Ellen Dissanayake, *Music as a Human Behavior: an Hypothesis of Evolutionary Origin and Function*. Unpublished paper presented at the Human Behavior & Evolution Society Meeting, Los Angeles, August 1990.
16. Alex Aronson, *Music and the Novel* (New Jersey: Rowman and Littlefield, 1980), p. 40.
17. William Pole, *The Philosophy of Music*, sixth edition (London: Kegan Paul, Trench, Trubner, 1924), p. 86.
18. Charles Darwin, *The Descent of Man*, quoted in Edmund Gurney, *The Power of Sound* (London: Smith, Elder, 1880), p. 119.
19. Leonard Williams, *The Dancing Chimpanzee* (London: Deutsch, 1967), p. 40.
20. Terence McLaughlin, *Music and Communication* (London: Faber & Faber, 1970), p. 14.
21. Maurice Cranston, *Jean-Jacques* (London: Allen Lane, 1983), pp. 289–90.
22. John Blacking, 'A Commonsense

View of All Music' (Cambridge: Cambridge University Press, 1987), p. 22.

23. Martin Heidegger, *Language*, quoted in Bruce Chatwin, *The Songlines* (London: Picador, 1988), p. 303.

24. Isaiah Berlin, *Vico and Herder* (London: Hogarth Press, 1976), pp. 46–7.

25. J. F. Mountford and R. P. Winnington-Ingram, 'Music', in *The Oxford Classical Dictionary*, second edition, edited by N. G. L. Hammond and H. H. Scullard (Oxford: Clarendon Press, 1970), pp. 705–13.

26. Julian Jaynes, *The Origin of Consciousness in the Breakdown of the Bicameral Mind* (Boston: Houghton Mifflin, 1976), p. 364.

27. Thrasybulos Georgiades, *Music and Language*, translated by Marie Louise Göllner (Cambridge: Cambridge University Press, 1982), p. 6.

28. Anton Ehrenzweig, *The Psychoanalysis of Artistic Vision and Hearing*, third edition (London: Sheldon Press, 1975), pp. 164–5.

29. Bruno Nettl, *The Study of Ethnomusicology* (Chicago: University of Illinois Press, 1983), p. 165.

30. Igor Stravinsky, *Poetics of Music* (New York: Vintage Books, 1947), p. 21.

31. Ellen Dissanayake, *What is Art For?* (Seattle: University of Washington Press, 1988), pp. 74–106.

32. Raymond Firth, *Elements of Social Organization* (London: Watts, 1961), p. 171.

33. John Blacking, op. cit., (1976), p. 51.

34. Béla Bartók, *Folk Song Research in Eastern Europe*, quoted in Paul Griffiths, *Bartók*

(London: Dent, 1984), p. 30.

35. John A. Sloboda, *The Musical Mind* (Oxford: Clarendon Press, 1985), p. 267.

36. Quoted in Isaiah Berlin, *Vico and Herder* (London: The Hogarth Press, 1976), p. 171.

37. Trevor A. Jones, 'Australia', *The New Oxford Companion to Music*, edited by Denis Arnold, Volume I (Oxford: Oxford University Press, 1983), pp. 117–9.

38. Bruce Chatwin, op. cit., p. 120

39. Bruno Nettl, op. cit., p. 156.

40. Edward O. Wilson, *Sociobiology* (Cambridge, Mass.: Harvard University Press, 1975), p. 564.

41. Leonard Williams, op. cit., pp. 39–40.

42. John Blacking, '*A Commonsense View of All Music*' (Cambridge: Cambridge University Press, 1987), p. 26.

43. Paul Farnsworth, *The Social Psychology of Music* (Iowa: Iowa State University Press, 1969), p. 216.

44. Saint Augustine, *Confessions*, translated by R. S. Pine-Coffin, Book 10 (Harmondsworth: Penguin, 1961), p. 239.

CHAPTER II

1. John Blacking, '*A Commonsense View of all Music*' (Cambridge: Cambridge University Press, 1987), p. 60.

2. John Blacking, *How Musical Is Man?* (London: Faber & Faber, 1976), pp. vi–viii.

3. G. Harrer and H. Harrer, 'Music, Emotion and Autonomic Function', in *Music and the Brain*, edited by Macdonald Critchley and R. A. Henson (London:

Heinemann Medical Books, 1977), pp. 202–16.

4. David Burrows, *Sound, Speech and Music* (Amherst: University of Massachusetts Press, 1990), p. 17.

5. Alfred C. Kinsey, Wardell B. Pomeroy, Clyde E. Martin, Paul H. Gebhard, *Sexual Behavior in the Human Female* (Philadelphia: W. B. Saunders, 1953), pp. 703–5.

6. Anthony Storr, *Freud* (Oxford: Oxford University Press, 1989), pp. 14–15, 45.

7. Anthony Storr, *Solitude* (London: Flamingo/Collins, 1989), pp. 42–61.

8. Marcel Proust, *Remembrance of Things Past*, Volume I, *Swann's Way*, translated by C. K. Scott Moncrieff and Terence Kilmartin (London: Chatto & Windus, 1981), p. 224.

9. Roger Brown, 'Music and Language', in *Documentary Report of the Ann Arbor Symposium: applications of psychology to the teaching and learning of music* (Reston, Virginia: Music Educators National Conference, 1981).

10. Peter Kivy, *Music Alone* (Ithaca: Cornell University Press, 1990), p. 153.

11. Igor Stravinsky and Robert Craft, *Dialogues and A Diary* (London: Faber & Faber, 1968), pp. 126–7.

12. Claude Debussy, 'Monsieur Croche the Dilettante Hater', in *Three Classics in the Aesthetics of Music*, translated by B. N. Langdon Davies (New York: Dover, 1962), p. 22.

13. Paul R. Farnsworth, *The Social Psychology of Music* (Iowa: Iowa State University Press, 1969), p. 214.

14. Yehudi Menuhin, *Theme and Variations* (New York: Stein and Day, 1972), p. 9.

15. Grosvenor Cooper and Leonard

B. Meyer, *The Rhythmic Structure of Music* (Chicago: University of Chicago Press, 1960), p. 1.

16. Paul Nordoff and Clive Robbins, *Therapy in Music for Handicapped Children* (London: Gollancz, 1971), p. 105.

17. Oliver Sacks, *Awakenings*, revised edition (London: Pan, 1981), pp. 56–7.

18. Ibid., p. 237.

19. Macdonald Critchley, 'Musicogenic Epilepsy', in *Music and the Brain*, edited by Macdonald Critchley and R. A. Henson (London: Heinemann Medical Books, 1977), pp. 344–5.

20. A. R. Luria, *The Working Brain*, translated by Basil Haigh (London: Allen Lane, 1973), pp. 142–3.

21. A. R. Luria, *The Man with a Shattered World*, translated by Lynn Solotaroff (London: Cape, 1973), pp. 154–5.

22. Howard Gardner, *Art, Mind and Brain* (New York: Basic Books, 1982), p. 328.

23. Oliver Sacks, *The Man Who Mistook His Wife for a Hat* (London: Duckworth, 1985), pp. 7–21.

24. Rosemary Shuter, *The Psychology of Musical Ability* (London: Methuen, 1968), p. 194.

25. John A. Sloboda, *The Musical Mind* (Oxford: Clarendon Press, 1985), p. 264.

26. G. Harrer and H. Harrer, 'Music, Emotion and Autonomic Function', in *Music and the Brain*, edited by Macdonald Critchley and R. A. Henson (London: Heinemann Medical Books, 1977), pp. 202–3.

27. Wilhelm Worringer, *Abstraction and Empathy*, translated by Michael Bullock (London: Routledge & Kegan Paul, 1963).

28. Plato, *The Republic of Plato*, third edition, translated by Benjamin

Jowett (Oxford: Clarendon Press, 1888), Book III, p. 88.

29. Ibid., pp. 84–5.

30. Aristotle, *The Politics*, translated by T. A. Sinclair, revised by T. J. Saunders (London: Penguin 1981), Book VIII, section v, p. 466.

31. E. R. Dodds, *The Greeks and the Irrational* (Berkeley: University of California Press, 1951), pp. 76–80.

32. Plato, *The Republic of Plato*, third edition, translated by Benjamin Jowett (Oxford: Clarendon Press, 1888), Book IV, pp. 112–3.

33. Ibid., p. 100.

34. Edward Gibbon, *The History of the Decline and Fall of the Roman Empire* (London: Methuen, 1897), Volume II, pp. 34–5.

35. Plato, *Timaeus and Critias*, translated by Desmond Lee (London: Penguin, 1977), p. 65.

36. Quoted in Lewis Rowell, *Thinking About Music* (Amherst: University of Massachusetts Press, 1983), pp. 40–1.

37. Quoted in J. P. Stern, *Hitler: The Führer and the People* (London: Fontana Press, 1975), p. 90.

38. Maurice Cranston, *Jean-Jacques* (London: Allen Lane, 1983), pp. 289–90.

39. Erich Fromm, *The Anatomy of Human Destructiveness* (New York: Holt, Rinehart and Winston, 1973), p. 420.

CHAPTER III

1. Alexander J. Ellis, 'On the Musical Scales of Various Nations', *Journal of the Society of Arts*, xxxiii (1885), pp. 485–527.

2. Hans Keller, *The Great Haydn Quartets* (London: Dent, 1986).

3. John Blacking, '*A Commonsense View of all Music*' (Cambridge: Cambridge University Press, 1987), p. 149.

4. Paul Hindemith, *A Composer's World* (New York: Anchor Books, 1961), p. 81.

5. William Pole, *The Philosophy of Music* (London: Kegan Paul, Trench, Trubner, 1924), p. 93.

6. William Pole, op. cit., p. 137.

7. Ferruccio Busoni, 'Sketch of a New Esthetic of Music', in *Three Classics in the Aesthetics of Music* (New York: Dover, 1962) pp. 90–91.

8. William Pole, op. cit., p. 102.

9. Charles Rosen, *Arnold Schoenberg* (New York: Viking Press, 1975), p. 28.

10. Charles Rosen, op. cit., pp. 24–5.

11. Igor Stravinsky, *Poetics of Music* (New York: Vintage Books, 1947), p. 40.

12. Deryck Cooke, *The Language of Music* (Oxford: Oxford University Press, 1959), p. 42.

13. Leonard Bernstein, *The Unanswered Question* (Cambridge, Mass.: Harvard University Press, 1976), p. 424.

14. Hugo Cole, private letter, 10 January 1991.

15. Deryck Cooke, *The Language of Music* (London: Oxford University Press, 1959), p. 55.

16. Leonard Bernstein, op. cit., p. 27.

17. Ibid., p. 29.

18. Ibid., p. 33.

19. Brian Trowell, private letter, 26 June 1990.

20. Jeremy Montagu, private letter, 12 July 1990.

21. Roger Sessions, *The Musical Experience of Composer, Performer, Listener* (New York: Atheneum, 1965), pp. 9–10.

CHAPTER IV

1. Felix Mendelssohn-Bartholdy, Letter to Marc-André Souchay, 15 October 1842, quoted in *The*

Musician's World, edited by Hans Gal (London: Thames & Hudson, 1965), p. 170.

2. Michael Hurd, 'Concert', *The New Oxford Companion to Music*, edited by Denis Arnold (Oxford: Oxford University Press, 1983), Volume I, pp. 452–3.

3. Jennifer Sherwood and Nikolaus Pevsner, *Oxfordshire, The Buildings of England* (Harmondsworth: Penguin, 1974), p. 217.

4. George Dyson, *The Progress of Music* (London: Oxford University Press, 1932), p. 174.

5. Charles Rosen, *Sonata Forms* (New York: W. W. Norton, 1980), p. 8.

6. Samuel Wesley, *Memoirs*, quoted in Arthur Searle, *Haydn and England* (The British Library, 1989), p. 24.

7. William Styron, *Darkness Visible* (New York: Random House, 1990), p. 66.

8. Kenneth Clark, *Leonardo da Vinci* (Harmondsworth: Penguin, 1958), p. 82.

9. Mendelssohn, op. cit.

10. Marcel Proust, *Remembrance of Things Past*, Volume III, *The Captive*, translated by C. K. Scott Moncrieff, Terence Kilmartin, and Andreas Mayor (London: Chatto & Windus, 1981), p. 260.

11. Jaroslav Vogel, *Leoš Janáček* (London: Orbis, 1981), p. 113.

12. Leonard Bernstein, *The Unanswered Question* (Cambridge, Mass.: Harvard University Press, 1976), pp. 136–9.

13. Alfred Einstein, *Mozart*, sixth edition (London: Cassell, 1966), p. 192.

14. Deryck Cooke, *The Language of Music* (London: Oxford University Press, 1959), p. 33.

15. Eduard Hanslick, *Music Criticisms, 1846–99*, translated and edited by Henry Pleasants, revised edition (Harmondsworth, 1963), pp. 26–7.

16. Igor Stravinsky and Robert Craft, *Expositions and Developments* (London: Faber & Faber, 1962), pp. 101–3.

17. Ibid., p. 58.

18. Paul Hindemith, *A Composer's World* (New York: Anchor Books, 1961), p. 42.

19. Ibid., p. 43.

20. Ibid., p. 51.

21. Ibid., p. 45.

22. Ibid., p. 57.

23. Susanne K. Langer, *Philosophy in a New Key* (Cambridge, Mass.: Harvard University Press, 1960), p. 222.

24. Donald Francis Tovey, *Symphonies, Essays in Musical Analysis* (London: Oxford University Press, 1935), Volume I, pp. 160, 117.

25. Frances Berenson, 'Interpreting the Emotional Content of Music', in *The Interpretation of Music: Philosophical Essays*, edited and introduced by Michael Krausz (Oxford: Clarendon Press, 1993), p. 64.

26. Joseph Kerman, *Musicology* (London: Fontana, 1985), p. 73.

27. Jacques Barzun, *Critical Questions*, edited by Bea Friedland (Chicago: University of Chicago Press, 1982), p. 97.

28. Alan Walker, *Franz Liszt* (London: Faber & Faber, 1989), Volume II, p. 305.

29. Barzun, op. cit., p. 77.

30. Donald Francis Tovey, *Essays in Musical Analysis*, (London: Oxford University Press, 1936), Volume III, p. 15.

31. Alex Aronson, *Music and the Novel* (New Jersey: Rowman and Littlefield, 1980), pp. 66–7.

32. Lewis Rowell, *Thinking about Music* (Amherst: University of Massachusetts Press, 1984), pp. 178–89.

33. Leonard B. Meyer, *Emotion and Meaning in Music* (Chicago: University of Chicago Press, 1956), p. 23.

34. Ibid., p. 155.

35. Hans Keller, 'Towards a Theory of Music', *Listener* (11 June 1970), p. 796.

36. Ibid.

37. Hans Keller, 'Closer Towards a Theory of Music', *Listener* (18 February 1971), p. 218.

38. Victor Zuckerkandl, *Music and the External World, Sound and Symbol*, Volume I, translated by Willard R. Trask (London: Routledge & Kegan Paul, 1956), p. 51.

39. Peter Kivy, *Music Alone* (Ithaca: Cornell University Press, 1990), p. 156.

40. Marcel Proust, op. cit., pp. 378–9.

CHAPTER V

1. Joseph Addison, 'A Song for St Cecilia's Day', *The Miscellaneous Works of Joseph Addison*, edited by A. C. Gulthkelch (London: G. Bell, 1914), p. 22.

2. Harry Freud, 'My Uncle Sigmund' (1956), in *Freud As We Knew Him*, edited and introduced by Hendrik M. Ruitenbeek (Detroit: Wayne State University Press, 1973), p. 313.

3. Sigmund Freud, *Three Essays on Sexuality*, translated and edited by James Strachey et al., Standard Edition, Volume VII (London: Hogarth Press, 1953), p. 182.

4. Sigmund Freud, *Formulations on the Two Principles of Mental Functioning*, translated and edited by James Strachey et al., Standard Edition, Volume XII (London: Hogarth Press, 1958), p. 218.

5. Sigmund Freud, *Introductory Lectures on Psycho-Analysis*, translated and edited by James Strachey et al., Standard Edition, Volume XVI (London: Hogarth Press, 1963), p. 376.

6. Sigmund Freud, *Formulations on the Two Principles of Mental Functioning*, translated and edited by James Strachey et al., Standard Edition, Volume XII (London: Hogarth Press, 1958), p. 224.

7. Sigmund Freud, *Civilization and its Discontents*, translated and edited by James Strachey et al., Standard Edition, Volume XXI (London: Hogarth Press, 1961), pp. 79–80.

8. Anthony Storr, *Freud* (Oxford: Oxford University Press, 1989), p. 80.

9. Heinz Kohut, 'Some Psychological Effects of Music and Their Relation to Music Therapy', *Music Therapy*, 1955, 5:17–20.

10. Pinchas Noy, 'The Development of Musical Ability', *The Psychoanalytic Study of the Child*, 1968, Volume XXIII, pp. 332–47.

11. Johan Sundberg, 'Computer synthesis of music performance', in *Generative Processes in Music*, edited by John A. Sloboda (Oxford: Clarendon Press, 1988), p. 52.

12. Edmund Spenser, *The Faerie Queene*, edited by Thomas P. Roche Jnr. and C. Patrick O'Donnell Jnr. (Harmondsworth: Penguin, 1978), Book 1, Canto IX, 40.

13. Sigmund Freud, *Civilization and its Discontents*, translated and edited by James Strachey et al., Standard Edition, Volume XXI (London: Hogarth Press, 1961), pp. 64.

14. Ibid., p. 65.

15. Marghanita Laski, *Ecstasy* (London: Cresset Press, 1961), p. 190.

16. Alexander Goehr, *Independent*, 1 June 1991.

17. Roger Nichols, *Ravel Remembered* (London: Faber & Faber, 1987), p. 58.

18. Walter de la Mare, 'Arabia', *Collected Poems* (London: Faber & Faber, 1942), p. 279.

19. Robin Maconie, *The Concept of Music* (Oxford: Clarendon Press, 1990), p. 24.

20. Ibid., p. 16.

21. Pinchas Noy, 'The Development of Musical Ability', *The Psychoanalytic Study of the Child*, 1968, Volume XXIII, pp. 332–47.

22. Frederick K. Goodwin and Kay Redfield Jamison, *Manic-Depressive Illness* (New York: Oxford University Press, 1990), p. 509.

23. David Cairns, *Berlioz, 1803–1832* (London: Deutsch, 1989), p. 287.

24. John Warrack, *Tchaikovsky* (London: Hamish Hamilton, 1989), p. 118.

25. C. G. Jung, *Memories, Dreams, Reflections*, edited by Aniela Jaffé, translated by Richard and Clara Winston (London: Collins and Routledge & Kegan Paul, 1963), p. 233.

26. Igor Stravinsky, *Poetics of Music* (New York: Vintage Books, 1947), p. 24.

27. John Blacking, '*A Commonsense View of All Music*' (Cambridge: Cambridge University Press, 1987), p. 118.

CHAPTER VI

1. Gioseffo Zarlino, *On Musica Humana*, quoted in Joscelyn Godwin, *Music, Mysticism, and Magic* (London: Penguin, 1986), p. 134.

2. H. C. Robbins Landon and David Wyn Jones, *Haydn: His Life and Music* (London: Thames & Hudson, 1988), p. 12.

3. Anthony Storr, *Solitude* (London: Flamingo/Collins, 1989).

4. Victor Zuckerkandl, *Sound and Symbol*, Volume II, *Man the Musician*, translated by Norbert Guterman (Princeton: Princeton University Press, 1973), p. 24.

5. Rollo H. Myers, *Erik Satie* (New York: Dover, 1968), p. 60.

6. Frances Berenson, 'Interpreting the Emotional Content of Music' in *The Interpretation of Music: Philosophical Essays*, edited and introduced by Michael Krausz (Oxford: Clarendon Press, 1993), p. 70.

7. Jacques Barzun, *Critical Questions*, edited by Bea Friedland (Chicago: University of Chicago Press, 1982), p. 87.

8. Jerrold Northrop Moore, *Edward Elgar: A Creative Life* (Oxford: Oxford University Press, 1984), p. vii.

9. Bernard Berenson, *The Italian Painters of the Renaissance* (London: Phaidon Press, 1959), p. 201.

10. Quoted in Rosemary Hughes, *Haydn* (London: Dent, 1970), p. 47.

11. Georg August Griesinger, 'Biographical Notes Concerning Joseph Haydn', in *Haydn: Two Contemporary Portraits*, translated by Vernon Gotwals (Madison: University of Wisconsin Press, 1968), pp. 54–5.

12. Albert Christoph Dies, 'Biographical Accounts of Joseph Haydn', in *Haydn: Two Contemporary Portraits*, translated by Vernon Gotwals (Madison: University of Wisconsin Press, 1968), p. 202.

13. Griesinger, op. cit., p. 57.

14. Rosemary Hughes, op. cit., p. 193.

15. Marcel Proust, *Remembrance of Things Past*, Volume III, *The Captive*, translated by C. K. Scott Moncrieff, Terence Kilmartin, and Andreas Mayor (London: Chatto

& Windus, 1981), p. 156.

16. Ibid.

17. Cecil Gray, *Musical Chairs* (London: Hogarth Press, 1985), p. 85.

18. Thomas Mann, 'The Sorrows and Grandeur of Richard Wagner', in *Pro and Contra Wagner*, translated by Allan Blunden (London: Faber & Faber, 1985), p. 100.

19. Ibid., p. 210.

20. Friedrich Nietzsche, *Daybreak*, translated by R. J. Hollingdale (Cambridge: Cambridge University Press, 1982), p. 145.

21. Mária Sági and Iván Vitányi, 'Experimental Research into Musical Generative Ability', in *Generative Processes in Music*, edited by John A. Sloboda (Oxford: Clarendon Press, 1988), p. 184.

22. Ibid., p. 186.

23. D. K. Antrim, 'Do musical talents have higher intelligence?' quoted in Rosamund Shuter, *The Psychology of Musical Ability* (London: Methuen, 1968), p. 244.

24. Plato, *Timaeus and Critias*, translated by Desmond Lee (London: Penguin, 1977), p. 65.

25. Edward Cone, *The Composer's Voice* (Berkeley: University of California Press, 1974), p. 157.

CHAPTER VII

1. Arthur Schopenhauer, *The World as Will and Representation*, translated by E. F. J. Payne, Volume II (New York: Dover, 1966), p. 448.

2. Peter Franklin, *The Idea of Music: Schoenberg and Others* (London: Macmillan, 1985), pp. 1–2.

3. David Pears, *The False Prison*, Volume I (Oxford: Clarendon Press, 1987), p. 5.

4. Arthur Schopenhauer, op. cit. Volume I, pp. 162, 164.

5. Arthur Schopenhauer, op. cit.

Volume II, p. 195.

6. Patrick Gardiner, *Schopenhauer* (Harmondsworth: Penguin, 1967), p. 60.

7. Arthur Schopenhauer, op. cit., Volume I, pp. 100–101.

8. C. G. Jung, *Memories, Dreams, Reflections*, edited by Aniela Jaffé, translated by Richard and Clara Winston (London: Collins & Routledge, 1963), p. 17.

9. C. G. Jung, 'Synchronicity: An Acausal Connecting Principle', in *The Structure and Dynamics of the Psyche*, Volume VIII, translated by R. F. C. Hull, *The Collected Works*, second edition (London: Routledge & Kegan Paul, 1969), p. 481.

10. F. David Peat, *Synchronicity: The Bridge Between Matter and Mind* (New York: Bantam Books, 1987).

11. Arthur Schopenhauer, op. cit., Volume I, pp. 263–4.

12. Plato, *The Republic of Plato*, translated by Benjamin Jowett, third edition, Book VI, (Oxford: Clarendon Press, 1888), p. 207.

13. Arthur Schopenhauer, op. cit., Volume I, p. 176.

14. C. G. Jung, *The Archetypes and the Collective Unconscious, The Collected Works*, Volume IX, Part 1, translated by R. F. C. Hull (London: Routledge & Kegan Paul, 1968), p. 79.

15. C. G. Jung, *Civilization in Transition, The Collected Works*, Volume X, translated by R. F. C. Hull (London: Routledge & Kegan Paul, 1964), p. 411.

16. Arthur Schopenhauer, op. cit., Volume I, pp. 234–5.

17. Ibid., pp. 184–5.

18. Wilhelm Worringer, *Abstraction and Empathy*, translated by Michael Bullock (London: Routledge & Kegan Paul, 1948), p. 24.

19. Arthur Schopenhauer, op. cit., Volume I, p. 198.

20. Ibid., p. 197.

21. Sigmund Freud, *Beyond the Pleasure Principle*, Standard Edition, Volume XVIII, translated and edited by James Strachey et al. (London: Hogarth Press, 1955), p. 38.

22. Alec Harman, Wilfrid Mellers and Anthony Milner, *Man and his Music* (London: Barrie and Rockcliff, 1962) p. 754.

23. Arthur Schopenhauer, op. cit., Volume I, p. 257.

24. Ibid.

25. Ibid., pp. 262–3.

26. Ferrucio Busoni, 'Sketch of a New Esthetic of Music', in *Three Classics in the Aesthetic of Music*, translated by Th. Baker (New York: Dover, 1962), p. 83.

27. Arthur Schopenhauer, op. cit., Volume I, p. 260.

28. Ibid., pp. 261–2.

29. Ibid., Volume II, p. 449.

30. Edward Cone, *The Composer's Voice* (Berkeley: University of California Press, 1974), p. 35.

31. Arthur Schopenhauer, op. cit., Volume I, p. 264.

32. Ibid., p. 261.

33. Quoted in Susanne K. Langer, *Philosophy in a New Key* (Cambridge, Mass.: Harvard University Press, 1960), pp. 221–2.

34. Ibid., p. 222.

35. Arthur Schopenhauer, op. cit., Volume I, p. 260.

36. Michael Tippett, 'Art, Judgment and Belief: Towards the Condition of Music', in *The Symbolic Order*, edited by Peter Abbs (London: The Falmer Press, 1989), p. 47.

37. Malcolm Budd, *Music and the Emotions* (London: Routledge & Kegan Paul, 1985), p. 103.

38. Constant Lambert, *Music Ho!* (London: Faber & Faber, 1937), second edition, pp. 89–112, 246–56.

39. John Blacking, *How Musical Is Man?* (London: Faber & Faber, 1976), pp. vi–vii.

40. Arthur Schopenhauer, op. cit., Volume I, p. 257.

CHAPTER VIII

1. Friedrich Nietzsche, *The Will to Power*, translated by Walter Kaufmann and R. J. Hollingdale (London: Weidenfeld & Nicolson, 1968), p. 432.

2. Roger Scruton, *Modern Philosophy and the Neglect of Aesthetics*, in *The Symbolic Order*, edited by Peter Abbs (London: The Falmer Press, 1989), p. 27.

3. C. G. Jung, *The Development of Personality*, *The Collected Works*, Volume XVII, translated by R. F. C. Hull (London: Routledge & Kegan Paul, 1954), p. 171.

4. Friedrich Nietzsche, *The Birth of Tragedy* and *The Case of Wagner*, translated by Walter Kaufmann (New York: Vintage Books, 1967), pp. 52, 141.

5. C. G. Jung, *Psychology and Religion*, *The Collected Works*, Volume XI, translated by R. F. C. Hull (London: Routledge & Kegan Paul, 1958), pp. 81–2.

6. Walter Kaufmann, *Nietzsche*, fourth edition (Princeton: Princeton University Press, 1974), p. 101.

7. C. G. Jung, *Psychology and Religion*, *The Collected Works*, translated by R. F. C. Hull, Volume XI (London: Routledge & Kegan Paul, 1958), pp. 85–6.

8. Friedrich Nietzsche, *Beyond Good and Evil*, translated by R. J. Hollingdale (Harmondsworth: Penguin, 1973), p. 93.

9. C. G. Jung, *Memories, Dreams,*

Reflections, edited by Aniela Jaffé, translated by Richard and Clara Winston (London: Collins, Routledge & Kegan Paul, 1963), p. 217.

10. Friedrich Nietzsche, *The Birth of Tragedy* and *The Case of Wagner*, translated by Walter Kaufmann (New York: Vintage Books, 1967), p. 59.

11. Friedrich Nietzsche, *The Will to Power*, translated by Walter Kaufmann and R. J. Hollingdale (London: Weidenfeld & Nicolson, 1968), pp. 434-5.

12. Walter Kaufmann, *Nietzsche*, fourth edition (Princeton: Princeton University Press, 1974), p. 131.

13. F. K. Goodwin and K. R. Jamison, *Manic-Depressive Illness* (New York: Oxford University Press, 1990), Ch. 14.

14. Quoted in Walter Kaufmann, *Nietzsche*, fourth edition, (Princeton: Princeton University Press, 1974), p. 130,n.

15. Friedrich Nietzsche, *The Gay Science*, translated by Walter Kaufmann (New York: Vintage Books, 1974), pp. 34-5.

16. Quoted in C. G. Jung, *The Seminars, Nietzsche's Zarathustra*, edited by James Jarrett, Volume II, Part 1 (London: Routledge & Kegan Paul, 1989), p. xiv.

17. Friedrich Nietzsche, *The Birth of Tragedy* and *The Case of Wagner*, translated by Walter Kaufmann (New York: Vintage Books, 1967), p. 164.

18. Friedrich Nietzsche, *The Will to Power*, translated by Walter Kaufmann and R. J. Hollingdale (London: Weidenfeld & Nicolson, 1968), p. 427.

19. Friedrich Nietzsche, *The Birth of Tragedy* and *The Case of Wagner*, translated by Walter Kaufmann

(New York: Vintage Books, 1967), p. 157.

20. Friedrich Nietzsche, *Beyond Good and Evil*, translated by R. J. Hollingdale (Harmondsworth: Penguin, 1973), pp. 168-9.

21. Arthur Schopenhauer, *The World as Will and Representation*, translated by E. F. J. Payne, Volume I (New York: Dover, 1969), p. 251.

22. Quoted in C. G. Jung, *The Seminars, Nietzsche's Zarathustra*, edited by James L. Jarrett, Volume II, Part 1 (London: Routledge & Kegan Paul, 1989), p. xviii.

23. Friedrich Nietzsche, *The Gay Science*, translated by Walter Kaufmann (New York: Vintage Books, 1974), pp. 324-5.

24. Friedrich Nietzsche, *Thus Spoke Zarathustra*, translated by R. J. Hollingdale (Harmondsworth: Penguin, 1969), pp. 61-2.

25. Friedrich Nietzsche, *The Will to Power*, translated by Walter Kaufmann and R. J. Hollingdale (London: Weidenfeld & Nicolson, 1968), pp. 427-8.

26. Friedrich Nietzsche, *The Birth of Tragedy* and *The Case of Wagner*, translated by Walter Kaufmann (New York: Vintage Books, 1967), pp. 55-6.

27. Friedrich Nietzsche, *The Will to Power*, translated by Walter Kaufmann and R. J. Hollingdale (London: Weidenfeld & Nicolson, 1968), p. 442.

28. Paul Valéry, *Pure Poetry: Notes for a Lecture*, quoted in *The Creative Vision*, edited by Haskell M. Block & Herman Salinger (New York: Grove Press, 1960), pp. 25-6.

29. Victor Zuckerkandl, *Man the Musician, Sound and Symbol*, translated by Norbert Guterman (New Jersey: Princeton University Press, 1973), p. 75.

30. Bertrand Russell, *History of Western*

Philosophy (London: Allen & Unwin, 1946), p. 731.

31. Friedrich Nietzsche, *On the Genealogy of Morals* and *Ecce Homo*, translated by Walter Kaufmann (New York: Vintage Books, 1989), p. 274.

32. Quoted in M. S. Silk and J. P. Stern, *Nietzsche on Tragedy* (Cambridge: Cambridge University Press, 1981), p. 247.

CHAPTER IX

1. D. E. Berlyne, *Aesthetics and Psychobiology* (New York: Appleton-Century-Crofts, 1971), p. 296.

2. William H. Calvin, *The Cerebral Symphony* (New York: Bantam, 1989), p. 145.

3. James J. Gibson, *The Senses Considered as Perceptual Systems* (London: Allen & Unwin, 1968), p. 93.

4. Victor Zuckerkandl, *Music and the External World, Sound and Symbol*, translated by Willard R. Trask, Volume I (London: Routledge & Kegan Paul, 1956), p. 15.

5. Fred Lerdahl, 'Cognitive constraints on compositional systems', in *Generative Processes in Music*, John A. Sloboda (Oxford: Clarendon Press, 1988), pp. 253–4.

6. Quoted in Walter Kolneder, *Anton Webern*, translated by Humphrey Searle (London: Faber & Faber, 1968), p. 61.

7. Victor Zuckerkandl, op. cit., p. 94.

8. Eduard Hanslick, *On the Musically Beautiful*, translated by Geoffrey Payzant, eighth edition, (Indiana: Hackett Publishing, 1986), p. 29.

9. Henri Bergson, 'The Perception of Change', in *The Creative Mind*, translated by Mabelle L. Andison (New Jersey: Citadel Press, 1946), p. 149.

10. Jack Kaminsky, *Hegel on Art* (Albany: State University of New York Press, 1962), p. 125.

11. Henri Bergson, ibid.

12. Heinrich Schenker, *Free Composition*, quoted in Nicholas Cook, *Schenker's Theory of Music as Ethics, Journal of Musicology*, Volume VII, No. 4 (1989) pp. 415–39.

13. Isaiah Berlin, *Vico and Herder* (London: Hogarth Press, 1976), p. 216, p. 175 (note 1).

14. Bertrand Russell, *The Autobiography of Bertrand Russell*, Volume I, 1872–1914 (London: Allen & Unwin, 1967), p. 36.

15. Ray Monk, *Ludwig Wittgenstein: The Duty of Genius* (New York: The Free Press, 1990), p. 44.

16. Alfred North Whitehead, *Science and the Modern World* (Cambridge: Cambridge University Press, 1928), p. 25.

17. Bertrand Russell, 'The Study of Mathematics', in *Mysticism and Logic* (London: Allen & Unwin, 1917), p. 66.

18. G. H. Hardy, *A Mathematician's Apology* (Cambridge: Cambridge University Press, 1940), pp. 24–5.

19. Alfred North Whitehead, op. cit., p. 28.

20. Malcolm Boyd, *Bach* (London: Dent, 1983), p. 208.

21. G. H. Hardy, op. cit., p. 70.

22. Roger Penrose, *The Emperor's New Mind* (London: Vintage, 1990), p. 126.

23. Quoted in Jacques Hadamard, *The Psychology of Invention in the Mathematical Field* (New Jersey: Princeton University Press, 1954), p. 15.

24. Igor Stravinsky and Robert Craft, *Expositions and Developments* (London: Faber & Faber, 1962), pp. 147–8.

25. Roger Penrose, op. cit., p. 127.

26. James Hillman, *Emotion* (London: Routledge & Kegan Paul, 1960), p. 126.

27. R. Murray Schafer, *The Tuning of the World* (New York: Knopf, 1977), p. 150.

28. Roger Sessions, *The Musical Experience of Composer, Performer, Listener* (New York: Atheneum, 1965), pp. 18–19.

29. Igor Stravinsky, *Poetics of Music* (New York: Vintage Books, 1947), p. 33.

30. Ibid.

31. Bayan Northcott, *Independent*, 25 May 1991.

32. J. W. N. Sullivan, *Beethoven* (London: Cape, 1937), p. 225.

Bibliography

Abbs, Peter (ed.), *The Symbolic Order* (London: The Falmer Press, 1989).

Adorno, Theodor, *In Search of Wagner*, translated by Rodney Livingstone (Manchester: NLB, 1981).

Arnold, Denis (ed.), *The New Oxford Companion to Music* Vols. I & II (Oxford: Oxford University Press, 1983).

Arnold, Denis, *Bach* (Oxford: Oxford University Press, 1984).

Aronson, Alex, *Music and the Novel* (New Jersey: Rowman & Littlefield, 1980).

Barzun, Jacques, *Critical Questions* (Chicago: University of Chicago Press, 1982).

Bergson, Henri, *The Creative Mind*, translated by Mabelle L. Andison (New Jersey: Citadel Press, 1946).

Berlin, Isaiah, *Vico and Herder* (London: Hogarth Press, 1976).

Berlin, Isaiah, *The Crooked Timber of Humanity* (London: John Murray, 1990).

Berlyne, D. E., *Aesthetics and Psychobiology* (New York: Appleton–Century–Crofts, 1971).

Bernstein, Leonard, *The Unanswered Question* (Cambridge, Massachusetts: Harvard University Press, 1976).

Blacking, John, *How Musical is Man?* (London: Faber & Faber, 1976).

Blacking, John, *'A Commonsense View of All Music'* (Cambridge: Cambridge University Press, 1987).

Bloch, Ernst, *Essays on the Philosophy of Music*, translated by Peter Palmer (Cambridge: Cambridge University Press, 1985).

Boethius, Anicius Manlius Severinus, *Fundamentals of Music*, edited by Claude V. Palisca, translated by Calvin M. Bower (New Haven & London: Yale University Press, 1989).

Boulez, Pierre, *Orientations*, edited by Jean-Jacques Nattiez, translated by Martin Cooper (London: Faber & Faber, 1986).

Boyd, Malcolm, *Bach* (London: Dent, 1983).

Brendel, Alfred, *Musical Thoughts & Afterthoughts* (London: Robson Books, 1976).

Brendel, Alfred, *Music Sounded Out* (London: Robson Books, 1990).

Brindle, Reginald Smith, *The New Music*, 2nd edn (Oxford: Oxford University Press, 1987).

Budd, Malcolm, *Music and the Emotions* (London: Routledge & Kegan Paul, 1985).

Bujić, Bojan (ed.), *Music in European Thought, 1851–1912* (Cambridge: Cambridge University Press, 1988).

Burrows, David, *Sound, Speech, and Music* (Amherst: University of Massachusetts Press, 1990).

Cairns, David, *Berlioz, 1803–1832* (London: Deutsch, 1989).

Cole, Hugo, *Sounds and Signs: Aspects of Musical Notation* (London: Oxford University Press, 1974).

Cole, Hugo, *The Changing Face of Music* (London: Gollancz, 1978).

Cone, Edward T., *Musical Form and Musical Performance* (New York: W. W. Norton, 1968).

Cone, Edward T., *The Composer's Voice* (Berkeley and Los Angeles: University of California Press, 1974).

Cook, Nicholas, *A Guide to Musical Analysis* (London: Dent, 1987).

Cook, Nicholas, *Music, Imagination, and Culture* (Oxford: Clarendon Press, 1990).

Cooke, Deryck, *The Language of Music* (London: Oxford University Press, 1959).

Cooke, Deryck, *Vindications* (London: Faber & Faber, 1982).

Cooper, Grosvenor and Meyer, Leonard B., *The Rhythmic Structure of Music* (Chicago: University of Chicago Press, 1960).

Cooper, Martin, *Beethoven: The Last Decade* (London: Oxford University Press, 1970).

Cooper, Martin (edited by Dominic Cooper), *Judgements of Value* (Oxford: Oxford University Press, 1988).

Critchley, Macdonald and Henson, R. A. (eds.), *Music and the Brain* (London: Heinemann Medical Books, 1977).

Dahlhaus, Carl, *Realism in Nineteenth-century Music*, translated by Mary Whittall (Cambridge: Cambridge University Press, 1985).

Dahlhaus, Carl, *Esthetics of Music*, translated by William W. Austin (Cambridge: Cambridge University Press, 1982).

Debussy, Claude and Busoni, Ferrucio and Ives, Charles E., *Three Classics in the Aesthetic of Music* (New York: Dover Books, 1962).

Dissanayake, Ellen, *What Is Art For?* (Seattle: University of Washington Press, 1988).

Dissanayake, Ellen, *Homo Aestheticus* (New York: The Free Press, 1992).

Dodds, E. R., *The Greeks and the Irrational* (Berkeley: University of California Press, 1951).

Dyson, George, *The Progress of Music* (London: Oxford University Press, 1932).

Dyson, George, *The New Music* (London: Oxford University Press, 1926).

Ehrenzweig, Anton, *The Psychoanalysis of Artistic Vision and Hearing*, 3rd edn (London: Sheldon Press, 1975).

Epstein, David, *Beyond Orpheus* (Oxford: Oxford University Press, 1987).

Evans, Martyn, *Listening to Music* (London: Macmillan, 1990).

Farnsworth, Paul R., *The Social Psychology of Music* (Iowa: Iowa State University Press, 1969).

Franklin, Peter, *The Idea of Music: Schoenberg and others* (London: Macmillan, 1985).

Gardiner, Patrick, *Schopenhauer* (Harmondsworth: Penguin, 1967).

Gardner, Howard, *Art, Mind and Brain* (New York: Basic Books, 1982).

Georgiades, Thrasybulos, *Music and Language*, translated by Marie Louise Göllner (Cambridge: Cambridge University Press, 1982).

Gray, Cecil, *Sibelius*, 2nd edn (London: Oxford University Press, 1934).

Gray, Cecil, *Musical Chairs* (London: Hogarth Press, 1985).

Godwin, Joscelyn, *Music, Mysticism, and Magic* (London: Arkana, 1987).

Griffiths, Paul, *The String Quartet* (London: Thames & Hudson, 1983).

Griffiths, Paul, *Bartók* (London: Dent, 1984).

Gurney, Edmund, *The Power of Sound* (London: Smith, Elder, 1880).

Hanslick, Eduard, *On the Musically Beautiful*, translated by Geoffrey Payzant (Indianapolis: Hackett, 1986).

Hanslick, Eduard, *Music Criticisms 1846–99*, edited and translated by Henry Pleasants (Harmondsworth: Penguin, 1950).

Harman, Alec and Mellers, Wilfrid, and Milner, Anthony, *Man and His Music* (London: Barrie & Rockcliff, 1962).

Hartshorne, Charles, *Born to Sing* (Bloomington: Indiana University Press, 1973).

Hillman, James, *Emotion* (London: Routledge & Kegan Paul, 1960).

Hindemith, Paul, *A Composer's World* (New York: Anchor Books, 1961).

Hollinrake, Roger, *Nietzsche, Wagner, and the Philosophy of Pessimism* (London: Allen & Unwin, 1982).

Kaminsky, Jack, *Hegel on Art* (Albany, New York: State University of New York Press, 1962).

Kaufmann, Walter, *Nietzsche*, 4th edn (Princeton: Princeton University Press, 1974).

Keller, Hans, *The Great Haydn Quartets* (London: Dent, 1986).

Keller, Hans, *Criticism* (London: Faber & Faber, 1987).

Kerman, Joseph, *The Beethoven Quartets* (London: Oxford University Press, 1967).

Kerman, Joseph, *Musicology* (London: Fontana, 1985)

Kivy, Peter, *Music Alone* (Ithaca: Cornell University Press, 1990).

Kivy, Peter, *Sound Sentiment* (Philadelphia: Temple University Press, 1989).

Kolneder, Walter, *Anton Webern*, translated by Humphrey Searle (London: Faber & Faber, 1968).

Lambert, Constant, *Music Ho!* (London: Faber & Faber, 1937).

McLaughlin, Terence, *Music and Communication* (London: Faber & Faber, 1970).

Maconie, Robin, *The Concept of Music* (Oxford: Clarendon Press, 1990).

Magee, Bryan, *The Philosophy of Schopenhauer* (Oxford: Clarendon Press, 1983).

Magee, Bryan, *Aspects of Wagner* (Oxford: Oxford University Press, 1988).

Mann, Thomas, *Pro and Contra Wagner*, translated by Allan Blunden (London: Faber & Faber, 1985).

Mellers, Wilfrid, *The Masks of Orpheus* (Manchester: Manchester University Press, 1987).

Mellers, Wilfrid, *Bach and the Dance of God* (London: Faber & Faber, 1980).

Mellers, Wilfrid, *Beethoven and the Voice of God* (London: Faber & Faber, 1983).

Menuhin, Yehudi, *Theme and Variations* (New York: Stein and Day, 1972).

Meyer, Leonard B., *Emotion and Meaning in Music* (Chicago: University of Chicago Press, 1956).

Meyer, Leonard B., *Music, the Arts, and Ideas* (Chicago: University of Chicago Press, 1967).

Meyer, Leonard B., *Explaining Music* (Berkeley: University of California Press, 1973).

Meyer, Leonard B., *Style and Music* (Philadelphia: University of Pennsylvania Press, 1989).

Moore, Jerrold Northrop, *Edward Elgar: A Creative Life* (Oxford: Oxford University Press, 1984).

Myers, Rollo H., *Erik Satie* (New York: Dover, 1968).

Nattiez, Jean-Jacques, *Proust as Musician*, translated by Derrick Puffett (Cambridge: Cambridge University Press, 1989).

Nehamas, Alexander, *Nietzsche: Life as Literature* (Cambridge, Massachusetts: Harvard University Press, 1985).

Nettl, Bruno, *The Study of Ethnomusicology* (Urbana & Chicago: University of Illinois Press, 1983).

Nichols, Roger, *Ravel Remembered* (London: Faber & Faber, 1987).

Nietzsche, Friedrich, *The Birth of Tragedy* and *The Case of Wagner*. translated by Walter Kaufmann (New York: Vintage Books, 1967).

Nietzsche, Friedrich, *The Gay Science*, translated by Walter Kaufmann (New York: Vintage Books, 1974).

Nietzsche, Friedrich, *The Genealogy of Morals* and *Ecce Homo*, translated by Walter Kaufmann (New York: Vintage Books, 1989).

Nietzsche, Friedrich, *Thus Spoke Zarathustra*, translated by R. J. Hollingdale (Harmondsworth: Penguin, 1969).

Nietzsche, Friedrich, *Beyond Good and Evil*, translated by R. J. Hollingdale (Harmondsworth: Penguin, 1973).

Nietzsche, Friedrich, *Daybreak*, translated by R. J. Hollingdale (Cambridge: Cambridge University Press, 1982).

Nietzsche, Friedrich, *The Will to Power*, translated by Walter Kaufmann and R. J. Hollingdale, edited by Walter Kaufmann (London: Weidenfeld & Nicolson, 1967).

Nordoff, Paul and Robbins, Clive, *Therapy in Music for Handicapped Children* (London: Gollancz, 1971).

Plato, *The Republic*, translated by B. Jowett, 3rd edn (Oxford. Clarendon Press, 1888).

Plato, *Timaeus and Critias*, translated by Desmond Lee (London: Penguin, 1977).

Pletsch, Carl, *Young Nietzsche* (New York: The Free Press, 1991).

Pole, William, *The Philosophy of Music* (London: Kegan Paul, Trench, Trubner, 1924).

Reti, Rudolph, *The Thematic Process in Music* (London: Faber & Faber, 1961).

Révész, Géza, *Introduction to the Psychology of Music*, translated by G. I. C. de Courcy (London: Longman, 1953).

Robbins Landon, H. C. and Jones, David Wyn, *Haydn: His Life and Music* (London: Thames & Hudson, 1988).

Rosen, Charles, *The Classical Style* (London: Faber & Faber, 1971).

Rosen, Charles, *Arnold Schoenberg* (New York: Viking Press, 1975).

Rosen, Charles, *Sonata Forms* (New York: W. W. Norton, 1980).

Rowell, Lewis, *Thinking About Music* (Amherst: University of Massachusetts Press, 1983).

Sacks, Oliver, *The Man Who Mistook His Wife for a Hat* (London: Duckworth, 1985).

Sadie, Stanley (ed.), *The New Grove Dictionary of Music and Musicians* (London: Macmillan, 1980).

Said, Edward W., *Musical Elaborations* (London: Chatto & Windus, 1991).

Schafer, R. Murray, *The Tuning of the World* (New York: Knopf, 1977).

Schopenhauer, Arthur, *The World as Will and Representation* translated by E. F. J. Payne, Vols. I & II (New York: Dover, 1966).

Scruton, Roger, *Art and Imagination* (London: Methuen, 1974).

Scruton, Roger, *The Aesthetic Understanding* (London: Methuen, 1983).

Sessions, Roger, *The Musical Experience of Composer, Performer, Listener* (New York: Atheneum, 1965).

Shuter, Rosemary, *The Psychology of Musical Ability* (London: Methuen, 1968).

Silk, M. S. and Stern, J. P., *Nietzsche on Tragedy* (Cambridge: Cambridge University Press, 1981).

Sloboda, John A., *The Musical Mind* (Oxford: Oxford University Press, 1985).

Sloboda, John A., *Generative Processes in Music* (Oxford: Clarendon Press, 1988).

Solomon, Maynard, *Beethoven* (New York: Schirmer, 1977).

Stern, J. P., *Nietzsche* (London: Fontana, 1978).

Stravinsky, Igor, *Poetics of Music*, translated by Arthur Knodel and Ingolf Dahl (New York: Vintage Books, 1947).

Stravinsky, Igor and Craft, Robert, *Expositions and Developments* (London: Faber & Faber, 1962).

Stravinsky, Igor and Craft, Robert, *Dialogues and A Diary* (London: Faber & Faber, 1968).

Sullivan, J. W. N., *Beethoven* (London: Cape, 1937).

Tovey, Donald Francis, *Essays in Musical Analysis* Vols. 1–6 (London: Oxford University Press, 1935–9).

Tovey, Donald Francis, *The Integrity of Music* (London: Oxford University Press, 1941).

Tovey, Donald Francis, *Musical Textures* (London: Oxford University Press, 1941).

Tovey, Donald Francis, *Essays in Musical Analysis: Chamber Music* (London: Oxford University Press, 1944).

Tovey, Donald Francis, *Musical Articles from the Encyclopaedia Britannica* (London: Oxford University Press, 1944).

Tovey, Donald Francis, *Beethoven* (London: Oxford University Press, 1944).

Wagner, Cosima, *Cosima Wagner's Diaries*, edited by Martin Gregor-Dellin and Dietrich Mack, translated by Geoffrey Skelton, Vols. I and II (London: Collins, 1978, 1980).

Warrack, John, *Tchaikovsky* (London: Hamish Hamilton, 1989).

White, Alan, *Within Nietzsche's Labyrinth* (New York: Routledge, 1990).

Winner, Ellen, *Invented Worlds: The Psychology of the Arts* (Cambridge, Massachusetts: Harvard University Press, 1982).

Wood, Alexander, *The Physics of Music* (London: Methuen, 1944).

Worringer, Wilhelm, *Abstraction and Empathy*, translated by Michael Bullock (London: Routledge & Kegan Paul, 1963).

Zuckerkandl, Victor, *Music and the External World, Sound and Symbol*, translated by Willard R. Trask, Vol. I (London: Routledge & Kegan Paul, 1956).

Zuckerkandl, Victor, *Man the Musician, Sound and Symbol*, translated by Norbert Guterman, Vol. II (Princeton: Princeton University Press, 1973).

Zuckerkandl, Victor, *The Sense of Music* (Princeton: Princeton University Press, 1959).

Index

About the Author

ANTHONY STORR is a Fellow of the Royal
College of Physicians, a Fellow of the Royal College
of Psychiatrists, and a Fellow of the Royal
Society of Literature. He is also an Emeritus Fellow
of Green College, Oxford, and Honorary
Consulting Psychiatrist to the Oxfordshire Health
Authority. He currently lives in Oxford, England.